CAMBRIDGE

Official Cambridge Exam Preparation

COMPLETE

FIRST

Teacher's Book
WITH DIGITAL PACK

Third edition

B2

Deborah Hobbs

ENGLISH FOR SPANISH SPEAKERS

CAMBRIDGE
UNIVERSITY PRESS & ASSESSMENT

Shaftesbury Road, Cambridge CB2 8EA, United Kingdom

One Liberty Plaza, 20th Floor, New York, NY 10006, USA

477 Williamstown Road, Port Melbourne, VIC 3207, Australia

314–321, 3rd Floor, Plot 3, Splendor Forum, Jasola District Centre, New Delhi – 110025, India

103 Penang Road, #05–06/07, Visioncrest Commercial, Singapore 238467

Cambridge University Press & Assessment is a department of the University of Cambridge.

We share the University's mission to contribute to society through the pursuit of education, learning and research at the highest international levels of excellence.

www.cambridge.org
Information on this title: www.cambridge.org/9788413224800

First published 2008
Second edition 2014
Third edition 2021

20 19 18 17 16 15 14 13 12 11 10 9 8 7

Printed in Spain by Pulmen

Legal Deposit: M-100-2021

A catalogue record for this publication is available from the British Library

ISBN 978-8-413-22480-0 Teacher's Book with Digital Pack
(English for Spanish Speakers edition)

Additional resources for this publication at www.cambridge.es/complete

Contents

CAMBRIDGE

Official Cambridge Exam Preparation

DEAR TEACHERS

I'm delighted that you've chosen our official preparation materials to prepare for a Cambridge English Qualification.

We take great pride in the fact that our materials draw on the expertise of a whole team of writers, teachers, assessors and exam experts. These are materials that you can really trust.

Our preparation materials are unique in many ways:

- They combine the skills and knowledge of the teams at Cambridge Assessment English, who create the tests, and the teams at Cambridge University Press, who create the English Language Teaching materials.
- They draw upon the experience of millions of previous exam candidates – where they succeed and where they have difficulties. We target exercises and activities precisely at these areas so that you can actively 'learn' from previous test takers' mistakes.
- Every single task in our materials has been carefully checked to be an accurate reflection of what test takers find in the test.

In addition, we listen to what you tell us at every stage of the development process. This allows us to design the most user-friendly courses, practice tests and supplementary training. We create materials using in-depth knowledge, research and practical understanding. Prepare for Cambridge English Qualifications with confidence in the knowledge that you have the best materials available to support you on your way to success.

We wish you the very best on your journey with us.

With kind regards,

Pamela Baxter
Director
Cambridge Exams Publishing

PS. If you have any feedback at all on our support materials for exams, please write to us at cambridgeexams@cambridge.org

The Complete Exam Journey

The unique exam journey in *Complete First* allows learners to build their confidence and develop their skills as they progress through each unit, ensuring they are ready on exam day. Along the journey there are ...

Full reading and Use of English, Listening, Writing and Speaking exam tasks in every unit, with step-by-step preparation exercises to ensure students have the skills necessary to understand and do the exam task.

Exam info and advice boxes with up-to-date exam information and advice, which are placed before every exam task in every unit, so students can apply the tips as they do the task.

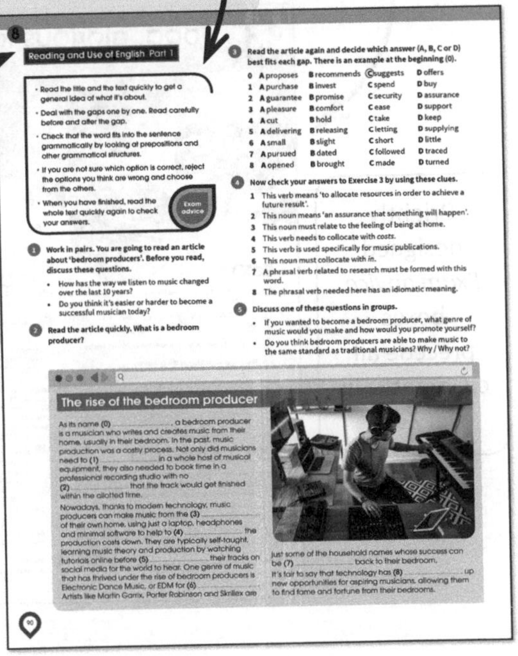

Opportunities to fine-tune and practise each exam task, confident in the knowledge that the materials are checked by the same team who writes the exams.

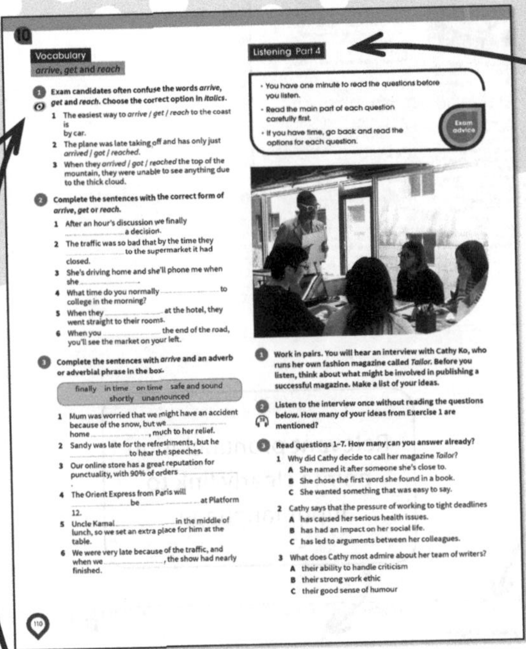

Exercises targeting common B2 First problem areas, using data from the Cambridge Learner Corpus, so students can overcome language areas of difficulty in time for the exam.

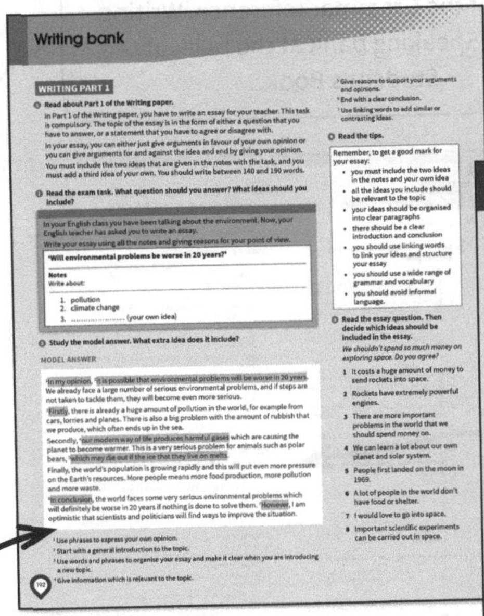

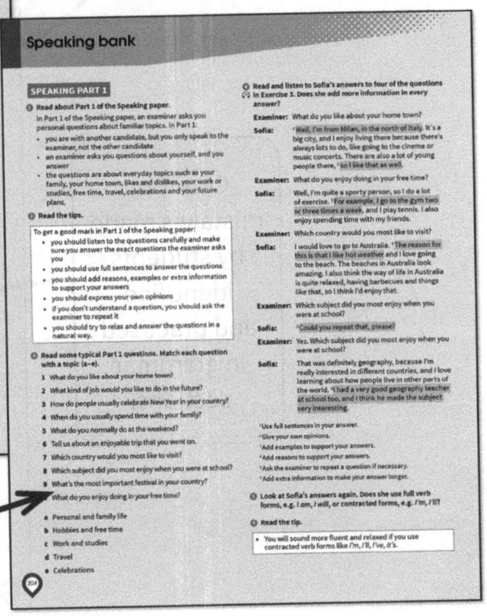

Extra practice sections for Writing and Speaking exam tasks at the back of the book, with preparation exercises and model exam tasks for students to follow

Student's Book overview

Eye-catching images in the *Starting off* section at the beginning of each unit get students interested in the unit topic.

All B2 First full Listening, Reading and Use of English, Speaking and Writing exam tasks have relevant and engaging topics.

Brightly designed *Exam advice* boxes precede all exam tasks in every unit.

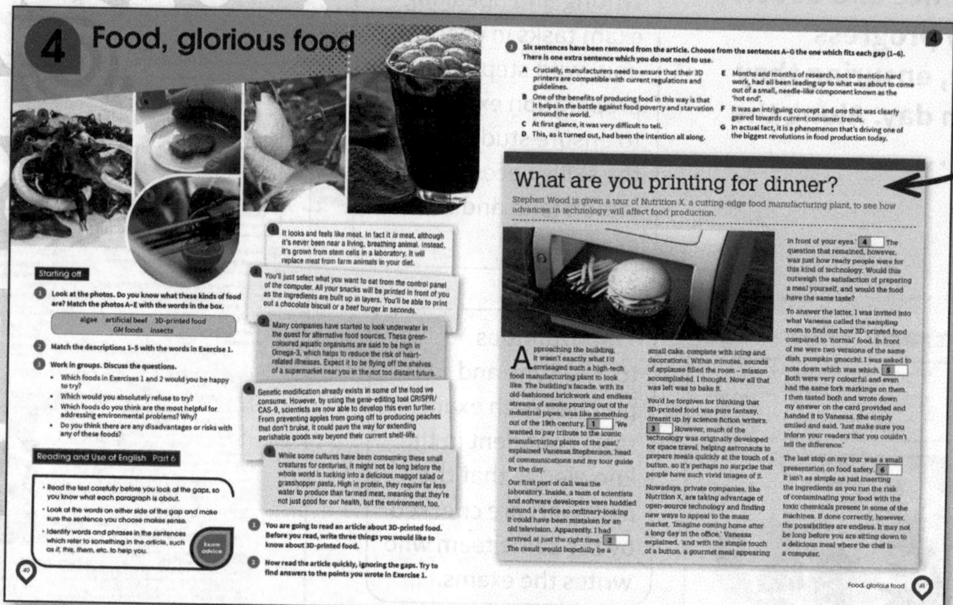

Clearly flagged signposts to the relevant sections of the Grammar reference, Writing bank and Speaking bank at the back of the Student's Book.

Relevant pronunciation points clearly link to input language.

Common mistakes made by students identified and practised in grammar sections.

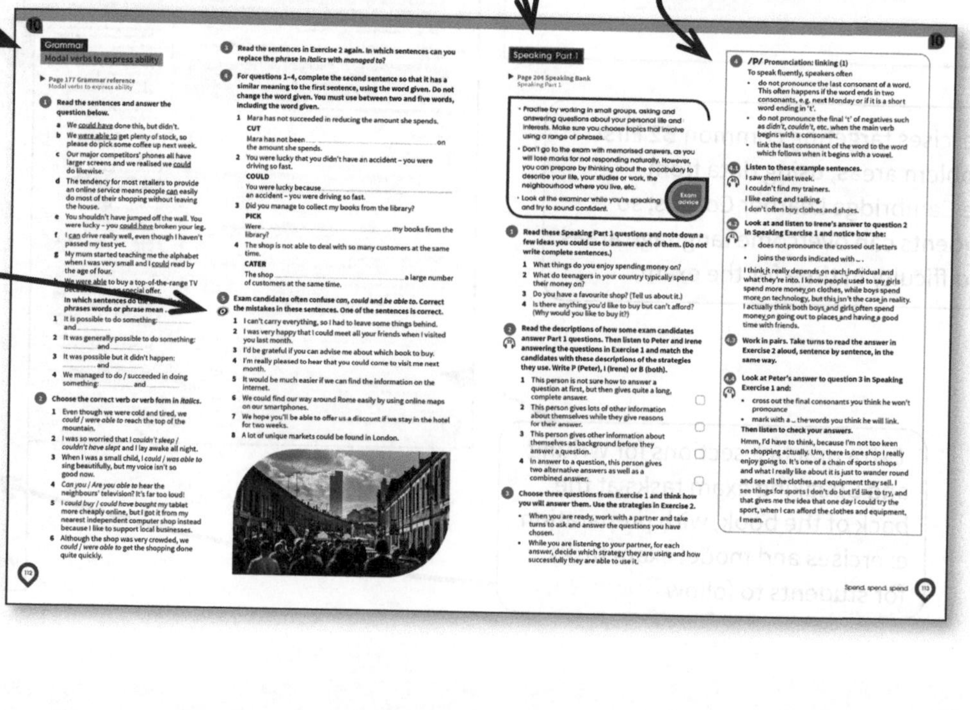

Communicative speaking activities encourage topic discussion.

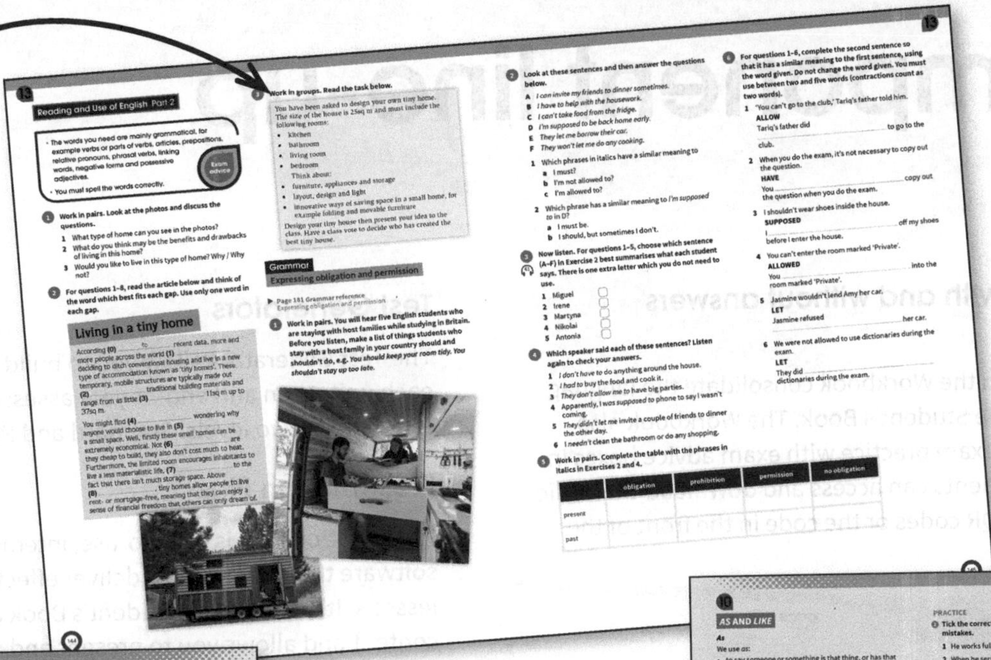

Unit *Vocabulary and grammar reviews* provide consolidation exercises.

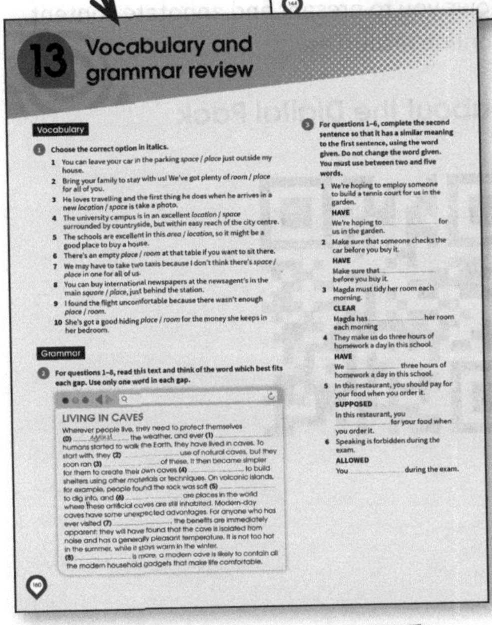

Unit-by-unit *Grammar reference* section provides further explanations and practice exercises.

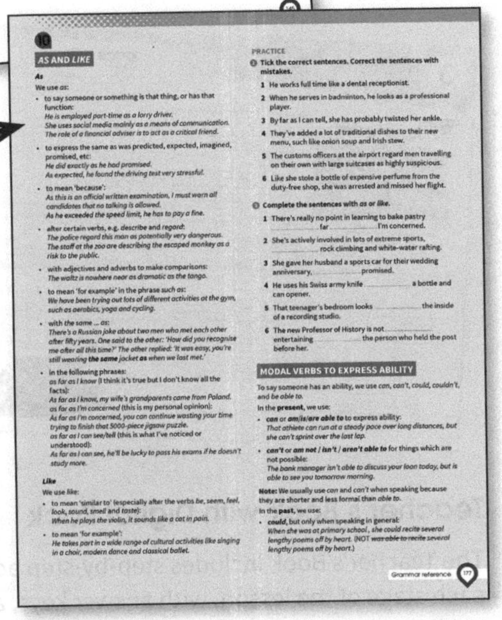

Exam task *Speaking bank* section includes practice exercises, useful language, photos and model answers.

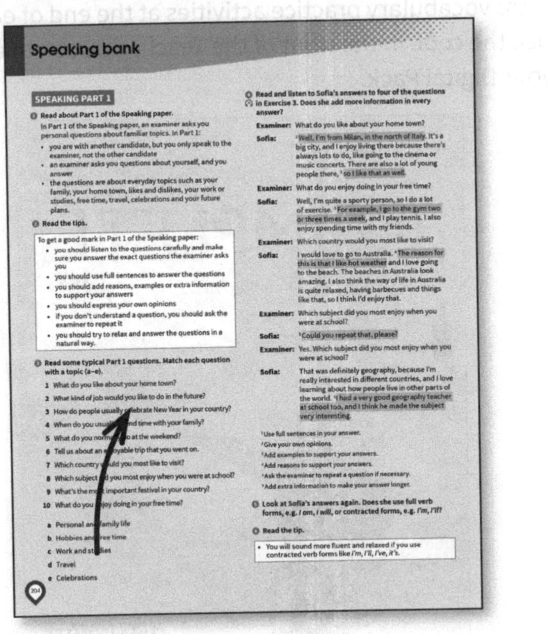

Exam task *Writing bank* section includes useful language, practice exercises and model exam answers.

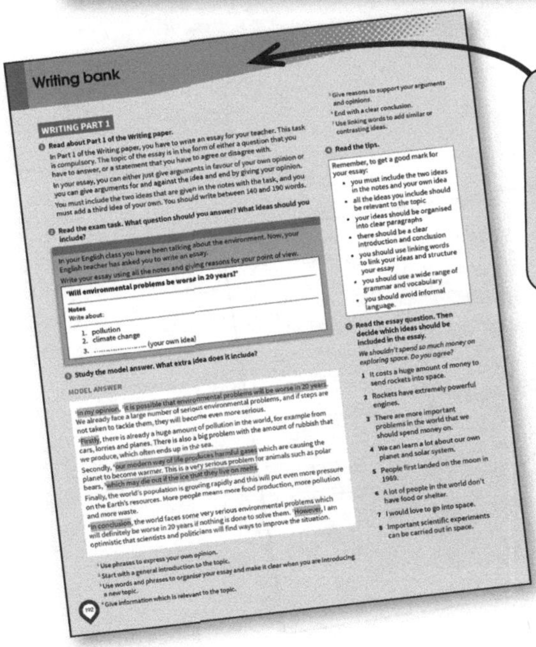

Extra grammar and vocabulary exercises for students can be found in *Practice Extra*.

Component line-up

Workbook with and without answers with Audio

The activities in the Workbook consolidate the language presented in the Student's Book. The Workbook also includes extra exam practice with exam advice boxes in every unit. Students can access and download the audio files using the QR codes or the code in the front of the Workbook.

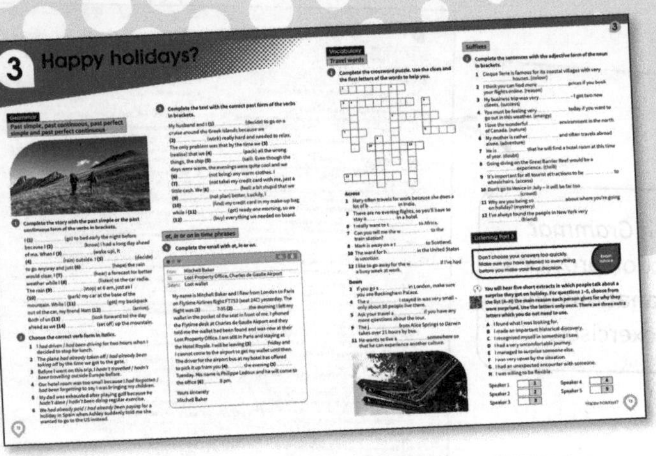

Test Generators

The Test Generators allow you to build your own tests for each unit, term and end-of-year assessment. Tests are available at two levels: Standard and Plus.

Presentation Plus

Presentation Plus is easy-to-use, interactive presentation software that helps you to deliver effective and engaging lessons. It includes the Student's Book and Workbook content and allows you to present and annotate content and link to the online resources.

Learn more about the Digital Pack

Teacher's Book with Digital Pack

The Teacher's Book includes step-by-step activities for each stage of the lesson, with answer keys, audioscripts, background information and extra activities. It also includes extra vocabulary practice activities at the end of each unit. Use the code in the front of the Teacher's Book to access your Digital Pack.

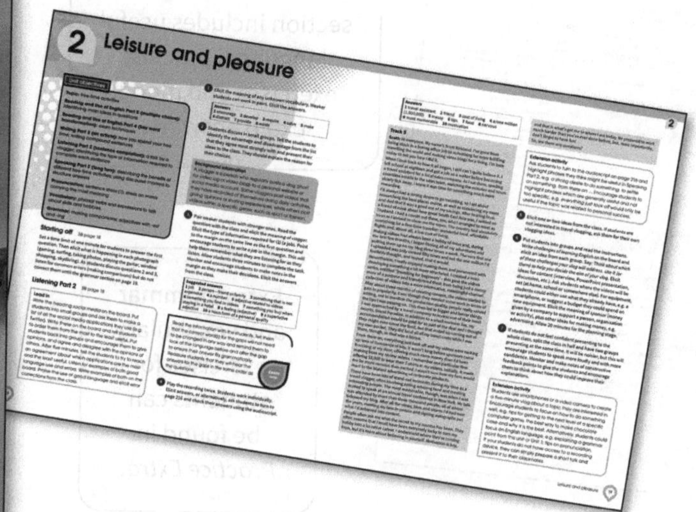

B2 First content and overview

Part/Timing	Content	Exam focus
Reading and Use of English 1 hour 15 minutes	**Part 1** A modified cloze text containing eight gaps and followed by eight multiple-choice items. **Part 2** A modified open cloze text containing eight gaps. **Part 3** A text containing eight gaps. Each gap corresponds to a word. The stems of the missing words are given beside the text and must be changed to form the missing word. **Part 4** Six separate questions, each with a lead-in sentence and a gapped second sentence to be completed in two to five words, one of which is given as a 'key word'. **Part 5** A text followed by six multiple-choice questions. **Part 6** A text from which six sentences have been removed and placed in a jumbled order after the text. A seventh sentence, which does not need to be used, is also included. **Part 7** A text, or several short texts, preceded by ten multiple-matching questions.	Candidates are expected to demonstrate the ability to apply their knowledge of the language system by completing the first four tasks; candidates are also expected to show understanding of specific information, text organisation features, tone, and text structure.
Writing 1 hour 20 minutes	**Part 1** One compulsory essay question presented through a rubric and short notes. **Part 2** Candidates choose one task from a choice of three task types. The tasks are situationally based and presented through a rubric and possibly a short input text. The task types are: • an essay • an article • a letter or email • a review • a report	Candidates are expected to be able to write using different degrees of formality and different functions: advising, comparing, describing, explaining, expressing opinions, justifying, persuading, recommending and suggesting.
Listening Approximately 40 minutes	**Part 1** A series of eight short unrelated extracts from monologues or exchanges between interacting speakers. There is one three-option multiple-choice question per extract. **Part 2** A short talk or lecture on a topic, with a sentence completion task which has ten items. **Part 3** Five short related monologues, with five multiple matching questions. **Part 4** An interview or conversation, with seven multiple choice questions.	Candidates are expected to be able to show understanding of attitude, detail, function, genre, gist, main idea, opinion, place, purpose, situation, specific information, relationship, topic, agreement, etc.
Speaking 14 minutes	**Part 1** A conversation between the examiner (the 'interlocutor') and each candidate (spoken questions). **Part 2** An individual 'long turn' for each candidate, with a brief response from the second candidate (visual and written stimuli, with spoken instructions). **Part 3** A discussion question with five written prompts. **Part 4** A discussion on topics related to Part 3 (spoken questions).	Candidates are expected to be able to respond to questions and to interact in conversational English.

1 A family affair

Unit objectives

Topic: family life

Reading and Use of English Part 6 (gapped text): understanding text structure

Reading and Use of English Part 2 (open cloze): phrases for common household chores

Writing Part 1 (an essay): technology and family life; expressing opinions; using *although, however, despite, that being said* and *whereas*

Listening Part 1 (multiple choice): people talking about friends and family

Speaking Part 1 (interview): talking about yourself, your friends and your family; giving extended answers

Pronunciation: word stress; stress in words with two or more syllables

Vocabulary: phrasal verbs to describe relationships; collocations with *make* and *do*

Grammar: present perfect simple and continuous

Starting off SB page 8

Lead in

With books closed ask students to think about their family. Ask students to write three adjectives, e.g. *honest, hard-working, quiet,* to describe one member of their family. Students tell a partner about their family member for one minute.

Look at the photos with the students. Elicit the different aspects of family life, e.g. siblings arguing over a tablet, a family sharing a meal together, a dad playing with his daughter, a family giving gifts. Elicit ideas from different pairs after they have discussed the questions.

Listening Part 1 SB page 8

Exam info

Read the information with the students, reminding them to listen to each extract individually as there is no connection between the eight recordings. Tell students they will hear the audio twice and should use the second listening to check their answers.

1 Elicit the answer to question 2 and point out that the main idea may be more than one phrase. Ask students to underline the main idea in questions 3 to 8 on their own before comparing their answers in pairs. Set a time limit of three minutes for this task.

Answers
2 sale of his family home / upsets him / parents' decision
3 her childhood / remembers / bedtime routine
4 working from home / how / feel about it
5 an article / family life / what point / making
6 new job / feel pleased about
7 buying presents / annoyed because
8 presentation / agree about the presenter

2 Before students listen, point out that candidates can be distracted by hearing words or phrases in the recording which appear in one of the incorrect options. As this is an exam task, set a time limit of 45 seconds for students to look at the questions before they do the listening exercise. Play the recording twice.

Answers
1 C **2** A **3**C **4**C **5**C **6**C **7**B **8**A

Track 2

Narrator: One. You hear a woman talking to her brother about an old family photo.

Woman: Hey! Look what I just found!

Man: No way! When was that taken?

Woman: About fifteen years ago, I reckon. You haven't changed a bit!

Man: Very funny – I can't believe our parents made us wear matching jumpers. We look ridiculous.

Woman: Ah, it's not that bad. It does help us to look more like brother and sister, I suppose, which is probably why they did it.

Man: You're right about that!

Woman: It would be so much better if you weren't sticking your tongue out, though.

Man: Yeah, I remember Mum and Dad not being too pleased about that.

Narrator: Two. You hear a man talking to a woman about the sale of his family home.

Woman: So I heard your parents are selling the house?

Man: Yeah, they're downsizing. I'd already cleared out my old room and moved everything to my flat, so I doubt I'll get sentimental about that. The one thing I might shed a tear over is the doorframe of the kitchen. Our parents used to mark our heights on it every six months, and it's quite sweet. I guess I'll just have to take a picture. My sister, on the other hand, is fairly upset about the location of the new house. It's only a one-hour drive to the city, but it does make it trickier to hang out with her friends who live there.

Narrator: Three. You hear a woman talking about her childhood.

Woman: The fondest memory I have of my childhood is playing football with my dad every evening before bed. Normally children get bedtime stories, but not me! My dad would grab a worn-out football made of foam and play with me in the tiny hall of the flat. We'd carry on playing for ages! I can't begin to tell you how many vases and other fragile objects we managed to break – it used to drive my mum mad! It was extremely effective though – I was exhausted after playing and I slept like a log. I guess I did get stories every now and again, but for some reason I found them more annoying than anything else.

Narrator: Four. You hear a woman talking about her experience of working from home.

Woman: I've been working from home for just over two weeks now. I certainly don't miss having to commute for two hours every day, waking up early to catch my train, that sort of thing. I thought I'd be more easily distracted than working in the office, but, amazingly, my productivity has actually gone up. I'm conscious of the fact I'm spending more time on my own, though, so I've organised daily virtual coffee breaks with people in the office, just to keep in touch, which has worked out really well.

Narrator: Five. You hear a journalist talking about an article he has written on family life.

Man: So my article on family life has been out in the public domain for about a week now. I didn't know if anyone would even read it at first, but it seems to have caused quite a stir online. Hardly surprising, I suppose, given the subject matter. Quite a few people have got in touch to say how helpful they found it, which is what I was counting on really, because a lot of the insights I gained into family life were based on other people's accounts rather than my own.

Narrator: Six. You hear a woman talking to her father about her new job.

Man: So, how's the new job?

Woman: I can't believe it's been three months already! The hours are long, but that's to be expected, really, as we're working on some really important projects at the moment.

Man: How are you getting on with your new colleagues?

Woman: They've been really supportive and have helped me get to grips with the new systems and processes. I couldn't have hoped for a nicer atmosphere in the office, either. I just hope I'll get the chance to book some time off for a holiday when the work starts to settle down. I'll have definitely earned it by then!

Narrator: Seven. You hear part of a conversation about buying presents.

Man: I'm so stressed out about having to buy all these presents. My family is way too big and it's such a hassle every year.

Woman: Tell me about it.

Man: I guess I've made some progress, but I'm still nowhere near done. The most irritating bit is having to get stuff for relatives who might not even be there. There are a few people in my family who think it's hilarious to say they're not coming, then turn up for lunch and go: 'Surprise!' They've caught me off guard a few times, so now I have to have a few extra presents, just in case, to avoid it turning into an embarrassing situation.

Narrator: Eight. You hear two friends talking about a presentation they've just attended.

Woman: What did you think about the presentation today, Sam? The presenter was good, wasn't he?

Man: Absolutely! The data he presented was so surprising; I thought he was making it up at first. I struggled to keep up with the more complex arguments, though. They could have been clearer.

Woman: Yeah, a lot of people have said the same. I personally thought he was quite easy to follow. And he was so passionate about the topic, you could see how interested everyone was.

Man: I couldn't agree more! It's just a shame he ran out of time at the end. I had so many questions to ask him.

Woman: That's true. We can always email him, I guess.

Extension activity

Students either listen again or use the audioscript to spot why the incorrect options are wrong. This will help students to understand how distractors are used in Listening Part 1. For example, Q1 C is correct because the woman says, 'It would be so much better if you weren't sticking your tongue out'; A is incorrect because it is the man who is making fun of the matching jumpers while the question asks what the woman is doing. B is incorrect because the woman says the jumpers made them 'look more like brother and sister', not that they had similar personalities (*alike*). Note that *alike* in the option is a 'word spot' for *more like* in the audioscript: remind students to be careful not to choose an option because they hear words or phrases in the recording which appear in one of the incorrect options.

3 Elicit the answer to question 1. Before students answer questions 2 to 7, remind them to think about word order for questions, question words and auxiliary verbs.

Answers
1 Do you have / **Have** you **got** any embarrassing family photos?
2 Have you ever moved house with your family?
3 What **did** your family **use** to do to make you fall asleep when you were a child?
4 What's the best present you have ever **received** from your friends or family?
5 Is there anything you do with your family every week?
6 Does anyone in your family **have** a really interesting job?
7 Did you use to fight with your siblings when you were children?

4 Students ask and answer the questions in pairs. For additional speaking practice, students either change partners, or ask the questions in a mingling activity. After three minutes, elicit whole-class feedback.

Vocabulary
Phrasal verbs SB page 9

Lead in
With books closed, write *At weekends I hang out with my friends.* on the board. Elicit and underline the phrasal verb. If students say *hang out* instead of *hang out with*, remind them that some phrasal verbs have one particle, and some have two. Elicit the meaning of *hang out with* (spend time with) and ask, *Who do you usually hang out with at weekends?* Students briefly discuss who they hang out with and what they usually do.

1 Allow students to discuss the vocabulary in pairs if they are unsure. Elicit the answers.

Answers
1 e 2 a 3 c 4 f 5 b 6 d

2 Students work on their own and then compare their answers in pairs. Elicit the correct answers.

Answers
1 make up 2 carry on 3 hang out with 4 turn up
5 count on 6 turn into

3 Students ask and answer questions in pairs. Encourage students to give reasons for their answers and to agree, disagree or ask questions about their partner's opinion. Listen for common errors and elicit corrections in whole-class feedback. Ask stronger students to present what they and their partner discussed.

Reading and Use of English Part 6 SB page 10

Lead in
With books closed, ask students to think of three adjectives – two positive and one negative – that a close friend would use to describe them. Invite students to write the adjectives on the board. Elicit the reasons why students think their friend would describe them this way and whether they agree or disagree and why.

1 Students do the exercise in pairs. Elicit the answers. For adjectives which could be either positive or negative, elicit example sentences for each sense.

Answers
usually positive: bright, considerate, enthusiastic, hard-working, mature, organised, polite, responsible, wise
usually negative: anxious, bad-tempered, bossy, dishonest, impatient, unreliable
could be either: quiet, reserved, sensitive

2 Students work on their own and then compare their answers in pairs. Elicit the correct answers.

Answers
unconcerned, unenthusiastic, immature, disorganised, impolite, irresponsible, insensitive

3 Put students into groups of three or four and ask them to discuss the questions. After five minutes ask one person from each group to present the groups' ideas to the class.

Background information
A wedding reception is a party that takes place after a marriage ceremony. It is usually held for those who have attended the wedding. A wedding reception features many traditions and often includes eating and dancing.

4 Remind students to read quickly, ignoring the gaps and any unknown vocabulary. Set a time limit of two minutes. Elicit the correct answer.

Answers
She has a problem with the seating arrangement at her wedding reception.

Exam info
Read the information with the students. Elicit parts of speech that will be useful in linking sentences in the text, e.g. pronouns and determiners such as *they, this, that*.

5 Ask students to underline the pronouns and determiners in the list of sentences A–G. For example, in sentence A students underline *this*. Tell students to make sure they find the things that these words refer to when checking they have the correct answer. For example, in question 5 *this* (in sentence A) refers to Laura wanting to sit next to her mum: 'they can be next to each other'. As this is an exam task, set a time limit of ten minutes. Allow students to compare answers before eliciting the correct answer.

Answers
1 F 2 B 3 E 4 G 5 A 6 C

6 Set a time limit of five minutes. Put students into groups of three or four. Assign a note-taker in preparation for presenting their ideas to the class. Point out that students will need to justify their ideas and not simply present a list of who will sit where.

7 Remind students that they need to explain their ideas by giving reasons and examples and allow one more minute for students to make sure they have done this. Ask them to choose one member from the group to present their ideas. The whole class vote on which group has come up with the best arrangement.

Extension activity
Put students into new groups. Write *our end-of-course dinner* on the board and ask students to imagine they are organising this event and to come up with a seating arrangement for the class. After five minutes, ask one person from each group to present their ideas. Students could recycle adjectives from page 10 Exercises 1 and 2 when giving reasons, e.g. *Paolo is quite quiet so we decided to sit him next to Sonya, who is sensitive and will make him feel comfortable.* Students decide which group came up with the best seating arrangement, and why.

Grammar
Present perfect simple and continuous

SB page 12

▶ **Page 162 Grammar reference**

Lead in
Write on the board *Why am I exhausted?* Tell students you are going to mime the answer and they must say the reason, using present perfect continuous. Mime why you are exhausted, e.g. working in the garden, sweeping the floor, cycling. Elicit the answer, checking for accurate use of the target grammar, and write it on the board (*You're exhausted because you've been working in the garden/sweeping the floor/cycling*). To prepare for the next exercise, draw a timeline under the sentence to show that the activity happened over a period of time.

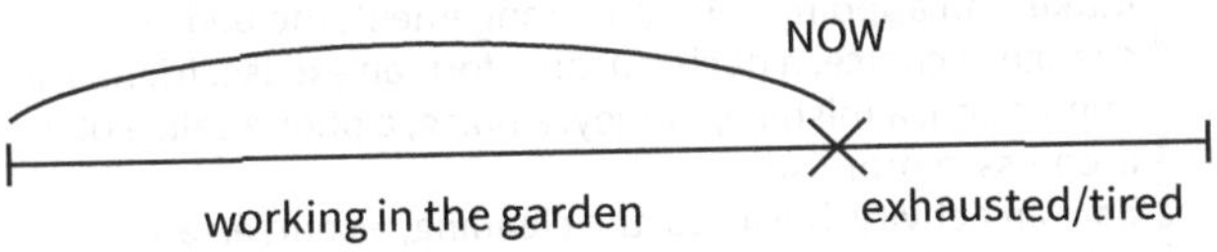

1 If students find this exercise challenging, tell them to draw a timeline for each sentence to help them. Elicit the answers.

Answers
1 **1** a **2** b
2 **1** b **2** a
3 **1** a **2** b

2 Tell students to look at the answers in Exercise 1 if they need help. After five minutes, ask students to check their answers in pairs. Elicit the answers. Look for any problem areas which could benefit from completion of Grammar reference Exercises 1–3 (you could set this as a homework task if you prefer).

Answers
2 've asked **3** 've cleaned **4** 's been playing **5** 've passed **6** 's only been working **7** 've spent **8** 've been cooking

Fast Finishers
Students write about a friend or family member using language from the unit so far, e.g. *I've been hanging out with my friend Tommy a lot more this year. We've been to a few football matches together …*

3 Read the rubric with the students. Students correct the mistakes on their own and then compare their answers in pairs. Elicit the correct answers.

Answers
2 ~~are~~ = have been
3 ~~learnt~~ = 've been learning
4 ~~I never met~~ = I've never met
5 ~~I've always been wanting~~ = I've always wanted
6 ~~read~~ = 've been reading

4 Students complete the gaps on their own and then discuss their answers with a partner. Alternatively, put the students into pairs and ask them to turn the statements into questions and interview their partner, e.g. *What TV series have you been watching recently?* Listen for common errors with the target structures and write down some examples. After five minutes, stop the students, write the example sentences on the board and elicit error correction from the class.

Extension activities
Repeat the Lead in miming activity, but this time ask students to mime why *they* are exhausted. Alternatively, students work in pairs and write three sentences with one present perfect simple or continuous grammar mistake in each for another pair to correct. If you choose the second option, you will probably need to monitor and help students to produce an error-free sentence which they can then change to include one mistake that is specific to the target language.

Reading and Use of English Part 2 SB page 13

Lead in
With books closed, write *household chores* on the board. Elicit the meaning of *chore* (a job or piece of work that is often boring or unpleasant but needs to be done regularly). Put students into small groups and ask them to brainstorm as many household chores as they can in one minute. Write these on the board.

1 If students are not sure, ask them to say the phrases out loud to try to hear if they sound correct. Elicit the correct answers and check unknown vocabulary.

Answers
1 e 2 d 3 b 4 g 5 f 6 a 7 c

2 Students discuss the questions in small groups for three minutes. For extra vocabulary and speaking practice, students include the chores from the Lead in exercise. Listen for errors, e.g. *I make the kitchen clean.* Do not stop the discussion, but elicit corrections afterwards.

3 Remind students to read quickly and ignore the gaps. Set a time limit of one minute.

Answers
the difference between the amount of housework done by men and women

Exam info
Read the information with the students. Remind them to read the word after the gap as well as the one before it. Tell the students that if they complete a gap with a verb it must agree with its subject.

4 Students work on their own. They should think of a word for each gap, but should not complete the answers until they do Exercise 5. Set a time limit of three minutes.

5 Students work on their own and use the clues to complete the answers. After eight minutes, ask students to compare their answers with a partner. If they have different answers, ask them to decide who they think has the correct answer. Elicit correct answers.

Answers
1 because **2** so **3** on **4** been **5** would **6** as **7** be **8** which

6 Students discuss in pairs. Tell students to give reasons and examples to support their ideas.

Extension activity
Students write a paragraph about who does the chores in their home. Tell them to include pronouns, determiners, articles and other function words (*this, these, that, the, a, his, she, my,* etc.) to avoid repetition and improve the style of their writing, e.g. *My mum does all the cooking, but my sister helps her with the washing-up.* Monitor and help individual students with error correction. Then ask students to re-write their paragraph, this time removing five different function words, e.g. *My mum does all ___ cooking but ___ sister helps with the washing-up.* to create a task for a partner to complete.

Vocabulary
Collocations with *make* and *do* SB page 14

Lead in
With books closed, write *make* and *do* on the board. Put students into small teams and tell them to write down as many collocations with *make* and *do* as they can think of (provide an example for each first, if necessary). Set a time limit of one minute. Give each team a board pen and tell them to select one team member to come to the front of the class and write their team's collocations on the board. Elicit corrections to any errors before declaring the winning team with the most correct collocations. Leave the collocations on the board in case you wish to use them for follow-up to Exercise 1.

1 If students are unsure of any items, tell them it may help to say the phrases out loud. Elicit the answers, including pronouns (*do (someone) a favour*). Tell students to look at the board and add to the table any collocations from the Lead in which were not included in Exercise 1.

Answers
make = an appointment, an arrangement, the bed, a change, a choice, a decision, an effort, an excuse, friends, an impression, a mistake, money, a noise, a phone call, a plan, progress, a promise
do = an activity, business, the cleaning, a course, (an) exercise, a favour, homework, housework, a job, the shopping, (a) sport, work

Fast finishers
One student says a common collocation and their partner must use the collocation in a sentence, e.g. Student A: *do the cleaning.* Student B: *I don't enjoy doing the cleaning at home, so sometimes I make up an excuse.*

2 Students work in pairs. Elicit answers. For personalisation, ask students to change the sentences so they are true for them, e.g. *My older brother usually does a lot more housework than me.*

Answers
1 do **2** make; do **3** make; make **4** made; making
5 do; make **6** doing; do

3 Students work in pairs then mingle and tell another two or three students. Listen for common errors but do not interrupt. After four or five minutes, write the errors on the board and elicit corrections from the class.

Extension activity
Students use collocations from Exercise 1 and write questions for their classmates to answer, e.g. Q1: *How often do you make your bed?*; Q2: *When was the last time you made an excuse for someone else?*

Speaking Part 1 SB page 14

▶ **Page 204 Speaking bank**

Lead in
Ask students to look at the photos and discuss where they would most like to live and why. *I'd prefer to live on the coast/at the seaside because …*

1 Students work in pairs. Elicit the answers plus an example answer for each question. Remind students that in spoken English we usually only use the phrase *in my opinion* when speaking in formal contexts.

Answers
1 *What do you like about the place where you live?* asks for a personal opinion. *Where are you from?* asks for personal information.
2 *Where are you from?* can be answered with a short phrase; *What do you like about the place where you live?* needs a longer answer.

2 Tell students they will listen to the recording twice. The first time, they should just listen without writing anything. The second time they should listen and make notes. When eliciting answers, ask students to give examples to support their ideas.

Suggested answers
Irene: she answers in sentences, not single words; she gives some extra details.

Track 3

Examiner: So, Irene, where are you from?
Irene: I'm from Llanes. It's a small town on the north coast of Spain, which becomes quite a busy tourist resort in the summer.
Examiner: And what do you like about Llanes?
Irene: Well, it's a fairly quiet place in the winter, so it has quite a relaxed atmosphere, but it's got wonderful beaches nearby and it's surrounded by lovely countryside. Also, I've got lots of friends in the area, so I have a very active social life. And of course, most of my family and relations live nearby, too.
Examiner: And you, Peter, where are you from?
Peter: Bremen, in northern Germany.
Examiner: And what do you like about Bremen?
Peter: My friends, the shops, the sports centre …
Examiner: Do you come from a large family?

Extension activity
Students improve Peter's answers.

3 Read the questions with the students and look at the photos. Elicit one or two examples of appropriate vocabulary, e.g. *a tourist destination*, *a bustling city centre*. Tell students it's important to use adjectives and noun collocations in the Speaking exam.

Answers
1
Photo 1: Bournemouth, England (b; c; l)
Photo 2: Stockholm, Sweden (e; f; g; h; i)
Photo 3: Mexico City, Mexico (a; f; g; i; j; k)

4 Weaker students can work in pairs. Monitor and help where necessary. Listen for common errors.

Answers
It is: a, c, d, e, f, k
It has: b, e, f, g, h, i, j, k, l

/P/ word stress (1)

5 Read the introduction with the students. If necessary, elicit the meaning of *syllable* (a single unit of speech) and remind students each syllable has a vowel sound. You may find that holding up your hand and using your fingers to count the syllables helps the students to understand. For example, *industrial* has four vowel sounds and therefore four syllables *in/dus/tri/al*. Hold up four fingers and say each syllable. Point to the second finger as you say the stressed syllable. Tell students to say the words out loud and, if they are unsure, to move the stressed syllable until they think it sounds correct.

Answers
industrial, relaxed, atmosphere, wonderful, important
business, impressive, historic, attractive, residential

Track 4

industrial	relaxed
atmosphere	wonderful
important	business
impressive	historical
attractive	residential

6 Allow students two minutes to think about their answers and tell them to make notes if they want to. For extra support refer them to the audioscript on page 215 of the Student's Book.

7 Students complete the task in pairs or, alternatively, work in groups of three with the third student observing and giving feedback to the 'candidate', e.g. *Well done for using the phrase 'a relaxed atmosphere' in your answer.* Set a time limit of five minutes.

8 Remind students to use adjective and noun collocations and elicit some appropriate vocabulary, e.g. *I have three younger siblings*. Monitor and listen for common errors. Elicit answers and correct errors.

Extension activity
If feasible, students record themselves answering the questions using their smartphones. Then in pairs they listen to their pronunciation, focusing on word stress.

Writing Part 1 (an essay) SB page 16

▶ **Page 192 Writing bank**

Lead in
Write on the board: *The piece of technology I cannot live without is … because …* Students discuss in small groups. Set a time limit of two minutes. Invite one or two students to share their ideas with the class.

1 Divide the class in half. Half the class discuss advantages (positive impacts), the other disadvantages (negative impacts). Set a time limit of three minutes. Tell students for each impact, they must think of an example, e.g. *One advantage of technology is communication. These days we can communicate easily and quickly with family members we don't live with by using video, emails or messaging.* Elicit ideas and write them on the board. Make pairs so that each student is sat with someone from the opposite group (a positive with a negative). Tell students they must discuss the advantages and disadvantages, giving examples and supporting their ideas. After five minutes, stop the students and hold a class vote on whether technology has a more positive or negative impact on families overall.

Exam info
Read the information with the students. Remind them they must write about three ideas (the two in the notes plus one of their own). Tell students that using an idea they are interested or experienced in will help them to write more effectively.

2 Read the task with the students. Ask: *Why is it important to underline the points you must include?* (to help them answer the question fully). Elicit the meaning of *largely positive* (almost completely positive). In pairs, students quickly brainstorm three ideas for the third note: *your own idea*.

Suggested answers
technology/positive impact/families/spending free time/talking together/own idea

3 Put students in groups. Ask them to brainstorm ideas using a spider diagram. If students find this difficult, groups can share ideas. When eliciting ideas from the class, ask students to give reasons why an idea would be a good or bad choice.

4 Students work on their own and then compare their ideas with a partner. Remind them to justify their ideas.

5 Ask students why it is important to make a plan. (It will help them stay focused on the question, answer the question more fully and get higher marks). Weaker students can work in pairs. Elicit the correct answers.

Answers
1 a 2 d 3 b 4 c 5 e

6 Ask students to underline the phrases. Students work on their own and then compare their answers. Elicit correct answers and ask: *Could these phrases be used in the speaking part of the exam?* (Yes.)

Answers
As far as I'm concerned (paragraph 1)
In my opinion (paragraph 2)
In my view (paragraphs 3 and 4)
I believe (paragraph 5)

7 Remind students to think about sentence structure and to read the sentence in full before making their choice. Weaker students can work in pairs.

Answers
1 Although 2 Whereas 3 That being said 4 Despite

8 As students often find this sort of task challenging, answer the first question with the students and allow them to work in groups. Elicit the correct answers.

Answers
1 whereas 2 Although 3 However 4 Although
5 whereas 6 However 7 Despite

9 As this is an exam task, set a time limit of 40 minutes. Ask students how long they should spend planning their answer (five to ten minutes). Tell students they should use four phrases to express their opinion, e.g. *as far as I'm concerned, … In my view …*; and four words to contrast ideas, e.g. *although, despite* in their essays.

Extension activity
In pairs, students read each other's essay and underline the four examples of phrases to express opinion and the four words to show contrasting points of view. Monitor to check if the target language has been used. If students have not included the target language, you could pair weaker with stronger students, tell them to choose one paragraph (from the weaker student's essay) and re-write (improve) it together.

Vocabulary

Phrasal verbs

hang out with
count on
turn into
make (something) up
carry on (doing something)
turn up

Adjectives

bad-tempered
bossy
bright
(un)concerned
(in)considerate
dishonest
(un)enthusiastic
hard-working
impatient
(im)mature
(dis)organised
(im)polite
quiet
reserved
(ir)responsible
(in)sensitive
unreliable
wise

Common household chores

do the ironing
do the washing-up
dust the furniture
get the dinner ready
hang the washing out to dry
lay/set the table
make the beds
sweep the floor

Collocations with *make* and *do*

make = an appointment, an arrangement, the bed, a change, a choice, a decision, an effort, an excuse, friends, an impression, a mistake, money, a noise, a phone call, a plan, progress, a promise

do = an activity, business, the cleaning, a course, (an) exercise, a favour, homework, housework, a job, the shopping, (a) sport, work

Language to talk about the place where you live

a large industrial city
a relaxed atmosphere
a busy tourist resort
in the middle of some lovely countryside
a pleasant residential district
an important business centre
some impressive architecture
a lot of historic buildings
a lot of attractive buildings
some pretty good shopping streets
a busy city centre
wonderful beaches nearby

Vocabulary activity 1

Put students into groups of three. Student A starts a story about any topic using words or phrases from the list. When Student A uses a word Student B ~~crosses it out~~. After one-minute, Student B must take over and continue telling the same story, using words from the list that Student A did not use. As Student B continues the story, Student C ~~crosses out~~ the words from the list that Student B uses. After one-minute, Student C continues the story and Student A ~~crosses out~~ the words that Student C uses. Telling the story may get harder as the words are crossed out and there are fewer words left to use, so if possible, choose a stronger student for C. The aim is for the group to use all the vocabulary items by the time they have finished their story (in three minutes). If Students A cannot think of story ideas, you could help with a few ideas: *A funny thing happened to me in my city recently. I met an interesting person while I was walking along the street. / A strange thing happened when I went to buy a washing machine with my mum.* Tell students that the stories do not need to be real and encourage them to be creative. Often, the more unrealistic the stories are, the more fun the students will have.

Vocabulary activity 2

Put students in pairs. One student describes a household chore, without saying the word, and the other has to guess what they are describing, e.g. Student A: *You do it after you have eaten.* Student B: *The washing-up.*

DIGITAL CLASSROOM

Practice Extra Unit 1

Test Generator Unit 1 test

Test and Train Exam Practice

2 Leisure and pleasure

Unit objectives

Topic: free-time activities

Reading and Use of English Part 5 (multiple choice): identifying main ideas in questions

Reading and Use of English Part 4 (key word transformation): exam techniques

Writing Part 2 (an article): how you spend your free time; writing compound sentences

Listening Part 2 (sentence completion): a talk by a vlogger; identifying the type of information required to complete each sentence

Speaking Part 2 (long turn): describing the benefits of different free-time activities; using discourse markers to structure answers

Pronunciation: sentence stress (1): stress on words carrying the most meaning

Vocabulary: phrasal verbs and expressions to talk about skills and hobbies

Grammar: making comparisons; adjectives with *-ed* and *-ing*

Starting off SB page 18

Set a time limit of one minute for students to answer the first question. Then elicit what is happening in each photograph (gaming, surfing, taking photos, playing the guitar, window shopping, skydiving). As students discuss questions 2 and 3, listen for common errors (making comparisons) but do not correct them until the grammar section on page 19.

Listening Part 2 SB page 18

Lead in

Write the heading *social media* on the board. Put students into small groups and ask them to make a list of all the social media applications they use (e.g. Twitter). Write these on the board and tell students to order them from the most to the least useful. Put students back into groups and encourage them to give opinions, and agree and disagree with the opinions of others. After five minutes, tell the students to try to reach an agreement about which applications are the most and the least useful. Listen for examples of both good language use and errors. Write examples of both on the board. Praise the use of good language and elicit error corrections from the class.

1 Elicit the meaning of any unknown vocabulary. Weaker students can work in pairs. Elicit the answers.

Answers
1 encourage **2** develop **3** require **4** solve **5** make **6** distract **7** provide **8** waste

2 Students discuss in small groups. Tell the students to identify the advantage and disadvantage from the list that they agree most strongly with and present their ideas to the class. They should explain the reason for their choices.

Background information

A vlogger is a person who regularly posts a vlog (short for *video log* or *video blog*) to a personal website or social media account. Some vloggers post videos that they have recorded of themselves doing daily activities, giving opinions or sharing experiences, while others post videos within a specific genre, such as sport or fashion.

3 Pair weaker students with stronger ones. Read the question with the class and elicit the meaning of *vlogger*. Elicit the type of information required for (1) (a job). Point to the margin on the same line as the first question and encourage students to write *a job* in the margin. This will help them remember what they are listening for as they listen. Allow students three minutes to complete the task. Monitor and encourage students to make notes in the margin as they make their decisions. Elicit the answers from the class.

Suggested answers
1 job **2** person – friend or family **3** something that is not expensive **4** a number **5** adjective related to videos **6** something you find in videos **7** something you buy when staying in a hotel **8** a feeling (adjective) **9** a superlative adjective **10** a noun form of a personal quality

Exam info

Read the information with the students. Tell them that the correct word(s) for the gaps will not need to be changed in any way and remind them to look at the language before and after the gap to ensure their answer fits grammatically. Reassure students that they will hear the answers for the gaps in the same order as the questions.

4 Play the recording twice. Students work individually. Elicit answers, or alternatively, ask students to turn to page 216 and check their answers using the audioscript.

Answers
1 travel assistant **2** friend **3** cost of living **4** a/one million (1,000,000) **5** messy **6** tips **7** food **8** nervous **9** most memorable **10** motivation

Track 5

Scott: Hi everyone. My name's Scott Kirkland. I've gone from being stuck in a boring office job to something far more fulfilling: travelling the world and making video blogs for a living. I'm here today to tell you how I did it.

When I look back to how it all began, I still can't quite believe it. I left school at eighteen and got a job as a waiter before becoming a travel assistant for a local sales company. As I sat there, sending countless emails to the sales team, watching the minutes and hours slowly tick away, I knew it was time for something much more rewarding.

I'd always had a strong desire to go travelling, so I set about researching the best places online, as well as convincing my mum and dad that it was a good use of my savings. After hearing from a friend of mine about how great South East Asia was, I settled on Thailand. I had a cousin out there, too, who I arranged to meet as soon as I arrived to show me the ropes. The country had absolutely everything for a first-time traveller: wonderful food, affordable flights and, above all, a low cost of living.

Making videos had always been a hobby of mine and, during the first few months, I began filming all of my adventures and putting them up on my blog three times a week. The very first one I uploaded was only viewed fifty times and not the one million I'd foolishly thought, and hoped, that it would.

Nevertheless, I really enjoyed making them and persevered with developing something a bit more structured. I created a mini-series, entitled 'Travelling for beginners' – this gave the videos more of a purpose and transformed them from being just a messy collection of videos into a more informative, meaningful channel.

After about three months of creating content, the videos started to gain in popularity. Even though they needed some work in terms of editing, not to mention the production quality, people really valued the tips I was passing on. This then led to bigger and better things. I was approached by a travel company to review one of their hotel resorts, Grand Paradise. In addition to a small reviewer fee, my accommodation would be paid for as part of the deal and I thought they might even cover the food, but that ended up coming out of my own pocket. They did fund all of my travel costs while I was there, though, so that was a bonus.

From there on, everything just took off and my videos were racking up tens of thousands of hits. It wasn't long before sponsors came knocking at my door, offering much more money than I'd been making from my review videos. I remember one particular firm offering $2,000 to wear their T-shirts in my videos. Initially, it made me far more nervous than excited. I wasn't sure how my fans would react to the blatant advertising of corporate products.

There have been lots of stand-out moments during my time as a travel vlogger, often involving eating amazing food and meeting interesting people. The most memorable, though, was when I was invited to speak at an annual travel conference in New York. My talk was attended by more than three thousand people, all of whom followed my blog. After all the views, likes and shares I'd had over the years, meeting my fans in person and signing autographs put what I'd achieved into context.

People often ask me what the secret to my success has been. They often assume that I must have been extremely lucky to turn my hobby into a lucrative career. I understand where they're coming from, but it's more about believing in yourself. Motivation is key, and that is what's got me to where I am today. Be prepared to work much harder than you've ever done before, but, most importantly, don't forget to have fun!

So, are there any questions?

Extension activity

Ask students to turn to the audioscript on page 216 and highlight phrases they think might be useful in Speaking Part 2, e.g. *a strong desire to do something, to settle on something, from there on …* Encourage students to highlight phrases which are generally useful and not too specific, e.g. *everything just took off* would only be useful if the topic was related to personal success.

5 Elicit one or two ideas from the class. If students are not interested in travel vlogging, ask them for their own vlogging ideas.

6 Put students into groups and read the instructions. Write *challenges of learning English* on the board and elicit an idea from each group. Say: *Think about which of these challenges your vlog will address. Use it (or them) to help you decide the aim of your vlog.* Elicit ideas for content (interview, PowerPoint presentation, discussion, etc.). Ask students where the videos will be set (at home, school or somewhere else). For equipment, students could either use what they already have, e.g. a smartphone, or suggest a budget they could spend on new equipment. Elicit the meaning of *sponsor* (money given by a company to support a person, organisation or activity), plus other ideas for making money, e.g. advertising. Allow 20 minutes for the planning stage.

7 If students do not feel confident presenting to the whole class, split the class in half and have two groups presenting at the same time. It will be noisier, but this will encourage students to speak more loudly and with more confidence. Monitor and make notes of constructive feedback points to give the students and encourage them to think about how they could improve their explanations.

Extension activity

Students use smartphones or a video camera to create a five-minute vlog about a topic they are interested in. Encourage students to focus on how to do something well, e.g. tips for getting to the next level of a specific computer game; the best way to make chocolate cake and why it is the best. Alternatively, students could focus on English language, e.g. explaining a grammar point from this unit or Unit 1; tips on pronunciation. If your students do not have access to a recording device, they can simply prepare a short talk and present it to their classmates.

Grammar SB page 19

Making comparisons

▶ **Page 163 Grammar reference**

Lead in

Put students into A and B pairs to review comparative and superlative forms. Students A close their books and Students B turn to page 163 (Grammar reference, making comparisons). Tell Students B they must say an adjective from the list to their partner, who must give them the comparative and/or superlative form of the adjective, e.g. B: *Tell me the comparative for **high**.* A: *It's **higher** and the superlative is **highest**.* After four adjectives, students swap and Student A tests Student B. Tell students you do not expect them to get them all correct. Listen for common errors which can be corrected, if necessary, after students have completed Exercise 2.

1 Students answer the questions individually and then compare their answers with a partner. Tell students to say the sentences out loud as the correct answer may be easier to identify aurally. After they have listened and checked their answers, ask students which questions they did not get correct. Make a note of common problem areas.

Answers
1 far more **2** much more **3** best **4** bit more
5 bigger; better **6** much **7** most **8** much harder; most

Track 6

1 I've gone from being stuck in a boring office job to something far more fulfilling: travelling the world and making video blogs for a living.
2 I knew it was time for something much more rewarding.
3 I'd always had a strong desire to go travelling, so I set about researching the best places online.
4 Nevertheless, I really enjoyed making them and persevered with developing something a bit more structured.
5 This then led to bigger and better things.
6 It wasn't long before sponsors came knocking at my door, offering much more money than I'd been making from my review videos.
7 The most memorable, though, was when I was invited to speak at an annual travel conference in New York.
8 Be prepared to work much harder than you've ever done before, but, most importantly, don't forget to have fun!

2 Students work on their own and then compare their answers, with a partner. Elicit the answers. Ask students to put an asterisk (*) next to the errors they typically make. Suggest they refer to these errors when they are reviewing their own writing exam practice tasks. Elicit the errors in whole-class feedback. Elicit corrections and review the relevant rules. Refer to the Grammar reference on page 163 for detailed explanations and additional practice.

Answers
1 ~~the healthier~~ the healthiest **2** ~~more cheaper~~ cheaper
3 ~~that~~ than **4** ~~more hardly~~ harder **5** ~~as often than~~ as often as
6 ~~the more risky~~ the riskiest / the most risky **7** ~~the less interesting~~ the least interesting / less interesting **8** ~~more good~~ better

3 Students work individually. Monitor and help individual students who are struggling. Elicit answers and corrections for any common errors noticed when monitoring.

Answers
1 more focused **2** lazier **3** as popular **4** better

4 Encourage students to justify their answers. If they need support with this, provide a model, e.g. *I disagree that teenagers are more focused on becoming online celebrities. Take me, for example: whilst I'm interested in reading about celebrities, I've no desire to become one because …*

Fast finishers

Students write two or three sentences about a classmate using comparative language. Another student has to guess which classmate is being described, e.g. A: *this student is the cleverest student in class. He or she works harder, and is usually much more focused on doing their homework than the rest of us. Who is it?* B: *I think that's Jacob.*

Extension activity

Divide the class into groups of five or six. One person from each group is a photographer and the others are students who want a group photograph taken. Ask the photographers to arrange their group of students ready for the photograph to be taken. Encourage them to think about height, hair colour, clothing, etc. when making their decisions. Tell the photographer to make comparisons between the students in their group when they are putting them into position, e.g. *The most interesting thing about this group is that everyone is wearing black, so I think I am going to ask you as the tallest student, Bella, to stand on the far right and Miranda, as the shortest, can you go on the far left? OK, so that arrangement looks a bit more structured than it did before …*

Reading and Use of English Part 5 SB page 20

Lead in

Write on the board *turtle, bobcat, snow leopard, kingfisher* and *grizzly bear*. Look at the photos with the students and ask them to use the clues in the photos to help them guess the animals they are not sure about, e.g. Student A: *I think the top photograph is the snow leopard, as it is the only picture which has snow in it.*

Student B: *I agree. I have no idea what a kingfisher is but I can see the word fish in its name, so I think it must the bird which is carrying a fish in its beak.* Ask students if they have ever seen any of these animals, or which they would like to see if they had the chance.

1 Students work in pairs. Ask them to give reasons for their choices and encourage them to make comparisons. For example, the kingfisher would be one of the most challenging to photograph because of the speed at which it flies. On the other hand, the grizzly bear would be the easiest as, whilst it is dangerous, it is slower and bigger than the others. Monitor and make notes of errors students make with comparative language. Elicit whole-class feedback and correct the errors you heard during the speaking activity.

Background information

Snow leopards, as their name suggests, are adapted to living in cold environments. With fur that can be five cms long on their back and sides and up to 12 cms long on their stomachs, they are well-protected from the cold. Snow leopards live at high altitudes, often around 4,000 metres, and have short front legs to help them move around on rocks and steep cliffs. Snow leopards can't roar like other big cats; instead they have what can be described as a 'yowl'. However, their yowl is very loud.

2 Put students into A and B pairs. Ask A to scan the article and underline animals which are included in the photos and B to underline the places where these animals were photographed (grizzly bears: Rocky Mountains, bobcats: Yosemite Park, snow leopards: Himalayas). You could also ask students to find the two animals which are not included in the photos (wolves, deer). Remind students to read quickly, ignoring unknown vocabulary for now, and set a time limit of two minutes. Ask students to compare their answers in pairs, then elicit them during whole-class feedback.

Answers

Animals mentioned in the article are:

1 grizzly bear – Dennis won a competition for a photograph he took of one. (Paragraph 1)

2 bobcats – Dennis failed to get a photograph of them because he forgot to take a camera that could take photos at night. (Paragraph 3)

3 snow leopard – Dennis visited the Himalayas to photograph them. He found them challenging to photograph because of the high altitude and freezing temperatures. They are known as 'the ghost of the mountains'. He enjoyed being close to them when he finally spotted one. (Paragraph 4)

Exam info

Read the information with the students and remind them that this part tests their detailed understanding of a text. Write on the board: *opinion, attitude, purpose, main idea, detail, tone, implication, gist* and ask students which might be tested (any of them might be tested). Check students' understanding of what these terms refer to, paying particular attention to *tone*, *implication* and *gist*. (*tone*: the authors use of words to convey their own or a character's attitude, e.g. *It was a terrible excuse*, where *terrible* indicates their negative opinion of the excuse; *implication*: the meaning is not stated directly but can be inferred from clues given in the text; *gist*: the general meaning or purpose of a text). Finally, point out the importance of understanding reference words like pronouns which help students to understand the links between sentences. Get students into the habit of reading through the text before looking at the options. This is because three of the four options are incorrect, so there is little value in reading them carefully beforehand.

3 Tell students to focus on the question stem, not the multiple-choice options (see advice above). Weaker students can work in pairs. Elicit the answers in whole-class feedback.

Answers

Suggested underlining

1 learn about Dennis, first paragraph **2** first became a professional photographer **3** compare; time in mountains; to; walk in the park **4** After; Himalayas for a while **5** they, line 67 **6** biggest disadvantage of his job

4 Ask students what is meant by *word spotting* (assuming an option is correct because the text contains the same word). For example, question 1 option A includes the word *climbing* and *where he learned how to climb* is in the first sentence of the text; however, as he could climb **before** he became a wildlife photographer, A is not the correct answer. Tell students they must focus on meaning and make sure the whole sentence matches what is written in the text. For weaker students, elicit the answer to the first question before asking students to work on their own or in pairs.

Answers

1 B **2** B **3** D **4** B **5** A **6** C

Extension activity

Students read the text again and decide why the incorrect options are incorrect. A second example for question 1 is option C, which includes *competition, prize* and *North America*. The text says *first prize* (line 7) and *North America* (line 9); however, C is incorrect because the photograph which **won first prize** was **taken** in North America. The text does not say what the prize actually was.

5 Set a time limit of 20 minutes. Encourage students to recycle language from the unit so far, particularly comparisons, e.g. ***By far the most** challenging thing about taking this photograph was … I've always thought this was the **most amazing** animal because … Beforehand I felt **considerably nervous** about …*

Vocabulary SB page 20

Phrasal verbs and expressions

Lead in

On slips of paper write down five to ten phrasal verbs you often use in class, e.g. *stand up, sit down, write down.* Cut the paper in half so that you have a verb on one slip and the particle on another. Mix them up. Hand them to the students who have to mingle and match the verb with its correct particle. Set a time limit of two minutes.

1 Tell students to cover the definitions while they attempt to work out the meaning. Remind them to read the whole sentence as this will help them to understand the context.

Answers
1 g **2** d **3** j **4** e **5** h **6** b **7** i **8** a **9** c **10** f

2 Students work individually and then compare their answers in pairs. Remind students that some phrasal verbs are separable, and some are not, e.g. *I threw myself into my studies,* not *I threw into my studies myself. I ended up going to the cinema* not *I ended going up to the cinema.*

Answers
1 threw themselves into **2** end up **3** come up against **4** came along **5** run out of **6** count on **7** go on **8** big break **9** comes across **10** tick all the boxes

3 Monitor correct and incorrect use of the target language and elicit the correct examples in whole-class feedback. Alternatively, students can work in small groups.

Grammar SB page 22

Adjectives with *-ed* and *-ing*

▶ **Page 164 Grammar reference**

Lead in

Write *My brother is annoying …* and *My brother is annoyed …* on the board. Put students in pairs and ask them to discuss briefly the difference between the two sentences. Set a time limit of one minute. Elicit the answer (my brother is an annoying person / my brother feels annoyed with someone, by something or because something happened), followed by possible endings for each sentence (*My brother is annoying when he borrows my new trainers without asking. / My brother is annoyed because he left his mobile phone on the bus.*)

1 Remind students that an adjective used to describe the characteristic of a person, place or thing ends in *-ing* and one which describes a feeling or emotion ends in *-ed*. If students find this difficult, tell them to locate the noun in the sentence which the adjective is describing. For example, in the first sentence, the noun is *he* (Dennis) so the answer is 1 *how Dennis felt.* In the second sentence, the noun is *difficulties* (spending a long time at high altitude and in freezing temperatures) so the answer is 2 *what made him feel like that.*

Answers
1 fascinated **2** challenging, frustrating

2 Again, tell students to locate the noun (person, place or thing) which the adjective is describing. For example, in sentence 1, the noun (place) is *it* (Disneyland) so, as the adjective is describing the characteristic of Disneyland, the answer is *entertaining.* In 2, the noun (thing) is *it* (friends arriving late) so the answer is *irritating*. This will help struggling students to focus on whether the adjective is describing feelings or characteristics. Point out that these are common errors made in the exam. Students work in pairs. Elicit answers.

Answers
1 entertaining **2** irritating **3** bored **4** annoying **5** embarrassing **6** excited

Fast finishers

Students rewrite the sentences in Exercise 2 using the alternative form of the adjective, e.g. 1: ***We** were more **entertained** than our kids when we went to Disneyland.* 2: ***I** get really **irritated** when my friends arrive late for a film.* This activity will help with Exercise 3, so the whole class can do it, if required.

3 Answer the first question with the students. Elicit the person, place or thing the adjective is describing (*Pietro's dancing*), then elicit the correct answer (*astonishing*). Point out that for question 1 it is *Pietro's dancing* that the adjective is describing, and not how Pietro feels. Students work individually and then compare their answers with a partner.

Answers
1 astonishing **2** puzzled **3** motivating **4** worried **5** amusing **6** exhausted

4 Students answer the questions in pairs, one asking the questions as the examiner and the other answering as the candidate, before swapping roles. Listen for common errors but do not interrupt. After two minutes, stop the students, write the errors on the board and elicit corrections. Refer students to Grammar reference page 164 if additional support is required.

5 Before listening, ask students to read the options (a–g) and, in pairs, think of one or two adjectives which could be used to describe each experience. Elicit ideas from the class and write these on the board as complete sentences, e.g. *Riding a motorbike was frightening. I was frightened when I rode a motorbike.* After listening, ask students to turn to the audioscript on page 217 to check their answers.

Answer
g

Track 7

Young woman: The whole experience was amazing, actually. I mean, I'd been working really hard, studying, so I was feeling pretty tired and nervous already. So when my boyfriend suggested I went along with him, I was, like, shocked – like 'No way!' – I mean the thought of breaking a bone or something even worse just before an exam was terrifying. But you know, he just kept on at me, so for the sake of a bit of peace, in the end I said yes. When we were up there in the sky, I was just so scared I can't tell you. I just wanted to get out of the plane. I felt trapped, but the only way to do that was to jump. And in fact, the jump itself was really thrilling. I'd love to do it again. And I didn't break a thing!

6 This exercise helps students understand why the other options in Exercise 5 were incorrect. Remind them that in the exam, listening for words (word matching) in the audioscript and matching them with the same words they have seen in the question may make them choose the incorrect answer.

Answers
2 tired, nervous **3** shocked **4** terrifying
5 scared, trapped **6** thrilling

Extension activity
Students underline phrases or words in the audioscript on page 217 which may have made them choose the incorrect answer. For example, *breaking a bone* in the audioscript word matches with d in the options, *before an exam* in the audioscript word matches with c in the options.

7 Students discuss in pairs, or small groups if preferred. Set a time limit of five minutes. Select one student from each pair or group to summarise the discussion. Correct errors during whole-class feedback.

Extension activity
Students write two paragraphs describing a recent experience. They must make at least three comparisons, e.g. comparing the experience to a different one, and use at least six adjectives (three *-ed* and three *-ing*). Allow students to refer to the Grammar reference (pages 163 and 164) and tell them to focus on grammatical accuracy. Allow 15–20 minutes.

Reading and Use of English Part 4 SB page 23

Exam info

Read the information with the students. Elicit why they shouldn't alter the key word (in capitals), for example by changing the form of the word (because they would not be awarded the marks). Ask why they should pay attention to any verbs in the final part of the second sentence (this often indicates the need for a plural or singular noun in the answer). Finally, point out that any contractions in their answer, e.g. *don't*, count as two words (do not). *Can't* (cannot) is one word.

1 Look at the example (0) with the students. Elicit that the two activities (sailing, swimming) are being compared, so this question is testing the ability to make comparisons between two things, using the word MORE. Point out that for practice purposes, this exercise is testing comparisons and adjective structures only, while the exam tests a range of language forms. Weaker students can work in pairs. Students check their answers using the Grammar reference (pages 163 and 164) before whole-class feedback.

Answers
1 the laziest person in **2** as good at cooking **3** one of the hardest **4** not as interested in **5** less beneficial than **6** such a strange

Speaking Part 2 SB page 24

▶ **Page 206 Speaking bank**

Lead in
Students write down their top three free-time activities, e.g. playing football, reading, playing computer games. They mingle and find classmates who have the same free-time activities as them. The aim is to find classmates with the most matches.

Exam info

Read the information with the students. Point out that they should talk about both the similarities and differences between the photos before answering the direct question. Tell them to pay careful attention to the instructions which follow the words *and say* and remind them they will not lose marks by asking the examiner to repeat the instructions.

1 Elicit the instruction (after *and say*) and remind students it will also be written above the photograph. Next, students work on their own and write four sentences – two comparing the similarities and two comparing the differences. Preparing sentences helps with grammatical accuracy and is useful at this stage; however, you should point out that this is for practice only as in the exam, students will not be given additional time to make notes. Refer students to the Grammar reference on page 163 for language ideas. Once students have prepared their sentences, they should tell their partner what they have written. Encourage students to speak for one minute each, adding more comparisons when speaking if they need to.

2 As this activity could generate a lot of writing, allow students to underline the relevant parts of the audioscript on page 217 instead of making notes, if they wish.

> **Suggested answers**
> Playing video games: they're laughing, which helps them relax; having fun together, which helps develop their friendship; breaks down social boundaries and gender stereotypes
> Canoeing in a river: doing a sport that uses up more energy and helps them get fit; talk about their problems, relax and enjoy their friendship.

Track 8

Examiner: In this part of the test, I'm going to give each of you two photographs. I'd like you to talk about your photographs on your own for about a minute, and also to answer a short question about your partner's photographs. Marta, it's your turn first. Here are your photographs. They show people doing different activities in their free time. I'd like you to compare the photographs, and say how you think the people can benefit from spending their free time doing these different activities. All right?

Marta: Well, in the first photo, there are two women playing video games in their home together. They don't seem to be taking the game too seriously and they seem to be enjoying themselves. I think they benefit from this in several ways. Firstly, they're laughing, which is always good for you because it helps you to relax. At the same time, they're having fun together, which is important because it builds up their social relationship and their friendship. Also, it's good to see these women doing something which is traditionally seen as a male activity, because I think it helps break down social boundaries and gender stereotypes.
In the second photo, there is a man and a woman canoeing in a river. They are more active than the people in the first photo because they're doing a type of sport and using up more energy and getting fitter. I think they also benefit because it looks like they are just doing it as a leisure activity rather than a race, and so they can perhaps talk about their problems, relax and also enjoy their friendship. Mm, all in all, I think they get a lot from—

Examiner: Thank you.

Marta: —from both activities.

3 Ask students who used the audioscript in Exercise 2 not to refer to it for this exercise. Students work individually and compare their answers with a partner. Elicit the answers and refer to the audioscript to review why Marta includes or excludes the checklist items for this part of the Speaking exam.

> **Answers**
> Yes: **3, 4, 5, 7** No: **1, 2, 6**

4 Students work in pairs to complete the sentences with a suitable phrase, then listen again to check their answers.

> **Answers**
> **1** Well, in the first photo **2** I think they benefit from **3** Firstly **4** At the same time **5** Also **6** I think they also benefit because

5 Students work in pairs to complete the exercise.

> **Answers**
> **a** 1 **b** 2 **c** 3, 4, 5

6 Weaker students can work in pairs. Elicit the answers and point out that in natural English we typically say *What's more* rather than *What is more*. Students may be unfamiliar with *besides*, so provide an example if necessary, e.g. *Do you play any other sports besides football?* or *There's plenty to do here besides visiting museums.*

> **Answers**
> **a/b** First of all, To start with
> **c** Besides, In addition, What is more

Extension activity
Students decide which phrase(s) from Exercise 6 could be used in Writing Part 1 essay. (Yes: *In addition, First of all*, No: *to start with, what's more* and *besides* are more typical in spoken English.)

/P/ Pronunciation: sentence stress (1)

7 Tell students to close their books. Read the introduction to the students and elicit the meaning of *stress* (saying a word loudly and strongly). Tell students you are going to say a sentence twice. The first time, students listen. The second, they must clap when you stress a word. You can exaggerate this for the purposes of the exercise. Read out the first sentence in Exercise 7.1.

7.1 In pairs, student take turns to say the sentences and underline the stressed words. Elicit the answers in whole-class feedback after listening.

> **Answers**
> See underlining in the recording script below.

Track 9

1 Firstly, they're getting some exercise, which is always good for you.

2 It's great for your health and helps you to relax.

3 At the same time, they're having fun together.

4 which is important because it builds up their social relationships and their friendships.

5 Also, it's good to see boys and girls doing a bit of sport together instead of separately.

6 I think it helps break down social boundaries between boys and girls.

7.2 Alternatively, sit students back-to-back (so they are facing away from each other). Student A says a sentence and Student B claps when they hear a stressed word. Students swap after three sentences.

8 Monitor and write down examples of use of the target language from Exercise 4, including any errors. During feedback, write the examples on the board and elicit error correction. If students have struggled with accuracy, you may wish to repeat the activity.

9 One student takes the role of the examiner and reads the instructions, while the other responds as the candidate. Students swap roles after one minute. Monitor and write down examples of correct and incorrect language use, with focus on comparisons, adjectives and phrasal verbs from the unit. Review this in whole-class feedback.

Writing Part 2 (an article) SB page 26

▶ **Page 196 Writing bank**

Lead in
Write on the board *free-time activities*. Elicit up to ten free-time activities from the class and write them on the board (canoeing, snooker, cooking, etc.). Then elicit useful vocabulary connected with these activities (paddle, cue, frying pan, etc.). Students work in small groups and discuss which they enjoy, don't enjoy or would/wouldn't like to try and why.

Read the information with the students and remind them that, where possible, they should choose a task that relates to their experiences and interests.

Exam info

1 Weaker students can work in pairs. Elicit the answers from the whole class including one or two free-time activities they could include (basketball, football, swimming, etc.)

Answers
Suggested underlining
international magazine, leisure-time activity, How did you get started?, Why do you enjoy it so much?

2 Ask students to work with someone they do not normally work with. If students are unsure, allow them two minutes to write down a few ideas in note form before speaking, e.g. *football – used to play with Dad in the garden … fun spending time together.* Encourage students to speak for at least one minute each.

3 Ask how many ideas should be included in a paragraph (one). Students work individually and then compare their answers with a partner. If students find this difficult, you could write the first paragraph on the board and underline the first sentence. Elicit the main idea (how the writer became interested). Point to the second sentence and ask *When did the writer become interested?* (when he/she was staying with his/her aunt). Next, point to the third sentence and ask *What did the aunt do?* (taught the writer how to make simple dishes). Elicit that in sentences two and three, the writer gives additional information to support the main idea in the first sentence. Weaker students work in pairs. Elicit the correct answers from stronger students.

Answers
1
Para. 1: I first got interested … simple dishes at first
Para. 2: I found I really enjoyed cooking … usually ate the food quite happily Para. 3: When I went back to school … enjoying a meal I've cooked Para. 4: I'd recommend … that anyone can do.

Suggested answers
2
Para. 1: how I started Para. 2: how I progressed
Para. 3: why I enjoy it Para. 4: why I'd recommend it

4 Remind students that a sentence must contain a verb and typically includes a subject and a verb phrase. For example, in question 3 students may write, *When friends come to my house, I often cook them something …* They have seen friends and assumed it is the subject of the sentence. If this happens, ask *Where is the subject in the first sentence?* To further explain re-word: *I often cook for my friends when they come to my house.* In this example, it is clear the subject of the sentence is I.

Suggested answers
1 I found I really enjoyed cooking. I was soon doing things which were more complicated.
2 My younger brother and sister complained about some of my dishes. They usually ate the food quite happily.
3 When friends come round to my house, I often cook them something. I find it really satisfying and relaxing.
4 I'd recommend it as a hobby. For me, it's one of the most creative and useful free-time activities that anyone can do.
5 When I went back to school after the summer, I decided to do cookery lessons. Now I think I'm quite a competent cook.

5 Students work individually. Set a time limit of three minutes. Elicit the correct answers in whole-class feedback.

Suggested answers
2 I got interested in flying when I was about 14 and my father took me to an airshow. **3** My parents don't want me to fly because they think it is / it's dangerous. **4** One of my friends is learning to fly and he's asked me to come with him because he thinks I'd like it.

6 Students work individually and then compare their answers in pairs. Elicit the correct answers in whole-class feedback.

Suggested answers
2 I was staying with my aunt. My aunt is a keen cook. **3** I was soon doing things. They / The things were more complicated. **4** I went back to school after the summer. I decided to do cookery lessons. **5** Friends come round to my house. I often cook my friends / them something. **6** For me, cooking is one of the most creative and useful free-time activities. Anyone can cook / do it.

7 Students work individually and then compare their answers in pairs. For additional challenge, ask students to personalise the statements so they are true for them, e.g. *I was x when I started x. My x, who's a keen x, encouraged me …*

Suggested answers
1 I was 17 when I started running seriously. / I started running seriously when I was 17. **2** My aunt, who is a keen athlete, encouraged me. **3** I go running most days when I've finished work. **4** Running is a sport which/that gets you really fit.

8 For additional speaking practice, students work in pairs and turn each statement into a question about an activity of their choice. Then they take it in turns to interview each other, e.g. A: *How old were you when you started (playing rugby)?* B: *Well, I was around 12 when I started. I remember because I was in England at the time.* A: *Who encouraged you to play?* B: *One of my English mates Robbie, who is a fantastic player, suggested I start …*

Suggested answers
1 I started windsurfing when I was 19 and I was staying with friends by the sea. **2** One of my friends, who is a keen windsurfer, encouraged me to start windsurfing because she thought I would enjoy it. **3** I kept falling into the sea to start with because it was a fairly windy day and there were a lot of waves. **4** I didn't enjoy it at first because I had to concentrate quite hard, but I carried on trying. **5** I started to windsurf quite fast, which was exciting, and I found it quite enjoyable.

9 Students work individually and then compare their answers in pairs. Tell students to look back at the article on page 26 and that they should focus on the second half of the article. During whole-class feedback, elicit the answer and discuss any problem areas. For example, students may think *competent* refers to the writer's feelings because they do not know its meaning (the ability to do something well.)

Answers
1 satisfying, relaxing, fascinating, wonderful
2 creative, useful **3** competent

10 Put students in small groups or pairs. Ask them to tell each other what the adjectives mean (they can guess if they are unsure). Then change groups and repeat. Elicit the meaning of the adjectives in whole-class feedback and concept-check as necessary. Once students have categorised the adjectives, ask them to decide if they are generally positive or negative.

Answers
Describes a person's opinion about an activity: astonishing, delightful, demanding, depressing, dreadful, entertaining, exhausting, incredible, irritating, superb, tremendous, unbelievable
Describes a fact about an activity: competitive, economical, popular, time-consuming

11 Students can work individually or pair stronger and weaker students together if you think some of your students may struggle. Refer them to Exercise 3 if they need help planning the paragraphs and main ideas. Encourage students to write about a free-time activity that they are familiar with, perhaps one they discussed in Exercise 2. Remind students they must answer both bullet points in the task from Exercise 1. If students are struggling to create a title, tell them they can write this at the end and that it only needs to be three to five words in length.

12 Remind students they must write between 140 and 190 words, that they should write in paragraphs and that each paragraph should contain one main idea. As this is an exam task, set a time limit of forty-five minutes.

Extension activity
Students read the articles they wrote in Exercise 12 and underline examples of language from the unit, e.g. adjectives used to express feelings and activities, including *-ed* and *-ing* endings, comparative language and complex sentences. They check grammatical accuracy in pairs, using the Grammar reference section if they wish. Then students choose one paragraph that could be improved to include more accurate language from the unit, or a greater variety of it, and rewrite the paragraph. At this point, you may also wish to explore how students felt about the time limit. For example, were they able to finish their writing? In what ways did their plan help them and how could they improve their plan next time?

Vocabulary

Expressions and phrasal verbs

big break
come across
come along
come up against
count on
end up
go on
run out of
tick all the boxes
throw yourself into

Adjectives with *-ed* and *-ing*

amusing
astonishing
demanding
depressing
entertaining
exhausted
fascinating
irritating
motivating
puzzled
relaxing
satisfying
thrilling
time-consuming
worried

Other adjectives

competent
competitive
creative
delightful
dreadful
incredible
popular
scared
superb
trapped
tremendous
unbelievable
useful
wonderful

Vocabulary activity 1

Students must think of a free-time activity and describe it using at least four adjectives. A partner has to guess what the free-time activity is, e.g. Student A: *It's very popular to watch; it's exhausting to play; it's thrilling if your team are winning and dreadful if they are losing.* Student B: *Are you thinking of football?* Student B: *I almost didn't do it because I was worried something would go wrong. But as I was doing, it I felt excited. A lot of people are too scared to try it. It's not relaxing but it is thrilling and a little bit dangerous.* (skydiving)

Vocabulary activity 2

This is a whole-class activity. Students are divided into two teams. One person from each team (the player) comes to the front of the class and sits with their back to the board. Tell the players they are not allowed to look at the board. Write one word on the board from the vocabulary list. The team members must describe the word without saying it (encourage them not to use synonyms either – see example below). The players must guess what it is, using the clues given, and say the word out loud. A point is given to the first player to say the correct word. A point is deducted if the team 'accidently' say the word written on the board. For example, if you have written *useful* on the board, the team members may say: *It's an adjective. It has two syllables. You could use it to describe an umbrella in rainy weather.*

DIGITAL CLASSROOM

Practice Extra Unit 2

Test Generator Unit 2 test

Test and Train Exam Practice

Vocabulary and grammar review Unit 1

Answers

1
1 turned up 2 to hang out with / hanging out with 3 turn into
4 count on 5 making up 6 carrying on

2
1 bossy 2 bad-tempered 3 hard-working 4 unreliable
5 anxious 6 sensitive 7 mature 8 concerned/anxious

3
1 do 2 make 3 do 4 doing 5 do 6 made 7 made
8 making

4
1 won 2 have/'ve arrived; have/'ve been expecting 3 have/'ve spent; has/'s turned up 4 have/'ve been having / have had; has/'s been telling / has/'s told; hasn't told; has/'s seen 5 has/'s lost / has/'s been losing; has/'s been getting 6 has/'s finished; have/'ve been waiting 7 has/'s eaten; hasn't left 8 has/'s been looking; has/'s been studying

Vocabulary and grammar review Unit 2

Answers

1
1 throws himself into 2 ticks all the (right) boxes 3 ended up
4 count on 5 big break 6 came across 7 came up against
8 ran out of 9 came along 10 go on

2
(Suggested answers)
1 Katya took up karate when she was seven years old because she was interested in it.
2 Her father, who is a professional karate instructor, taught her, so she progressed quickly.
3 She did karate with other children who were the same age as her, but none of them was as good as her, so she felt dissatisfied.
4 Last year, she participated in the national championship, but she did not win because she was injured during one of the matches.
5 She hopes to become a professional karate instructor and work in the same sports centre as her father because he has too many students.
6 Some of her father's students have been studying karate for several years, and her father thinks they would benefit from a different teacher because they are too familiar with his style of karate.

3
1 motorbike made more noise than 2 are not as/so dangerous
3 is the best player 4 as stressed as 5 much more clearly than
6 more comfortable than any of

4
1 amazing 2 exhausting 3 puzzling 4 disappointed
5 motivated 6 astonished

3 Happy holidays?

Unit objectives

Topic: holidays

Reading and Use of English Part 3 (word formation): forming adjectives and adverbs with affixes

Reading and Use of English Part 7 (multiple matching): reading for specific information, detail and opinion

Writing Part 2: structuring a report

Listening Part 3 (multiple matching): listening for the general idea being expressed, details, attitudes, opinions or purpose

Speaking Part 3 (collaborative task): phrases to involve partners in a discussion; strategies for dealing with the second section of Part 3

Pronunciation: intonation (1); indicating that you have finished or have more to say

Vocabulary: *travel, journey, trip* and *way*; forming adjectives and adverbs with suffixes

Grammar: past simple, past continuous and *used to*; *at, in* and *on* in time phrases; past perfect simple and continuous

Starting off SB page 30

Lead in
Put students into pairs. Ask them to talk about their most memorable holiday. Students ask each other questions about where they went and what they did.

1 Give students a minute to look at the words and phrases individually before categorising them in pairs. As students work, tell them to make notes, e.g. the difference between *a hostel* (a place where people, especially young adults, can stay cheaply when they are travelling, often sharing a room) and *a hotel*, and elicit examples during whole-class feedback.

Answers
types of holiday: backpacking, a beach holiday, a city break, a cruise, a ski trip, a tour of a country
holiday accommodation: a cabin, couch-surfing, a hostel, a hotel
holiday activities: going sightseeing, meeting new people, relaxing, sunbathing, taking selfies by landmarks, trying local delicacies

Background information
Couchsurfing is the practice of travelling around the world and staying with people you don't know. Typically, hosts advertise available rooms in their homes online.

2 Allow students a minute to look at the questions before putting them into new pairs. Tell students they should justify their answers by giving reasons. As an alternative, and for additional Speaking Part 2 practice, students could choose two photos to compare and contrast as they did in the lead-in activity.

Listening Part 3 SB page 30

Exam info
Read the information with the students. Tell them to use the time given in the exam to read through the questions so they have a clear idea of what they are listening for. As students are allowed to listen twice, point out that they should use the second listening to check any answers they are not sure about.

1 Ask students what the main subject of the listening is (a holiday the speakers have been on). Elicit the answer to B. If students say 'variety of activities', point out that they must also listen for how these activities made the holiday special so special should also be underlined. Allow weaker students to work in pairs.

Answers
Suggested underlining
B variety of activities / special
C better than I'd expected
D wasn't / first time / this type of holiday
E disappointed / trip had to end
F saw everything / wanted
G unable to visit a place / ruined my holiday
H regret choosing / cheapest travel option

2 Although this is an exam task, at this early stage of the course you could allow a weaker class to read the audioscript on page 219 as they listen. This will help them develop the skill of identifying the correct answer as they hear it. During the second listening, tell students to underline the phrases in the audioscript which give them the correct answer, e.g. for Speaker 1 *I felt pretty low when it was all over and I was on my way back … I didn't want it to stop.*

Answers

Speaker 1: E	Speaker 2: F	Speaker 3: D
Speaker 4: A	Speaker 5: C	

Track 10

Narrator: Speaker 1

Male: Last year I had a gap year and went travelling on my own. I had no experience of international travel, so it was an incredible opportunity. I really appreciated the chance to visit all the main European attractions, landmarks and ruins, but the places that stuck with me the most were perhaps those off the beaten track, such as the ice caves in Austria and the Diapontia Islands in Greece – they were great. I felt pretty low when it was all over and I was on my way back, though. I didn't want it to stop. I remember looking through all the photos I'd taken and thinking how lucky I was to have such special memories.

Narrator: Speaker 2

Female: I'd always wanted to visit Iceland for as long as I could remember. I managed to scrape enough money together and booked a cheap hostel just on the outskirts of the capital, Reykjavik. I knew it would be beautiful and it didn't fail to live up to my expectations. Even though I was only there for a few days, I ticked everything off my list, including seeing the Northern Lights, which were breathtaking. The only thing I regret about it, though, was not taking enough pictures of all of the places I'd visited.

Narrator: Speaker 3

Male: Growing up, I was fortunate enough to go on a wide variety of holidays, from ski trips in the winter to beach holidays in the summer. When I was eighteen, my friends and I decided to go skiing in Bulgaria. Given the fact that we were students, we booked the cheapest accommodation we could find, which turned out to be a youth hostel which we shared with fifteen other people. As I'd done a bit of skiing before, I spent the first few days giving my friends lessons. They were much better than I'd expected and by the third day, we were all going down the same slopes together.

Narrator: Speaker 4

Female: Most people choose exotic locations for their honeymoon, but we wanted to keep it simple – and cheap. We hopped on a low-cost flight to Berlin, where we'd first met. Everything looked the same. Or so we thought. One day, we were checking out a café in our old neighbourhood when we started to get a strange feeling that we'd been there before. As it turns out, we were sitting in what was, a few years ago, our local grocery shop! It broke my heart. We had such fond memories of it. It's a shame the shop went out of business, and this spoiled our holiday somewhat.

Narrator: Speaker 5

Male: I was pretty anxious about my last holiday. When I was a kid, my family used to travel to Ireland by ferry and I always dreaded the journey because I used to get terribly seasick, so I was worried it would just be 12 days of that. I needn't have worried in the end. The sea was calm and the cruise ship was so big you didn't feel like you were at sea at all. We sunbathed in the morning, ate a big lunch, went sightseeing in the afternoon and got back at 6 pm every day. Too bad we weren't able to see Malta. We were running behind schedule and they informed us last minute that, in order to catch up, we wouldn't be able to stop.

Extension activity

Using the audioscript on page 219, ask students to underline words and phrases which may have distracted them from choosing the correct answer (word spotting). For example, Speaker 1's line *no* *experience of international travel* is a distractor for statement A *I had a sad experience …*

3 Allow students to use the audioscript on page 219 and encourage them to use the context of the script rather than a dictionary. As students work together, write down a few example statements using *off the beaten track* (e.g. *I prefer going off the beaten track when I'm on holiday, rather than visiting the famous places everyone goes to.*). Elicit example statements so that you can check understanding during whole-class feedback. Point out that *off the beaten **path*** has the same meaning.

Grammar
Past simple, past continuous and *used to*

SB page 31

▶ **Page 165 Grammar reference**

Lead in

Write on the board: *What were you doing at 7 am on Saturday morning?* Elicit answers using the past continuous tense from a couple of students, e.g. *I was taking a shower. / I was eating my breakfast. / I was waiting for a train. / I was sleeping …* Students ask and answer the question in a 'find someone who' activity using different times of the day. The aim is for them to find someone who was doing what they were doing when they were doing it. Monitor and write down common past continuous errors. Elicit corrections during whole-class feedback.

1 Students work individually. Elicit that *used to* is used for repeated actions, habits or situations in the past which are no longer true. Students compare their answers in pairs before listening. During whole-class feedback ask students to write a question that Speaker 2 may be answering, e.g. *How **did you use to** travel to Ireland?* If students make errors with *used to*, review the relevant Grammar reference section on page 165 with the class.

Answers
1 were checking out; started **2** used to travel

Track 11

1 One day, we were checking out a café in our old neighbourhood when we started to get a strange feeling that we'd been there before.

2 When I was a kid, my family used to travel to Ireland by ferry.

2 Weaker students can work in pairs and use the Grammar reference section on page 165 to help them.

Answers
1 was walking **2** used to spend **3** got; jumped; rode
4 used to visit **5** were walking; began **6** used to visit; was

3 Allow students five minutes to make notes before they tell their story in pairs or small groups. Monitor and make notes of errors made with the target language, plus examples of correct language use. Invite one or two stronger students to come to the front of the class and tell their stories.

4 Students work individually and then compare their answers in pairs.

Answers
1 C **2** A **3** B **4** C **5** B **6** D **7** C

5 Students work in pairs. Students often pronounce *-ed* endings incorrectly, so as they do the exercise, encourage them to say the *-ed* words out loud. Listen and check the *-ed* endings are being pronounced correctly with /t/, /d/ or /ɪd/.

Answers
developed, enjoyed, happened, liked, mentioned, occurred, opened, planned, preferred, stopped, studied, travelled (BrE) / traveled (AmE), tried

Vocabulary SB page 32
travel, journey, trip and *way*

Lead in
Write on the board: *How was your journey to school/class today?* and elicit a few answers from the class, e.g. *My journey was terrible. I got stuck in traffic and it took twice as long as it normally does.*

1 Students work individually and then compare their answers in pairs. During whole-class feedback, remind students that *travel* in this example is a noun, but it is also commonly used as a verb. Elicit one or two sentences using *travel* as a verb, e.g. *My mum used to travel to England when she was working as a travel agent.*

Answers
1 trip **2** Way **3** travel **4** journey

2 Encourage students to refer to Exercise 1 if they need a reminder. Weaker students can work in pairs.

Answers
1 trip **2** way **3** trip **4** journey **5** travel **6** journey
7 trip **8** journey **9** way

3 Students work individually or in pairs. Allow them to use a dictionary to help them with unknown vocabulary. As students work, write one or two additional examples, including question forms and *used to* (e.g. *The outward trip was far easier than the homeward one; coming back was a nightmare! I often used to stay overnight in a hotel when I visited the London office; Would you be happy in a job that involved frequently staying away from home on business trips?*). Elicit the answers plus additional examples.

Answers
1 pleasant/safe/successful **2** business **3** outward
4 shopping **5** sightseeing/day **6** overnight

Fast finishers
Students write five sentences using the words and phrases from the box in Exercise 3 so that they are true for them.

4 Students work in pairs to complete the gaps before changing partners to ask and answer the questions.

Answers
1 travel **2** trip **3** way **4** trips

5 Students work in pairs. Alternatively, tell students to compare and contrast the photos as they would in Speaking Part 2 (long turn) and encourage them to try to speak for one minute each. Monitor and write down examples of correct use of this lesson's target vocabulary for review during whole-class feedback.

Extension activity
Individually, students write a Speaking Part 2 direct question prompt – *I'd like you to compare the photographs and say …* – for the photos in Exercise 5 and take turns to answer them, e.g. *… and say where you think the people are going;*
… and say what the people are enjoying about travelling this way;
… and say why the people might not enjoy travelling this way.

Reading and Use of English Part 3 SB page 33

Lead in
Write *forming adjectives* on the board and tell students that adjectives can often be identified by their endings. Remind students that they studied two common endings in Unit 2 and elicit *-ed* and *-ing* (e.g. *excit<u>ed</u>, excit<u>ing</u>*). Tell students you are thinking of eight more endings. Put them in groups and give them three minutes to write down as many endings as they can, plus an example adjective for each. Select students to write examples on the board, e.g. -able/-ible: *understandable, incredible*; -al: *functional*; -ful: *beautiful*; -ive: *attractive*; -ic: *terrific*; -less: *harmless*; -ous: *dangerous*; -ly: *friendly*. Point out that while adverbs often end in *-ly*, some adjectives do too.

1 Put students into small groups and set a time limit of five minutes. Encourage students to guess the adjective if they are not sure, before they check their answers in a dictionary. Prepare some example sentences using all forms of the word, particularly for words you think students might not know, and underline the words directly before the target word. (*We had some adventures (n) when we lived in Egypt.*; *I'm trying to be more adventurous (adj) with my choice of holiday destination.*) During whole-class feedback, check the meaning of any unknown vocabulary, asking a stronger student to give the class an example sentence, or use examples you prepared when students were doing the exercise.

Answers
2 adventurous **3** friendly **4** memorable **5** mysterious **6** risky **7** crowded **8** thrilled/thrilling **9** doubtful/doubtless **10** successful **11** remarkable **12** accessible

2 Read the rubric with the students. Put them into groups of three or four and give each group a large piece of paper. Divide the nouns, allocating three or four nouns to each group. Ask each group to write as many adjectives and adverbs as they can in one minute. When the minute is up, tell the students to pass their paper to another group, who then have a further minute to add more adjectives and adverbs to the list. Collect the students' work and review it as a whole class.

Answers
artist – artistic, artistically; caution – cautious, cautiously; colour – colourful, colourless, colourfully; educate – educational, educated, uneducated; emotion – emotional, emotionally, unemotional, unemotionally; energy – energetic, energetically; mass – massive, massively; predict – predictable, predictably, unpredictable, unpredictably; reason – reasonable, reasonably, unreasonable, unreasonably; respond – responsible, responsibly, irresponsible, irresponsibly; storm – stormy; thought – thoughtful, thoughtless, thoughtfully, thoughtlessly; wealth – wealthy

Exam info

Ask students to read the information. Remind them the word they need might be the negative form, so they should not automatically write a related word they know well. Instead they should read the words before and after the gap carefully before making their decision. Point out that the internal part of the word may also change, e.g. *wide* may become *width*.

3 Before students answer the questions, tell them to read the text quickly, paying attention to the words before and after the gap, and identify the form of the word they need for each. For example, in the example answer (0), the words before and after the gap are *one of the most* and *roads*, which tells the students that an adjective is needed in the gap. Give students two minutes to do this. (1 = noun; 2 = adjective; 3 = verb; 4 = adjective; 5 = noun; 6 = adverb; 7 = adverb; 8 = noun). Next tell them to complete the gap with the correct form of the word. As this is an exam task, set a time limit of ten minutes. Allow students to compare their answers before eliciting in whole-class feedback.

Answers
1 heights **2** uncomfortable **3** discourage **4** alternative **5** motorists **6** undoubtedly/doubtlessly **7** dramatically **8** attraction

Background information
The Yungas Road, one of the world's most dangerous roads, is about 70 km long and links the capital city of Bolivia, La Paz, and the Yungas region. On one side there are towering cliffs, whilst on the other, there is a deep abyss which drops around 600 metres. The surface of the road is often muddy and most of it is no wider than three and a half metres. The road attracts around 25,000 tourists annually and, surprisingly, is still used by some buses and lorries, even though a safer route has been available for some years.

4 Allow students two or three minutes to prepare their arguments before the speaking exercise. You might do this by initially sitting all student As together and student Bs together so they can brainstorm or compare their ideas.

Grammar SB page 34

at, *in* and *on* in time phrases

▶ **Page 166 Grammar reference**

Lead in
Write these questions on the board and tell students to discuss them in small groups:
What did you do at the weekend?
Where do you usually go in the summer holidays?
What will you do on your next birthday?

1 Weaker students can work in pairs. Allow students to check their answers by referring to the Grammar reference on page 166.

Answers
1 in **2** at **3** on

2 Write the sentence for question 1 on the board. Elicit and underline the error then elicit the correction. Students work in pairs and check their answers using the Grammar reference section on page 166, before whole-class feedback.

Answers
1 ~~on July~~ in July **2** ~~In weekends~~ At weekends*, ~~on the afternoon~~ in the afternoon **3** ~~in 9.00~~ at 9.00 a.m. **4** correct **5** ~~at 2019~~ in 2019 **6** correct **7** ~~in certain times~~ at certain times **8** ~~In a typical day~~ On a typical day, ~~at the morning~~ in the morning, ~~at the evening~~ in the evening
*Note: *on the weekends* is correct in American English.

Fast finishers
Practise Exercise 1 on page 166 (Grammar reference).

3 As an alternative to working in pairs, students work in small groups or, if you want more repetition of the target language, students could ask and answer the questions in a mingling activity. If you choose the latter, tell students to have a pen and paper ready so they can write down some of the responses they hear. You may wish to point out that mingling encourages students to speak with peers they are less familiar with, which is something they may need to do in the speaking exam. After five minutes, select students to present the responses they heard to the class, e.g. *Rosa said she likes relaxing in her free time because … while Billy said he …*

Answers
1 in **2** at (BrE)/on (AmE) **3** on **4** In **5** in

Reading and Use of English Part 7 SB page 34

Read the information with the students. Point out that because the reading is quite long (500–600 words), they must practise two reading skills: *skimming* (reading quickly) and *scanning* (finding information in a text).

Exam info

1 Elicit one or two examples before students work in pairs, e.g. accommodation being double-booked; a tour being cancelled by the tour operator.

2 As you elicit the key words, remind students to think about meaning. To check students understand the meaning of each question, ask them to paraphrase the question (say it in another way), e.g. 1: Part of the reason (the person) travelled was to help someone else.

Answers
Suggested underlining
1 partly, sake of someone else **2** in order, have, new experience **3** didn't mind, mistake **4** issues, transport **5** regretted decision, earlier **6** provided assistance, emergency **7** let down, physical abilities **8** expected, do more, activity **9** visited a location, second time **10** technology, unreliable, their location

3 As this is an exam task, tell students to work individually and set a time limit of twelve minutes. As with the other exam tasks, remind students to be aware of word spotting. After twelve minutes, allow students to check their answers with a partner. During whole-class feedback, ask students to tell you why a particular part of the reading text matches with a question.

Answers
1 D **2** A **3** B **4** D **5** C **6** A **7** C **8** B **9** D **10** A

4 Encourage students to justify their answers by giving reasons, and to use comparative forms (Grammar reference pages 163 and 164). Select one or two stronger students to present their ideas to the class.

Extension activity
Tell students to underline phrases from the reading text that would be useful in the speaking part of the exam. Then ask them to say the phrases so that they are true for them. For example, in line 1 of A, students could underline I used to take it easy on holiday and change it to: *When I was younger, I used to take it easy when I went on holiday, for example I'd sit on the beach, but now I prefer something a little more exciting like skiing.*

Grammar SB page 36

Past perfect simple and continuous

▶ **Page 166 Grammar reference**

1 Read the rubric with the students and elicit the grammar tenses (*we saw another couple* = past simple. *The man had sprained his ankle* = past perfect simple.). Elicit one or two additional examples of the students' own examples if they are unsure, or refer them to Grammar reference on page 166.

Answers
1 b
2 past perfect (had sprained)
3 In the first extract, the man sprained his ankle before Sally saw the couple. In the second, Sally saw the man sprain his ankle.

2 As an alternative to using all the texts, give students one text each to look at before getting them to tell a partner the examples they found, e.g. Student A looks at Fiona, Student B looks at Patrick and Student C looks at Tim. As there is only one example in Patrick's text, you may prefer slower, or weaker students to tackle this one. During whole-class feedback, invite students to say which event happened first.

Answers
Fiona – Paris
I'd been learning the language via an app **I'd downloaded** in preparation for the holiday ...
the only time I did order in French I got a strawberry ice cream instead of the raspberry one I thought **I'd ordered**.

Patrick – Mongolia
I'd been planning this trip forever, mainly because I needed some time alone ... At the airport I rented out a battered old jeep that **had done** about 300,000 kilometres.

Tim – Rome
... the very place my wife and I **had been** to on our honeymoon.
... we got to the airport on the way back and found out that our flight **had been cancelled**.
When we got home, **he'd been crying** for so long that he fell asleep straight away.

3 Tell students to find the two activities described (e.g. in 1 they should find *eat lunch* and *were still feeling hungry*) and remind them to think about which activity happened first, using any clues or context given to help them (the clue in 1 is *an hour before*). For weaker students, elicit the answer to the first question before allowing them to work in pairs.

Answers
1 had eaten **2** had never been **3** arrived; had lost
4 had started **5** recognised; had never spoken
6 had damaged

4 Read the rubric with the students and elicit the answers from the class. Elicit from students that the continuous tense focuses on something which happens over a period of time. If students are confused, allow them five minutes to read the Grammar reference (page 167) and encourage them to write one or two of their own examples, e.g. *I'd been studying English for six months before I took my first exam. I'd been playing the piano for a few years before Mum and Dad bought me the piano I wanted.*

Answers
1 b
2
a past perfect simple
b past perfect continuous

5 Students work individually and then compare their answers in pairs or small groups. Monitor and help weaker students. Elicit answers during whole-class feedback.

Answers
1 had been living **2** had been walking **3** had already finished **4** had only been speaking **5** had been walking

6 Tell students that each sentence includes a common error made by an exam candidate. So, when completing the exercise, they should asterisk (*) the questions which include a common error they make themselves. You could elicit why this is helpful (students can use this knowledge to check their written work in the exam).

Answers
1 ~~have done~~ had done **2** ~~forgot~~ had forgotten **3** ~~didn't go~~ hadn't been **4** ~~had bought~~ bought; ~~always wanted~~ had always wanted **5** ~~she just finished~~ she had just finished
6 ~~I have been cleaning~~ I had been cleaning

7 For personalisation, tell students to think about a real holiday they've had. Then tell them to make a list of all the things (activities) they did, but not to worry about the grammar at this stage, e.g. *swim in the sea; sunbathe on the beach, eat sandwiches for lunch, play beach volleyball, eat in an expensive restaurant*. After they have done this, tell them to write paragraphs showing the order of the activities by using the correct tense, e.g. *I remember a fantastic holiday I had in Majorca, Spain. The water was warm and crystal clear. I remember that one day, I'd been swimming in the sea for so long that when I finally got out to sunbathe my brother and sister had eaten all the sandwiches ...*

Extension activity
Students make a list of the things they did last weekend (in any order) and ask and answer questions using the past perfect, past perfect continuous and past simple. For example, Student A writes: *dinner with friends, shopping with Mum, homework, help Dad in garden.* Student B looks at Student A's list and says: *I think you'd had dinner with your friends before you went shopping with your mum. Is that right?* Student A replies, *No, I'd gone shopping with my mum, and bought a lovely new skirt before I had dinner with my friends.*

Speaking Part 3 SB page 37

▶ **Page 209 Speaking bank**

Lead in
With books closed, put students into pairs and tell them to talk about their most and least favourite school trip. Tell them they should give reasons for their answers and speak for one minute.

Exam info
Read the information with the students. Ask: *Are you expected to discuss all the prompts in the time allowed?* (no) *Can you choose the order in which you discuss the prompts?* (yes). Tell students that as the task is opinion based there is no right or wrong answer. However, they must justify their opinions. Point out that they will not be penalised if they fail to reach a decision, as long as they have attempted to negotiate one.

1 Read the examiner's instructions with the students and allow them fifteen seconds to look at the question and options. Point out that in the exam, a list of phrases will not be given as is here. Choose one trip with the students and elicit one or two benefits from them. Make sure they justify their ideas. Set a time limit of two minutes for students to discuss their ideas in pairs. Monitor and write down examples of errors but do not correct until after Exercise 3.

2 As this is a listening rather than a note-taking exercise, allow students to tick the benefits from the box in Exercise 1 that Miguel and Antonia mention.

Answers
A city sightseeing tour: you learn about architecture and history, other cultures and visit somewhere different.
A weekend camping trip in the mountains: you have exciting experiences and adventures, learn to be independent, learn to work together to solve problems, learn teamwork, and it's educational.
A beach activity day: learn something from doing new and different sports and activities.

Track 12

Miguel: Shall we start with this one?
Antonia: OK.
Miguel: How do you think doing a sightseeing tour of a city might be good for students?
Antonia: I think you can learn a lot about architecture and history and things like that.
Miguel: Yes, and you can also visit somewhere very different and learn about other cultures.
Antonia: Right. What about this sort of activity holiday in the mountains? I think it can give young people exciting experiences and adventures – things they don't get in their everyday lives.
Miguel: Yes, and they learn to be more independent because they're away from home and their families, don't you think?
Antonia: I think that's right. Also, they learn to work together to solve problems, so it's good for learning teamwork.
Miguel: That's an important point, because if the school's organising the trip, it should be educational, shouldn't it? I mean, students have got to be learning something. And the beach activity day – what about that?
Antonia: It sounds great, doesn't it? And I think just by doing sports and activities they don't normally do at school, students learn something.
Miguel: I agree.

3 Students work in pairs. Encourage students to say the questions out loud as they work, reminding them that it can sometimes be easier to identify the correct sentence by listening rather than reading. After they have listened, allow students to check their answers using the audioscript on page 220.

Answers
1 Shall; this one **2** think **3** What about **4** don't you
5 about that

/P/ Pronunciation: intonation (1)

4 Read the pronunciation information with the students. As an example, say: *On holiday, I visited the museum and the beach and I went shopping.* Ensure that your intonation rises clearly on *museum* and *beach*, and drops on *shopping*. Point out why your intonation rose on *museum* and *beach* (the list of places you visited was not complete) and dropped on *shopping* (the end of the list).

4.1 Students can practise saying the sentences before they listen and again, after they listen.

Answers
1 good for students
2 architecture, history, things like that
3 different, cultures
4 activity, mountains
5 experiences, adventures, lives

Track 13
See page 38 of Student's Book for audioscript.

4.2 If students are unsure, encourage them to try different intonation patterns to help decide which sound they think is correct for English. Alternatively, demonstrate the correct intonation and ask the students to listen and repeat (drill).

4.3 It can be difficult for teachers and students to identify the stressed words in a sentence. Typically, the content words (the words which have meaning) are stressed, e.g. nouns, verbs, adjectives and adverbs. The grammatical words (words which help structure a sentence) are not stressed. So, in the following statement, *The School will be closed next Thursday.* we would typically stress *school / closed / Thursday.* As this is neither a question nor a list the intonation will fall.

5 Allow students time to look at the questions (Exercise 3) and task (Exercise 1) before putting them into pairs. Encourage them to use the phrases in the box on page 37. Set a time limit of two minutes before telling the students to find a new partner and repeat the exercise. For stronger students, tell them to cover the box when they do the exercise for the second time.

6 Tell students that the final question asked by the examiner encourages them to summarise their discussion and work towards a negotiated decision. Remind them once again, that they will not lose marks if agreement is not reached, but they *are* assessed on how well they negotiate and collaborate, so it is important that they agree and disagree with each other politely and take turns to speak. Tell students to think about this when they discuss the strategies. During whole-class feedback, you may want to elicit the answers from stronger students, making sure they justify their ideas.

Answers
Suggested answers
1 N, there isn't time – you need to reach a decision in one minute.
2 Y, it gets the discussion started and your partner involved.
3 N, it prevents further discussion.
4 Y, this is a possible way of creating more discussion.

5 Y, it creates further discussion.
6 N, you only have a minute and you'll get higher marks if you can have a natural conversation.

7 You may wish to allow the students to read the audioscript on page 221 as they listen and encourage them to underline the language used to agree, disagree and negotiate, e.g. *Well Antonia … What do you think? I think your suggestion would be fine if the weather is good, but …* Point out that Miguel uses Antonia's name in his response. Ask students if they think this would be helpful in the exam and why? (yes: it might help students to feel more relaxed when they are speaking).

Answers
Miguel = 2 Antonia = 4 Irene and Nikolai = 5

Track 14

Miguel and Antonia

Miguel: Well, Antonia, in my opinion, the best choice for the trip is the camping and walking activity in the mountains, because it'll be an adventure for everyone, and if it goes well, everyone will enjoy it. What do you think?

Antonia: Hmm, I think your suggestion would be fine if the weather is good, but no one will enjoy it if it rains all the time, and it's a lot of responsibility for the teachers who are supervising the trip. I think the beach activity trip is a better option because at least the kids will be staying in a hostel if the weather turns bad.

Irene and Nikolai

Irene: OK, I think we should choose the theme park because all teenagers enjoy the thrill of a theme park, and it gives everyone plenty to talk about and discuss before and after they go.

Nikolai: Yes, I think you're right, but I think we should also consider the visit to the museum because that might be more popular with the teachers, and we have to take their preferences into consideration as well.

Irene: Hmm, you might be right, but I think we should put the students' tastes first because it is their trip.

Nikolai: Maybe, but they can go to a theme park in their own time.

Irene: Yes, of course they can, but sometimes it's important to do these activities as a school group.

8 Students can work individually or in pairs. If students work in pairs, tell them to say the phrases out loud and practise correct word stress or intonation.

Answers
1 a **2** a **3** b **4** e **5** e **6** d **7** c

9 You could encourage students to disagree with each other at least once to help develop the discussion. As an alternative, put students into groups of three with one student listening to the discussion and ticking the phrases that they hear (from Exercise 8). Encourage students to give feedback to each other after they have spoken, e.g. *I heard you say … and I thought your intonation was very good. Maybe next time you could try asking me what my opinion was.*

Extension activity
Once students have practised the speaking activity (Exercise 9), tell them to record themselves using their mobile phones. Then ask them to listen using earphones and give each other feedback. If recording devices are not available, students could repeat Exercise 9 but in different groups, which can help build confidence through working with students they are less familiar with.

Writing Part 2 (a report) SB page 39

▶ **Page 198 Writing bank**

Lead in
Ask students to think about the differences between writing an email to a friend and writing a report for a teacher, colleague, etc. Elicit a few examples (report: more neutral tone; avoid informal language, etc.).

Exam advice
Read the exam advice with the students. Point out the report is normally written for a superior or peer group, for example a teacher or club members. Remind students of the importance of structuring their report clearly, including both an introduction and conclusion.

1 Elicit the answers from the class.

Answers
Suggested underlining
one-day excursion, local place of interest, what you did, why, a success

2 Allow students two minutes to read the question and write down some notes before discussing with a partner. Allow students to decide which points they would like to include, but tell them they must justify their choices.

3 Students work individually. Monitor and make a note of students who are having difficulties with the grammar. For homework you could refer them to the relevant Grammar reference section for additional practice. Alternatively, tell students to compare their answers with a partner. Tell them they must discuss the options when they do not agree, rather than simply change an answer because it is what their partner has.

Answers
1 took **2** went **3** was **4** had been **5** rode **6** were
7 took **8** had operated **9** was **10** were **11** enjoyed
12 learnt **13** had **14** found

4 Students work in pairs before you elicit the answers from the class. Alternatively, tell the students to cover Exercise 4 and highlight examples in the model answer of things a report needs. For example, they should highlight the title and the headings. Tell students to look at the exam question and underline examples in the model answer for each idea they underlined in Exercise 1. Then allow them to check their ideas with the list given in Exercise 4 before eliciting feedback from the class.

Answers
1 yes, Excursion to London
2 three, each has a heading: Purposes of trip, What we did, Comments
3 three: a break from normal lessons, to see the London Eye and do a tour of the Globe Theatre
4 The activities were interesting, different, everyone enjoyed something, they learned a lot, the day was well planned, plenty of opportunities to practise English, motivating.

5 Exam candidates often worry about the report writing task, so remind them to focus on writing a plan that covers each point in the question, is well structured and includes headings. Refer students to the Writing bank on page 198 if you think they would benefit from looking at a second model answer before attempting the task. Allow students five to ten minutes to write a plan and encourage them to share their plans so that weaker students are supported.

6 As this is an exam task, set a time limit of forty-five minutes. After students have completed the writing, tell them to read what they have written and correct any mistakes with spelling and grammar that they can identify themselves before handing it in to be marked or corrected.

Vocabulary

Holiday types, destinations and activities

backpacking	a hostel
a beach break	meeting new people
a cabin	relaxing
a city break	a ski trip
couch-surfing	sunbathing
a cruise	taking selfies by landmarks
going sightseeing	a tour of a country
a hotel	trying local delicacies

Commonly confused words

travel	trip
journey	way

Collocations with *journey* and *trip*

a(n) homeward / outward / hard / dangerous **journey**
a business / sightseeing / shopping / day / round / successful **trip**
a(n) outward / pleasant / safe / extended / overnight **journey**/ **trip**

Benefits of trips

become more self-confident	get a real thrill
become more independent	have new experiences
learn to work in a team	appreciate other cultures
cope in another language	learn teamwork
educational	tough conditions
make a change from their everyday lives	get away from their daily routine

Vocabulary activity 1

In small groups students choose a country or city they would like their class to visit.
Plan how they would get there.
Plan the activities they would do when they got there and why they have chosen these activities. Each group presents their proposal (plan) to the class. After every group has presented their proposal, the whole class decides which trip the class should go on.

Vocabulary activity 2

Divide the class into travel agents and tourists. This is a role-play activity where travel agents persuade tourists to buy the trip they are selling. First, allow students time to think about ideas, e.g.

travel agents – the type and length of the trip; accommodation; meals; activities on offer.
tourists – what type of experiences they want and do not want; how much money they are prepared to spend, etc.
After students have prepared, tell each travel agent to stand next to a tourist and try to persuade them to book their trip while the tourist raises objections (*the hotel you are offering is far too expensive, I'd prefer to stay in a hostel*). Every two minutes, the travel agent must talk to a different tourist until every travel agent has spoken to every tourist. At the end of the activity, each tourist decides which tour they are going to book and the winning travel agent is the one that has sold the most tours. Here are some ideas but you, or your students, can come up with your own.

- Trekking in the Himalayas
- Diving with great white sharks
- Spending a week in a jungle with no food or shelter
- Backpacking in Europe

DIGITAL CLASSROOM
Practice Extra Unit 3
Test Generator Unit 3 test
Test and Train Exam Practice

4 Food, glorious food

Unit objectives

Topic: food

Reading and Use of English Part 6 (gapped text): identifying referencing words; recognising cohesive development

Reading and Use of English Part 1 (multiple-choice cloze): exam technique

Writing Part 2 (a review): using descriptive adjectives

Listening Part 4 (multiple choice): an interview

Speaking Part 4 (discussion – topics related to Part 3 task): supporting opinions with reasons and examples

Pronunciation: grouping words and pausing (1)

Vocabulary: *food, dish* and *meal*; adjectives to describe restaurants

Grammar: *so* and *such*; *too* and *enough*

Starting off SB page 40

1 Tell students to look at the photos but cover the descriptions. Elicit one or two ideas (e.g. *photo A looks like insects*) before getting students to match the photos with the words. Elicit the answers and tell students not to worry about the meaning of unknown words as they may be explained in the next exercise.

Answers
A insects **B** artificial beef **C** GM foods **D** algae
E 3D-printed food

2 Match the first description with the students before putting them into pairs to complete the exercise. Elicit the answers from the class and concept-check any new vocabulary. You may wish to point out that they would not be expected to know technical abbreviations, e.g. *CRISPR*, before allowing them an additional five minutes to check new vocabulary, e.g. *aquatic*, *modification*, in a dictionary.

Answers
1 artificial beef **2** 3D-printed food **3** algae
4 GM foods **5** insects

3 Students discuss for five minutes. Remind them to justify their responses with reasons and examples. Select students to present their groups' opinions to the class.

Extension activity

Put students into pairs and tell them to take turns to compare and contrast two of the photos as they do in Speaking Part 2. Tell students they must each speak for one minute. For more authentic and extended practice, write the following prompt on the board: *I'd like you to compare the photographs and say which of these types of food you think might be useful in the future.*

Reading and Use of English Part 6 SB page 40

Exam advice

Read the exam advice with the students. Tell them that in addition to noticing referencing language, they need to recognise the cohesive development of a text. This means how a text develops logically. Point out how this is achieved by the use of words and phrases that contrast arguments, show cause and effect, etc. For example, *in actual fact* (sentence G).

1 Elicit ideas from the class, e.g. *Can you actually eat it? How is food printed? Is it healthy?* and write them on the board. Alternatively, put students into small groups and give them three minutes to brainstorm their ideas.

2 Students work individually. Set a time limit of five minutes then tell students to compare the answers they found with a partner. To practise paraphrasing skills (saying or writing something using different words) during whole-class feedback, encourage students to refer to the part of the text in their own words rather than reading it word for word.

3 Remind students to pay attention to referencing words and look carefully either side of the gap before telling them to complete the task individually. As this is an exam task, allow students ten minutes to do the exercise before eliciting the answers from the class.

Answers
1 D **2** E **3** G **4** F **5** C **6** A

Extension activity

Put students into groups and tell them to justify why each answer is correct or incorrect. This works well if students have come up with different answers to the same question.

Alternatively, add this step to Exercise 3, before eliciting the answers in whole-class feedback.

Vocabulary SB page 42

food, *dish* and *meal*

Lead in
In pairs students look at the photo and name as much of the food as they can in one minute: sausages, scrambled egg, yoghurt, smoked salmon, avocado, peppers, grapefruit, bread, milk, coffee, etc., before telling their partner which they do, and do not, enjoy eating.

1 Write *food*, *dish* and *meal* on the board along with an example sentence for each, e.g.
I had a great *__meal__* *at a local restaurant last night – the main course and pudding (dessert) were particularly good.*
I'm having dinner at my friend's house tonight and she's trying out a new chicken *__dish__* *– it's her gran's recipe.*
I don't really enjoy going *__food__* *shopping, so I don't appreciate having to do it every week.*

Tell students to look at the sentences and in pairs discuss how *food*, *dish* and *meal* are different. Elicit answers: *meal* – an occasion when food is eaten or the whole of a meal itself; *food* – the word for the broader, general category; *dish* – food prepared in a particular way as part of a meal. Students do the exercise individually and then compare their answers in pairs. Elicit the answers.

Answers
1 meals **2** dish **3** food

2 Students can work individually or in pairs. Allow five minutes for this exercise. Elicit the answers from the class.

Answers
2 ~~meals~~ dishes **3** ~~food~~ dish **4** ~~meat~~ food **5** ~~meals~~ food
6 ~~food~~ dish **7** ~~dishes~~ meals

3 Weaker students work in pairs. Allow students to use an English to English dictionary to check their answers before eliciting the answers from the class.

Answers
1 food **2** food **3** meal/dish **4** meal

Fast finishers
Students choose three collocations and write questions using them, then ask and answer them in pairs, e.g. *What would you do if there was a food shortage in your/our city? Why do you think organic food is so expensive?*

4 Students work individually and then compare their answers in pairs.

Answers
1 food **2** dish(es) **3** food **4** organic/convenience
5 elaborate **6** shortages

5 Set a limit of five minutes. Monitor and write down examples of common errors. Write the examples of common errors on the board and elicit error correction.

Extension activity
After error correction (Exercise 5), tell students to walk around the room (mingle) and ask and answer the questions. If students do not change partners, stop them every minute and say: *Change partner or mingle.* Monitor and write down examples of correct language use as well as persistent common errors.

Grammar SB page 43

so and *such*

▶ **Page 167 Grammar reference**

Lead in
Write the following on the board: *I had such a ___ meal last night I'm never going back. My tofu dish was so ___ I returned it to the kitchen immediately.* Tell students to think of as many words for the gaps as they can in one minute (e.g. *terrible, awful, disgusting meal; the dish was so awful, terrible, bland, dry.* Ask students to write two short sentences using *food*, *dish* and *meal*, and *so* and *such*. Invite one or two stronger students to write their sentences on the board.

1 Allow weaker students to work in pairs. Encourage students to check their answers using the Grammar reference on page 167 before eliciting feedback.

Answers
1 such a **2** so **3** such

2 Elicit the answer to the first question from the whole class. Students work individually. Monitor and support weaker students by eliciting correct answers.

Answers
1 such **2** so **3** such a **4** so **5** so **6** such a

3 Point out that these are real errors made by exam candidates. After students have completed the exercise they could asterisk (*) sentences which include errors they commonly make (they may have mistakenly thought a sentence in the exercise was correct) and use this information to check errors with *so* and *such* in their future written work.

Answers
1 ~~such~~ so 2 ~~a so much~~ such 3 correct 4 ~~so~~ such
5 ~~so~~ such a 6 ~~such a~~ so/such 7 correct 8 ~~so~~ such

4 You may prefer to set this as an exam practice task with a time limit of ten minutes. Alternatively, allow weaker students to work in pairs and/or use the Grammar reference on page 167. Elicit the answers in whole-class feedback.

Answers
1 never eaten such a good
2 so quickly that we
3 answered the question so well/excellently
4 with so little food
5 had so much fun at
6 make so much noise

Extension activity
Students write sentences using *so* and *such* about a personal topic, e.g. a place where they had a good experience, or a time they had a memorable meal.

Listening Part 4 SB page 44

Lead in
With books closed, write: *The food industry* on the board and elicit some food industry jobs or careers from the class, e.g. restaurant manager, private party caterer, chef, food critic, farmer, nutritionist.

Exam info
Read the information with the students. Tell them that they should read the question stems before they listen and the options as they listen. Remind them that because only one option is correct for each answer, trying to read all the options before they listen is a waste of their limited time.

1 Allow students time to look at the questions and think about their responses before they discuss in pairs.

2 Do the first question with the students before telling them to work individually. Make sure students understand that the question referred to is the numbered question and not the options A–C. Set a time limit of two or three minutes. Students compare their answers in pairs before you elicit from the class.

Note: If students find this challenging, it may help if you encourage them to think about how they would answer each question if it was asked of them. For example, for Q1 their answer would include <u>why</u> they <u>moved</u> from <u>London</u> and <u>why</u> they chose to <u>start</u> a <u>business</u>.

Answers
Suggested underlining
1 Why, start, business, moving from London
2 decided, set up, market stall, because
3 What change, make, menu, first few months
4 What type of advertising, most effective
5 When, moved into private catering, found it difficult
6 How, feel about catering for, Turkish ambassador
7 What, plan, do next, her business

3 Play the recording twice. After completing the task, students discuss the reasons for the answers in small groups, comparing the language that identified the correct answers with any distractors. For weaker students, you could allow them to do this by using the audioscript on page 222.

Answers
1 B 2 C 3 B 4 C 5 A 6 B 7 C

Track 15

I: So, Alina, you own a successful catering business called Anatolia. Why did you decide to start this business?

A: I've always been a big fan of travel and food from different countries. I'd thought about starting my own catering business for a while, but it wasn't until we moved to a small town on the south coast of England that it became a real possibility. It would have been too costly to start a business living in London with two school-age children to support. My husband and I probably would have stayed in London if he hadn't been offered a more senior role in his company elsewhere, so it seemed like it was meant to be.

I: It certainly sounds like it. So how did your business start out?

A: Well, one weekend, while I was walking around the local food market, I quickly noticed there wasn't much variety of food available, unlike in London. I felt a stall offering something different would be quite appealing to locals, so I sent in an application for a new market stall specialising in Turkish street food. To my surprise, the application was accepted in no time at all. I then set about developing dishes that were not only affordable for customers but would also allow me to earn enough money to make a profit.

I: And was the menu at the market stall an instant success?

A: It wasn't an immediate hit with the locals, but after a few months I had a good number of loyal customers, most of whom were quite well-travelled and were familiar with Turkish cuisine. The great thing about market stalls is that you have direct interaction with the people buying your food, so I got to know what was missing from my current menu and adapted it accordingly. Customers said there was too much fast food at the market, so I concentrated on healthier options. This helped to bring in more business and meant that I could justify charging a little more than other food stalls around me as the dishes became more sophisticated.

I: How did you advertise your business to more people?

A: To start with, most people found out about us via word-of-mouth, which worked very well in such a small town. Later on, I placed adverts in the local paper and on the town's website, though by that time, I already had plenty of customers.

I: This then led to you starting your own private catering business. How did this come about?

A: Well, I started by handing out fliers advertising my catering service to customers at the market. Nothing happened in the first few weeks until, one day, someone asked if I'd cater for their wedding. There were sixty guests to cater for in total. It meant getting a different licence, which I didn't have any trouble with. I needed extra staff to support me and I quickly realised it was far from straightforward. The thing is, you're hiring people for individual jobs, rather than full-time employment, which limits your options significantly. In the end, I had to ask my husband to help out and, fortunately, the wedding was a big success. But for the first few months in the new business, I had too much work and not enough people to help.

I: I heard that you once catered for the Turkish ambassador. What was that like?

A: Well, I didn't really have time to get nervous as I was so focused on getting everything right. I discovered that manti, a type of dumpling, was the Ambassador's favourite, so I served that. They're notoriously difficult to make, so I was pleasantly surprised when he came into the kitchen to thank me personally.

I: That's a great story! So what does the future hold for you?

A: Well, I'll probably continue with the catering company for the time being, but eventually I'd like to set up something bigger. I'd like to encourage people to learn to make Turkish food themselves, using the right ingredients. I plan to try and publish my recipes first and then, if the book's a success, open a small shop selling my books and ingredients to cook with.

4 As an alternative to pairs, students work in groups. Encourage students to use *so* and *such* when they are talking. Students could also take this opportunity to practise language for making comparisons from Unit 1, e.g. *I think street food is far more delicious than restaurant cuisine because …*

Background information
Street food is ready-to-eat or 'fast' food sold by a vendor in a street or other public place, such as a fair or local market. Typically, though not always, street food is simple and less expensive than restaurant food. Some people believe that eating street food is a great way to experience local dishes and specialities.

Grammar SB page 44

too and *enough*

▶ **Page 168 Grammar reference**

Lead in
If you have access to the internet, you could show students a photograph of a famous football player. Alternatively, draw a stick man playing football on the board. Say, or write: *I earn over £150,000 a week kicking a ball.* Tell students to respond to your statement (give their opinion) using *too* and *enough*, e.g. *You earn far too much money. I think that's enough money for anyone. That's enough money to buy anything you want. I don't think doctors earn enough; they deserve to earn that amount more than footballers do.*

1 Allow weaker students to work in pairs. Tell students to check their answers using the audioscript on page 222. Use the Grammar reference on page 168 if the students are unsure about the grammar structures, and for additional practice as necessary.

Answers
1 too **2** too much **3** enough **4** too many; enough

2 If you have a stronger group of students, you could tell them to turn the statements into questions and then ask and answer them in pairs, e.g. *Are you a fan of Asian cuisine, like curry, or do you find it a bit too spicy? Do you think supermarkets waste too much food and use too many plastic containers for their products? Why? Why not?*

Answers
1 too **2** too much; too many **3** enough **4** too much
5 enough

3 Point out that these are common errors made by exam candidates. Once they have completed the task and you have elicited the answers, you could ask students to asterisk (*) the sentences which include common errors they make themselves.

Answers
1 ~~the food wasn't enough~~ there wasn't enough food
2 ~~not too much good~~ not very good
3 ~~money enough~~ enough money
4 ~~enough comfortable~~ comfortable enough
5 ~~too much long~~ (much) too long
6 ~~doing too hard work~~ working too hard / doing too much hard work
7 ~~too much tasty~~ very tasty
8 ~~too much expensive~~ (much) too expensive

Fast finishers
Students write down three additional sentences with an error in each for their partner to correct, e.g. *I didn't like the restaurant as there wasn't choice enough.* If this is too challenging, tell students to go to the Grammar reference on page 168, choose three *correct* sentences and change them so they are *incorrect*.

4 Students work individually. Set a time limit of five minutes. Allow students to compare answers and check the Grammar reference on page 168 before you elicit answers from the class.

Answers
1 is too expensive for
2 enough petrol to reach
3 was too astonished by
4 was not / wasn't warm enough for

5 This task will help students prepare for the writing task on page 48. Remind them to use language from the unit so far (*enough, too, so, such, meal, dish, food*) and, if necessary, refer them to the content in this section that models language they could use for this topic (Exercise 2 q1; Exercise 3 q1, 5, 7, 8; Exercise 4 q1).

Speaking Part 4 SB page 46

▶ **Page 211 Speaking bank**

With books closed, put students into groups and tell them you are going to write four statements about Speaking Part 4 on the board. Tell them to discuss each statement and decide whether it is true or false. If false, they should say why it is false.
1. *In Speaking Part 4, the examiner will ask questions about a topic which is unrelated to the topic in Speaking Part 3* (F it will be connect to Part 3 but in a general way).
2. *The examiner may ask you to discuss questions with the other candidate.* (T)
3. *You should agree with everything the other candidate says* (F you should react to the other candidate's opinions with your own, so you may disagree).
4. *As long as you give an opinion, you don't need to justify it by giving reasons and examples* (F you should justify your opinion).
Elicit ideas from the students but do not correct them. Instead, tell the students to check their ideas by reading the exam information.

Exam info

1 In pairs, encourage students to read the answers out loud so they can start practising pronunciation. As students do the activity, write down a few additional example sentences with the language, which you can add to the board if necessary when you check meaning at the end of the exercise, e.g. *I try to eat a* ***balanced diet*** *with lots of fresh fruit and vegetables. Eating too much* ***junk food****, like burgers, can be bad for your health.* Elicit the answers and check meaning by eliciting some additional sentences from the students. Write these on the board and correct any errors the students made. Use the sentences you prepared earlier if necessary.

Answers
b balanced diet **c** cut down on **d** junk food
e dairy products **f** live on **g** lifestyle

2 Remind students to look at the words before and after the gap. Lower level students could read the audioscript on page 222 as they listen and check their answers.

Answers
1 in other words **2** because **3** On the other hand
4 then **5** but **6** which **7** what

Track 16

Examiner: Do you think fast food is bad for you?
Martyna: I think it depends. I think the most important thing / is to have a balanced diet, / in other words, you eat a variety of / vegetables, / meat, / cereals and so on. I'm not sure it matters so much / how long it takes to prepare, / because I think fast food is / just / food which is prepared quickly. On the other hand, / if you just live on / what's it called / junk food, / for instance hamburgers and pizzas and things like that, / then you probably need to cut down / and have a more balanced diet.
Examiner: And Miguel, / what do you think?
Miguel: I agree with Martyna. / I think it's fine to eat fast food occasionally, / but you have to balance it with other things like / fresh fruit and / vegetables which are in season and / cut down on dairy products and fat. / Also I think that what you eat is only one part of a / healthy lifestyle.
Martyna: I agree.

3 Ask stronger students if they can add one or two more phrases or words that could be used for each function in the list, e.g. *1 what I mean is …; 2 as a result of -ing …; 3 to illustrate this …; 4 on the flip side …*

Answers
1 in other words **2** because **3** for instance, like
4 but, on the other hand

/P/ Pronunciation: grouping words and pausing (1)

4 Read the paragraph to the students. As you do, group the words to emphasise the point the paragraph is making. Then ask the student to take turns to read the paragraph, pausing where you did:
When we speak /,
we say words in groups /
which form a meaning together /,
almost like one word, /
and we pause slightly /
between these groups of words.

Note: grouping may vary from person to person, depending on how precisely they interpret their own argument and what they wish to emphasise in it. You may wish to point out to students that the main objective here is to make a decision about where the main ideas could be divided and make pauses at those places.

4.1 Put students in pairs and tell them to read the audioscript out loud. Ask them where they think they will hear the pauses and to mark them (/) before they listen and check their answers. This is quite a challenging task for teachers and students, so tell them not to worry if they put their pauses in the wrong place at first. Reassure students their skills at grouping and pausing effectively will improve the more they practise.

> **Answers**
> See Track 17 recording script for answers.

Track 17

Examiner: How can families benefit from eating together?

Miguel: Well, / the important thing is not eating, / it's spending time together / so that they can talk about what they have been doing during the day. / They get the chance to exchange opinions / and make plans as well, / because everyone can contribute / and that's what makes a rich, / meaningful family life. / Children learn ideas and attitudes from their parents, / while parents keep up to date with their children / and what they are thinking and doing.

Examiner: And Martyna, / do you agree?

Martyna: Yes, I do. / And also I think people cook better / when they are cooking for several people / than when they are just cooking for themselves, / so as a result, / people who eat together / eat more healthily.

4.2 Encourage students to emphasise the pauses. Remind them they may think they sound unnatural, but that they will sound more natural the more they practise. Once students are more confident, ask them to stand up before reading the audioscript again.

4.3 Put students into new pairs for this exercise. They may feel more comfortable working with a partner than reading the audioscript out loud on their own.

> **Answers**
> See Track 16 recording script for answers.

4.4 If students have already read Martyna's and Miguel's answers out loud, they could mark the pauses (/) in the sentences from Exercise 2 or 3 on page 45, e.g. Q1:

I'm not a big fan /
of Asian cuisine /
like curry /
as I find it /
a bit too spicy /

Writing each chunk on a new line (as above) may help the students to do this activity.

5 Give students time to look back through the unit and remind themselves of the language they should use (*meal, dish, food, such, so, enough, too*, etc.) before they do this task. Weaker students can work in pairs. If in pairs, make sure both students write down the answer even if they only gave one, so that they can change pairs for Exercise 6.

6 Students change pairs if necessary. Monitor and write down examples of common errors, with focus on language from the unit. Ask one or two students to share their ideas before writing the errors you noted on the board and eliciting error correction from the class.

7 Allow students three minutes to read the questions and think about their answers. As an alternative, put the students into groups of three and ask one student to listen and write down examples of language from the unit that they hear. (A asks, B answers, C listens and makes notes). Encourage Student C to give feedback before they swap roles. (B asks, C answers, A listens)

Reading and Use of English Part 1 SB page 47

Lead in

Ask: *Do you have any pets?* (If you have a pet you could say: *I've got a pet x, it's such a lovely animal. Do you have any pets?* Or: *I used to have a pet parrot – it was so badly behaved. Do/Did you …?*) Elicit one or two responses from the class before putting students in pairs to talk about their pets, or if they don't have a pet, whether they want one in the future or had one in the past. Encourage students to use *so, such, too*, and *enough*, plus language from previous units (*used to*, etc.) and respond to each other.

Read the exam advice with the students. Remind students that different forms of words are tested, e.g. nouns, verbs, etc. Point out that they should be careful of words which have a similar meaning, e.g. *high* and *tall*. Tell students that when they learn new vocabulary they should also try to learn and record its use in groups of related words and phrases, and in collocations (collocations are words which are naturally used together in specific combinations that might not be obvious to language learners, e.g. *high mountains* vs *a tall man*). You could also draw attention to the example answer in Exercise 2 at this point and elicit the reason why C is correct here (*selection* takes the meaning of *choice* in this collocation, which is correct for the context, and the other options either don't collocate with *snacks* or have the wrong sense).

Exam info

1 Set a time limit of one minute to encourage students to read the article quickly and avoid pausing when they reach a gap. Tell students to underline the part of the text which gives them the answer. When eliciting the answer from the class, encourage students to paraphrase.

> **Answers**
> Spending time with cats is good for people's well-being; they find it relaxing; it is good for physical health.

2 If you did not draw attention to the example when you read the advice, do this now. Remind students that they must think about the meaning of the word in context and pay attention to the words after the gap as well as before it. As this is an exam task, set a time limit of ten minutes before eliciting the answers from the class.

Answers
1 D **2** A **3** C **4** B **5** D **6** C **7** A **8** B

Extension activity
Put students into groups and tell them to brainstorm collocations for the words given in the options, e.g. *a collection of books, an arrangement of flowers, a selection of cakes, a family gathering.* Allow them to use an English to English dictionary to help them. Select students to write their phrases on the board.

3 As with previous activities, encourage students to recycle (use) language from the unit, e.g. *I'd feel too uncomfortable to visit a cat café as I'd be worried it wasn't clean enough …*

Background information
A cat café is a themed café where customers can watch, and often play with, cats. Some cat cafés charge an entry fee while others are free to enter. Cat cafés have become very popular with both tourists and locals. In Japan, for example, there are around 150. While they can be popular, some people and organisations are against cat cafés because of concerns over animal welfare.

Writing Part 2 (a review) SB page 48

▶ **Page 200 Writing bank**

Lead in
Dictate five questions about reviews, e.g. *Have you ever written a bad review about something? Do you often read reviews about a product before you buy it? Would you visit a restaurant that had received terrible reviews? Why are people more likely to write bad reviews rather than good ones? Do you think you can trust reviews which have been posted on social media?* Students discuss the questions in small groups for five minutes.

Exam info
Read the information with the students. Ask them what a review should include (positive and/or negative opinions, and a recommendation). Point out that students will also need to know how to use a range of adjectives effectively. Finally, encourage students to read real reviews in English, particularly reviews about restaurants, holidays, television programmes and other topics likely to appear in the exam.

1 As students have done this type of activity a few times now, ask them to work individually before eliciting answers from the class.

Answers
Suggested underlining
local English-language newspaper, recommend, local restaurant, café or snack bar, review, what, place, food, are like, why, family, enjoy eating there

2 There are no right or wrong answers here. However, students should justify their ideas. To make this activity specific to the question, you could tell students that they should only include the features which directly relate to the question in Exercise 1 and encourage them to explain those connections during whole-class feedback, e.g. Student A: *I'd choose feature a because the question includes a point about the place and what it is like. However, I wouldn't choose feature x because …*

3 Students work individually and then compare their answers in groups. Accept different answers from those suggested below as long as students use the adjective in the correct context and can justify their ideas. You could allow students to use an English to English dictionary to check new vocabulary; this will encourage them to learn the word in context because example sentences, including common collocations, are often given.

Answers
Suggested answers
the waiters / the service: cheerful, exceptional, informative, rushed, satisfactory, superb, welcoming, wonderful
the interior: airy, attractive, cheerful, colourful, cosy, elegant, modern, original, welcoming
the food and menu: attractive, colourful, delicious, delightful, elegant, exceptional, fresh, original, raw, satisfactory, satisfying, superb, tasty, well-balanced, wonderful
the price: competitive, reasonable
the restaurant in general: attractive, colourful, delightful, elegant, exceptional, exclusive, modern, original, superb, welcoming

Extension activity
Students add affixes to make the positive adjectives negative (*unexceptional, unwelcoming, unreasonable, unsatisfying*, etc.) or, if the adjective does not have an appropriate affix, students try to come up with a negative alternative (*colourful/colourless, cosy/cramped, fresh/stale, modern/old-fashioned, delicious/disgusting*, etc.).

4 As students have completed this type of task before, allow them to do it individually before eliciting answers from the class.

Answers
Suggested underlining
college magazine, favourite restaurant, café or snack bar, review, 'Free Time' section, what it is like, why, recommend it to our students

5 Ask students why it is important to write a plan (it helps them to stay focused on the question and answer all parts of the question fully). Tell students to include five adjectives from Exercise 3 in their plan.

6 You could encourage students to share their plans in groups, or even as a class, and provide feedback to each other. Provide model language for feedback if necessary, e.g. *I like the way you organised your plan because it includes an idea for each point in the question. You used a spider diagram to brainstorm your ideas – I'm going to try that.*

7 Set a time limit of forty minutes. Remind students to follow their plans. Point out that once they start writing, it is easy to ignore the plan and omit an important point they had intended to include.

Vocabulary

Describing food / a restaurant

airy	modern
attractive	original
cheerful	raw
colourful	reasonable
competitive	rushed
cosy	satisfactory
delicious	satisfying
delightful	superb
elegant	tasty
exceptional	welcoming
exclusive	well-balanced
fresh	wonderful
informative	

Commonly confused words

dish / food / meal

Vocabulary activity 1

Put students into pairs. One student is an unhappy restaurant customer, the other is the restaurant manager. Tell the customer to complain to the manager about the food, the meal, a specific dish or the restaurant, using both the vocabulary and the grammar (*so, such, too, enough*) from the unit. Tell students that as most of the adjectives here are positive, they will need to add affixes to make them negative. (*unreasonable, dissatisfied, unoriginal*, etc.). You may also wish to provide some suggestions for things to complain about, for example:

The food/meal/dish: the temperature, the taste, the price

Restaurant: the length of time waiting, the atmosphere, the cleanliness, the staff

Example:
A: *I understand you would like to speak to me, Sir/Madam.*
B: *Yes. I'm sorry to say that my meal was completely* ***unsatisfactory****. Not only was the chef's fish* ***dish undercooked****, it was also very* ***bland****. And when I told the server …*

Vocabulary activity 2

Students work in pairs. One student chooses an adjective from the list and the other has to give an example sentence using the word, e.g.

Student A: *airy*
Student B: *I loved the restaurant as it was really airy. There was a lot of space and loads of big windows letting the light in.*

DIGITAL CLASSROOM

Practice Extra Unit 4

Test Generator Unit 4 test

Test and Train Exam Practice

Unit 3 vocabulary and grammar review

1
1 journey 2 trip 3 travel 4 way 5 journey 6 way 7 trip 8 journey
2
1 while I was visiting 2 I had lost 3 used to go to school 4 she was still going to 5 had never met 6 used to be more
3
1 considerable 2 luxurious 3 dramatic 4 unacceptable 5 disorganised 6 unhelpful 7 remaining 8 preferable

Unit 4 vocabulary and grammar review

1
1 meal 2 food 3 dish 4 food 5 dish 6 food / meal 7 meal 8 food
2
1 too hot (for us) to 2 slowly enough (for us) to 3 was so full (that) 4 such delicious food that 5 cook well enough 6 such a long time / so much time
3
1 filling 2 convenience 3 increasingly 4 organisations 5 discourage 6 balanced 7 disappearance 8 choice

5 Study time

Unit objectives

Topic: education

Reading and Use of English Part 7 (multiple matching): exam techniques

Reading and Use of English Part 3 (word formation): nominalisation

Writing Part 1 (essay): writing opening paragraphs

Listening Part 1 (multiple choice): focusing on meaning

Speaking Part 1 (interview): giving reasons and offering several possible ideas

Pronunciation: syllable stress; shifting word stress

Vocabulary: phrasal verbs connected with education and study, *find out, get to know, know, learn, teach and study; attend, join, take part* and *assist*

Grammar: zero, first and second conditionals

Starting off SB page 52

Lead in

Look at the photos with the students. Ask them which learning situations they have experienced and elicit one or two answers from the class. You might like to briefly explore how students believe the ways we learn will change over the next five to ten years.

1 Encourage students to give and justify their opinions. As an alternative, you could split the class before putting them into groups, with half discussing the advantages and the other half the disadvantages. At the end of the exercise, elicit ideas from each group before the class decides which type of learning offers the most and least advantages and why.

Listening Part 1 SB page 52

1 Students cover the definitions and discuss the meanings of 1–9 while you monitor without interruption. This will help you understand which words students already know. After students have completed the exercise and you have elicited the correct answers, you may wish to elicit from them those words which are both verbs and nouns (research, mark, pass) together with example sentences, e.g. *I was thrilled when I passed the test. I was reading an interesting piece of research last night about …*

Answers
1 h 2 d 3 b 4 a 5 i 6 e 7 f 8 c 9 g

Exam advice

Select a student to read the exam advice to the class. Remind them not to be distracted by hearing words in the transcript which appear in an incorrect option.

2 Students work individually. Remind them to focus on the context sentences and question stems only. Set a time limit of three minutes. Students compare their ideas before you elicit the answers from the class.

Answers
Suggested underlining
1 assignment, have to do, what does woman say
2 value, studying abroad, main benefit
3 new online course, students have to do
4 exam, both most worried about
5 new course, hasn't, made a final decision, apply for
6 chemistry teacher, career, why, become a teacher
7 amount of homework, why, unhappy
8 lecture, what, disagree about

3 Play the recording twice. Students work individually. Allow students time to check their answers using the audioscript on page 223 before eliciting the answers from the whole class.

Answers
1 B 2 C 3 A 4 C 5 A 6 B 7 C 8 C

Track 18

Narrator: One. You hear two students talking about the assignment they have to do.

Man: Nicky, have you thought about this term's final assignment yet?

Woman: I've looked at the instructions and read the text, but not much more than that so far. I think it's related to the homework we completed last Monday, so I'm just waiting for our teacher to mark that and give me the comments on it. I don't want to have to change everything later as that wouldn't be the best use of my time. I know it's due in very soon and you probably think it's a bit last-minute, but I'll easily be able to submit it on time.

Narrator: Two. You hear a student talking about the value of studying abroad.

Man: I've just come back from six months' studying in the Netherlands. The placement is available to all students and there's a wide variety of universities to choose from. It's one of the best experiences I've had. I think it'll be really useful to my future career, primarily due to all the new friends I've made who are hoping to work in international development, like me. I'm sure this will be useful when I've graduated and start looking for work. Studying abroad can also help to boost your job prospects in other ways. Employers really appreciate people with experience of living overseas, especially if you've immersed yourself in the culture and learnt the language along the way.

Narrator: Three. You overhear two people discussing a new online course.

Man: What's the new course like, Mariam?

Woman: Well, most of the teaching happens online via videos. A lot of research has gone into creating these types of courses, and it seems that students are finding it really motivating. You need a lot of self-discipline – it's a course requirement to watch and complete the whole list of videos and tasks supplied. You can also use the library to read around your subject more generally if you have the time. The tutors and course organisers train us to use the institution's virtual learning environment. This is really important, as there are a lot of educational resources available there to help you develop, as well as the opportunity to ask questions via the interactive forum.

Narrator: Four. You hear two students talking about an exam.

Man: How are you feeling about the exam next week?

Woman: OK, I guess. I'm quite concerned about how little time we've had to prepare for it, though.

Man: I see what you're saying, but don't forget that it's our final exam, so we can dedicate all our time to preparing for it. I just hope that we're not tested on topics we haven't covered during the course, like last year.

Woman: I couldn't agree more! It also doesn't help that they're doing some building work right next to the exam centre all this week and next.

Man: I'm sure they'll be asked to stop during exam hours, though. They can't ask us to sit an exam with that going on – it would be too distracting.

Woman: I hope you're right. If not, I'm going to demand that they lower the mark needed for a pass!

Narrator: Five. You hear a son talking to his mother about the new course he is applying for.

Mother: Michael, have you made your final choices for university yet?

Son: Almost, Mum. I've chosen three, but I'm still trying to decide where else I could go. Applying for admission to a highly-respected university might be a little overambitious, so I'm trying to be more realistic with my choices. I know you want me to go to a famous institution like you did, which is a lot to live up to. I just don't want to submit an application and get rejected – that'd be a wasted choice. I suppose I could go to a university with lower fees, although you did say that the cost isn't that important.

Narrator: Six. You hear a chemistry teacher talking about her career.

Woman: I can't remember a time when I didn't want to be a teacher, to be honest. I always loved learning and, according to my teachers and lecturers, I was very creative and enthusiastic – two qualities that are vital in teaching. I love the fact that my lessons can have a positive impact on my students and hopefully inspire them to go on to bigger and better things. Admittedly, I do have to try a bit harder as a science teacher, as my students aren't always as passionate about the subject as I am.

Narrator: Seven. You overhear a student talking to her friend about the amount of homework she has to do.

Man: Have you finished that piece of homework due in on Friday?

Woman: Don't remind me about that! I haven't even started it yet! I hate the fact that we have to do homework every day – there's no flexibility at all. Why don't they understand that some learners do things differently? I don't think it teaches us the discipline needed to study effectively if the teacher tells us what to do all the time. I think teachers should coach us to be more independent as learners by setting longer-term study goals and allowing us to choose when we complete each step – as long as we meet the final deadline.

Narrator: Eight. You hear two students talking about a lecture they have just attended.

Man: That was a great lecture, wasn't it?

Woman: Did you think so? I guess the presenter was very easy to follow and he clearly knew what he was talking about.

Man: That's hardly surprising, I suppose, given the fact he's been doing this for over thirty years. I was glad to see that people weren't constantly looking at their phones or talking to each other.

Woman: Actually, I did spot a few people doing that. You must just have been more immersed in the talk than I was. Still, we did learn a lot of great stuff.

Man: There's no doubting that!

Extension activity

In groups, students underline the part of the audioscript on pages 223 and 224 where they heard the correct answer and discuss reasons why the other options are incorrect. For example, in question 1 the line *I know it's due in very soon and you probably think it's a bit last-minute, but I'll easily be able to submit it on time* indicates the correct option, B. The distractor for option A is *that wouldn't be the best use of my time*: *time* in the audioscript is a word spot for *waste of time* in the option, and she's not saying the assignment itself is a waste of time; for option C the distractor is in the line *I've looked at the instructions and read the text*,… *the homework we completed last Monday*: whilst the reference in the option to *already written* has a similar meaning to *I've looked at … and …we completed* in the distractor, the speaker isn't referring to the assignment.

Vocabulary SB page 53
Phrasal verbs

Lead in

With books closed, tell students you are going to mime five phrasal verbs for them to guess. Mime a number of activities (e.g. *stand up, tidy up, turn on the light, turn off the light*). Alternatively, give students five commands using phrasal verbs (e.g. *stand up, sit down, put your* hand up ...). You may wish to remind students of the structure of phrasal verbs (a verb plus a particle or two particles) and that some are separable (*put down the book, put the book down*) but others are not (*take care of the baby* not ~~*take care the baby of*~~). If you choose to cover this aspect, point out that when a phrasal verb is separable and the noun is replaced with a pronoun, the pronoun must go between the verb and the particle (*put it down* not ~~*put down it*~~). This latter point is an error that students often make.

1 Tell students to cover the descriptions and tell a partner what they think the phrasal verbs mean before using the descriptions to check their answers. During feedback, you may wish to elicit which are separable (*hand (sth) back, put (sth) off, point (sth) out*) and which are not (*get over, live up to, get away with, turn out, look back*). For those that are separable, asking students to replace the noun with a pronoun will help them practise avoiding this common error (*I handed the pen back, I handed it back, I handed back the pen*). Explain that some phrasal verbs have multiple meanings and may be separable for one and inseparable for another, e.g. *the plane* <u>*took off*</u> (meaning *the plane left the ground* – inseparable) and *I* <u>*took*</u> *my coat* <u>*off*</u> (meaning *I removed my coat* – separable). Finally, point out that phrasal verbs with two particles (e.g. *get away with*) are always inseparable.

Answers
1 c **2** a **3** e **4** g **5** h **6** b **7** d **8** f

2 Students work in pairs before comparing their answers with a different partner. Elicit the answers and encourage students to practise the correct structure of separable phrasal verbs by saying the sentences in a different way (e.g. Q3 – *What does 'it' refer to? The test: Julia's teacher handed the test back to Julia; Julia's teacher handed back Julia's test*).

Answers
1 put off **2** gets away with **3** handed ... back; gets over
4 live up to; looks back **5** turned out; pointed out

find out, get to know, know, learn, teach and *study*; *attend, join, take part* and *assist*

3 Point out that these are common errors made by exam candidates. After feedback, ask students to asterisk (*) the questions which they answered incorrectly and make a note of them to review when revising for the exam.

Answers
1 Study **2** Get to know **3** Attend **4** taught **5** Take part
6 joining **7** Learn **8** know **9** find out

4 Allow students five minutes for this task. As an alternative, you could ask students to compare and contrast studying abroad with studying in their own country. This would give them the opportunity to use the language from the exercise whilst recycling complex comparative language necessary for a higher score in Speaking Part 2. You might also wish to encourage them to use language to give opinions or reach agreement, required for Speaking Part 3.

5 Students work individually and compare their answers in pairs.

Answers
1 learn **2** got to know **3** study **4** learnt **5** find out
6 know **7** taught **8** assist **9** joined **10** taken part

Fast Finishers
Students imagine the statements in Exercise 5 are answers to questions they have asked and write down the question which the statement answered. (*1 Dimitri, what do you need if you want to study in Seville next year? 2 Have you got to know a lot of interesting people while doing this course? 3 What do you hope to study next at university, Maria? 4 What did you learn at summer camp, Karen? 5 What's the best way to find out the answer to this question? 6 Why don't you ring Kevin, if you know his number?* etc.). This exercise will encourage students to recycle the language whilst practising question forms.

Grammar

Zero, first and second conditionals

SB page 54

▶ **Page 168 Grammar reference**

Lead in
Write the following question on the board: *If you could live anywhere in the world, where would you choose?* Elicit answers from the class, encouraging students to give reasons for their answers.

1 You could point out that the further the tense moves from the present, the further it moves away from reality, i.e. zero conditional is present tense + present tense (generally true), first conditional is present tense + *will* (possible, probable) and second conditional is past simple tense + *would* (imagining, improbable). Students work on their own before comparing their answers in pairs.

Answers
a 3, 5, 6 **b** 2, 4 **c** 1

2 Students often make mistakes when using *unless*, so you should check they understand its meaning before they start the exercise. To do this, you could point out that *unless* is used instead of *if* and *not*, e.g. ***Unless** you finish your homework, you can't go out.* = ***If** you **don't** finish your homework, you can't go out.* Students complete the exercise in pairs. Monitor and help weaker students before eliciting the answers from the whole class.

Answers
1 h **2** f **3** j **4** g **5** a **6** e **7** c **8** d **9** i **10** b

3 Students work individually. Ask them not to compare answers before feedback so that the corpus-focused follow-up is most effective. As exam candidates often make mistakes using conditional structures, you could ask students to asterisk (*) the questions which they answered incorrectly. Then refer them to the Grammar reference section (page 168). Tell students to read the advice and rules about the errors they made, making notes of the key points in their notebooks.

Answers
1 said **2** lived; 'd/would cycle **3** did; 'd/would be
4 have **5** have; ask **6** stopped; would be

Extension activity
To practise language and skills for Speaking Parts 2 and 3, students discuss how far the ideas in Exercise 3 might be true for them in small groups. They should give an opinion, justify it and agree and disagree with the opinions of others. If students don't have much to say, it may help if you first elicited the topic areas, e.g. in Q1 the effect technology has on studying, Q2 cycling infrastructure in cities, Q3 the advantages and disadvantages of studying with a friend.

4 Read the rubric with the students. Draw students' attention to the fact that this exercise is similar to Reading and Use of English Part 3 before they complete the task individually. Set a time limit of eight minutes. To encourage peer correction, you could put the students into groups to discuss and justify their answers before eliciting the correct answers in whole-class feedback.

Answers
1 you assist (us) with **2** if you join **3** would take part
4 will have to put off **5** better unless your teacher pointed
6 I get over my cold / I get better

5 As an alternative to pairwork, you could set this up as a mingling activity where students form two lines, face a partner, and have one minute to ask and answer the questions, before one line moves one place left and asks and answers the questions with a new partner (for another minute). This continues until students are facing their original partner (and have spoken to half the students in the class). If you choose this option, you could allow students to read the questions from the Student's Book when speaking to their first two partners and then ask the questions from memory for the remainder. Monitor and write down examples of common errors with conditional structures (when students are not using their books) and elicit error correction in whole-class feedback.

Reading and Use of English Part 7 SB page 56

Lead in
Look at the photos with the students. Ask students to name the cities or countries and elicit them from the whole class (page 56: Helsinki, Finland; page 57: London, UK; Windsor, Canada; Melbourne, Australia). Ask students which cities they might consider studying in and why. Encourage responses using conditional structures. (*If I could, I would study in Helsinki because …*)

1 Set a time limit of three to five minutes. Elicit answers from the class. As students have encountered this type of activity several times, after elicitation you might like to ask them to think about (or discuss in pairs) how they would respond to the ideas in the questions and then elicit one or two examples from stronger students. For example, the idea in Q1 is *educational experience*, so students say what educational experience they would be looking for, e.g. facilities, teaching methods, distance from campus to the city centre, transportation to and from campus. As we can see, several of these points are mentioned in the correct answer D. For Q2 you could ask students *Easier to get to from where?* (home) and *how?* (plane), and they may also add how long it might take them to travel home for holidays, etc. Thinking about the language and ideas they are likely to read in the text can help students find the correct answers more quickly and easily.

Answers
Suggested underlining
1 wanted, experience, specific way of learning
2 chose place, easier to get to
3 felt, choice, important for future career
4 surprised, approach to teaching and learning
5 considered, starting a career, chosen location
6 difficult, adapt, new environment
7 different experience to, originally expected
8 got to know, local area before, studies began
9 disappointed, aspects of their experience
10 pleased, studying, large city

Read the exam advice with the students. Remind them to focus on one section at a time, but not to spend too long on each section as this may waste time. If they are unsure, they could write down (in the margin) the question number(s) they think the section answers, followed by a question mark (?) and return to the section once they have matched the other questions.

Exam advice

2 As this is an exam task, set a time limit of fifteen minutes. Allow students to discuss and justify their answers in small groups before eliciting in whole-class feedback.

Answers
1 D **2** C **3** A **4** B **5** C **6** D **7** A **8** B **9** C **10** A

Extension activity
As the text includes examples of sentences using conditional structures, you might like to ask students to find and underline them (e.g. *If I wanted to enjoy something more typically British, I'd choose a smaller location*). You could then put students in pairs and ask them to identify which conditional it is (in the example above it's the second conditional) and say whether it refers to something which is generally true, possible, imaginary or improbable. (Exercise 1 page 54).

3 Encourage students to use the language from the unit so far in their response, with particular focus on conditional structures (page 54 and Grammar reference page 168), commonly confused words (ex 3 page 54) and phrasal verbs (page 53). Allow students ten minutes to look back through the unit and make notes before setting a time limit of 15 minutes for them to write the email. When they have finished, ask students to swap emails and underline examples of the target language.

Reading and Use of English Part 3 SB page 58

Lead in
Remind students of the importance of knowing different forms of the same stem word for Reading and Use of English Part 3. Put students in pairs and give each pair a list of longer (3+ syllables) words (nouns work well but so do adverbs and adjectives) and ask them to write down whether the word is a noun, adverb or adjective and then divide it into its prefix/affix, stem and suffix (e.g. *irregularity* – *ir|regular|ity* (noun), *uncomfortable* – *un|comfort|able* (adjective), *alteration* – *alter|ation* (noun). Once they have done this, tell them to look for patterns in prefixes and suffixes. As students will focus on nouns in this section, encourage them to focus on the common suffixes for nouns: *-ity*, *-ty -ance*, *-ence*, *-ism*, *-ist*, *-ment*, *-ness*, *-ship*, *-sion*, *-tion*. For stronger students, you could ask pairs to brainstorm the suffixes for nouns that they know before giving them the list of words.

1 Students work individually before comparing their answers in pairs. As an alternative, students could be paired A/B. A closes their book while B says the verb and asks A to tell them the noun. Students swap after six. Elicit the answers. Alternatively, you could allow students to look up any new words in the dictionary and encourage them to record them (preferably in the context of a phrase, collocation or sentence) in their notebooks.

Answers
2 intention **3** response (responsibility) **4** adjustment
5 comparison **6** existence **7** demand **8** development
9 behaviour **10** advice/advisor **11** appearance
12 knowledge

2 Students work individually before checking their answers by using an English to English dictionary. If dictionaries are not available, students could compare their answers with a different partner than in Exercise 1, before you elicit from the class.

Answers
2 assess **3** feel **4** involve **5** investigate **6** confuse
7 prefer **8** approve

Extension activity
Students could form adverbs and adjectives, where possible, from the words in Exercises 1 and 2. For additional challenge they could form negatives (e.g. *intentional, unintentional, intentionally, unintentionally*) and then create sentences using different forms (*I intend to study abroad next year, it is my intention to study abroad next year, I have intentionally chosen to study abroad next year because I'd like to learn about a new culture …*).

Read the exam advice with the students. You may wish to remind them that in addition to prefixes and suffixes, internal changes to the word stem may be required, e.g. *long* becomes *length*.

Exam advice

3 As this is an exam task, set a time limit of ten minutes. Allow students to compare their answers before eliciting them from the class. You may wish to point out that the answer to question 4 is a negative form and elicit from a stronger student who answered correctly, what, in the text, told them the negative form was required (the linker *but*, the preposition *from* rather than *to* after the gap, the overall meaning of the sentence).

Answers
1 completely **2** punishment **3** offenders **4** discouraged **5** willingness **6** guidance **7** educational **8** creativity

4 Allow groups ten minutes to brainstorm their ideas. You may wish to provide them with a list of subtopics which will be debated, and tell them they must think of at least one reason for each. This may help the flow of the debate later on. Examples of sub-topics include: project work, revision, collaboration, research, autonomy, time, connectivity, cost, student inclusion, role of the teacher, etc. Tell students that they should practise language to agree, disagree and give opinions and that they should look back through the Student's Book (Units 3 and 4, Speaking Parts 3 and 4) and/or Speaking bank pages 209–213 (Speaking Parts 3 and 4) to remind themselves of key phrases (*Yes, that's true, I can see what you mean but …, Would you agree that …?, I think there are some advantages to …*, etc.). During the debate, monitor and note examples of common errors with key language. After the class vote, elicit error corrections from the class.

Speaking Part 1 SB page 59

▶ **Page 204 Speaking bank**

Lead in
Put students into pairs and ask them to compare and contrast their most and least favourite subject at school/ when they were at school. Encourage them to use complex language to make comparisons, e.g. *by far the most/least interesting subject is/was x*. Do not tell students to give reasons to support their ideas as this is covered in Exercise 3. As you typically monitor for common errors, and students have practised complex comparative structures several times, it may be motivating to monitor for examples of correct language use and feed them back after the task.

1 As an alternative to pairwork, students could read the audioscript out loud, working in threes (each student reading a different speaker). As they read, they must try and add in the missing word. This may encourage them to more naturally complete the extract as they hear what they are saying. As the part of the teacher has no gaps, you may prefer this speaker to be read by weaker or very strong students who do not need the scaffolding.

Answers
1 because **2** if **3** when **4** who **5** if **6** and

Track 19

Teacher: Nikolai, what is your favourite subject at school?
Nikolai: I find biology very interesting. That's because I enjoy all science subjects a lot and if I can get good enough marks in my final exams, I'll study medicine when I go to university. Also, I've got a really excellent biology teacher, who makes the subject much more fun.
Teacher: And you, Martyna, how do you think you'll use English in the future?
Martyna: Well, I think English is an absolute necessity now and you just can't get by without it. It'll help me to find a job, and if my work involves travelling, it'll be an essential skill. I'd like to work in business, and I think English is a really big advantage for that, too.
Teacher: Thank you. Nikolai, can you …

2 You could let students listen a second time before they answer the questions and allow them to check their answers by underlining the relevant parts of the audioscript.

Suggested answers
1 two (he enjoys all science subjects; he has an excellent teacher)
2 three
3 Candidates receive marks based on their ability to manage grammar and longer units of discourse. Candidates also achieve a higher score for longer, more complex sentences.
4 It creates a good, positive impression.

3 Although the first part of this task is similar to the Lead in, the students focus on giving and justifying opinions rather than comparing and contrasting. Monitor and listen for common errors for giving opinions and elicit corrections during whole-class feedback.

Extension activity
In pairs, students compare and contrast language teaching now with how language teaching might be ten years in the future. If necessary, suggest subtopics such as: the role of the teacher, English language smart phone applications, online learning, translator applications, hearables (wireless in-ear accessory), the continued (or not) use of English as a lingua franca, etc.

/P/ Pronunciation: syllable stress

4.1 Students practise saying the words and underline which syllable they think is stressed before they listen.

Answers
necessary, necessity

Track 20
necessary necessity

4.2 Encourage students to say the words out loud and hear how the words sound when they move the stressed syllable, before underlining which syllable they think is stressed.

> **Answers**
> See Track 21 audioscript below.

4.3 After completing this exercise, you may wish to point out that typically neither suffixes nor prefixes are stressed, e.g. *unnecessary*.

> **Answers**
> The stress is always on the syllable before the suffix (*-tion*, *-ity*).

Track 21

satisfying/satisfactory	possible/possibility
educate/education	prefer/preference
exam/examination	refer/reference
explain/explanation	relative/relation
graduate/graduation	institute/institution

4.4 Students work in pairs. One student says the word and the other claps when they hear the stressed syllable. This will encourage students to emphasise the stressed syllable.

5 Allow students a few minutes to choose their words and prepare their ideas.

6 As an alternative to pairwork, you could put students into groups of four. Two students act as observers, listening to one student each. As the students speak, the observers write down examples of correct and incorrect word stress. After three minutes, ask the observers to give feedback to the speakers before they swap roles. When giving feedback, students should be encouraged to give examples of words they heard stressed correctly (at least two) as well as ones they think were incorrectly stressed. As it is probably more motivational and comfortable for students to provide both positive and critical feedback, you may wish to avoid them focusing only on incorrectly stressed words.

> **Exam advice**
> Read the exam advice with the students. Point out that they should give full answers to the questions, rather than yes, no, or very short answers. Say that even if the examiner does not ask *why?* they should still give reasons. Finally, remind students that they will not lose marks by asking the examiner to repeat a question as long as they ask for repetition correctly (e.g. Could you say that again, please? Did you mean …?). They should not say, e.g. What? Repeat please? at this level.

7 Set a time limit of five minutes for students to prepare their answers. Whilst preparing, encourage students to use the Speaking bank (page 204) for language examples and fluency ideas (e.g. Exercises 5 and 6: using contracted forms to sound more fluent).

Writing Part 1 (an essay) SB page 60

▶ **Page 192 Writing bank**

> **Lead in**
> In pairs, students discuss the challenges of learning English (or another foreign language). Encourage them to give opinions and agree and disagree with each other, as well as give reasons for their answers. For example, they should not simply say *the grammar is difficult*, but rather give reasons why they believe this to be the case, e.g. by saying what structures they find the most challenging, comparing English grammatical structures with their first language, and describing how these differences or similarities affect their use of English (either positively or negatively).

1 As an alternative to a pair discussion, you could split the class in half with half of the pairs discussing reasons why all young people should learn a foreign language and the other reasons why they should not. They should focus on the two points in the exam task plus an additional point they choose. Monitor and elicit one or two reasons from students who are struggling. After three minutes, reorganise the pairs so that *should* and *should not* are sat together. Students could then discuss the question in line with the rubric. At the end of five minutes, elicit ideas from the class and write them on the board. When eliciting, include ideas for (your own idea).

2 Ask students to cover Marina's plan (Exercise 3) before you do this task. Remind them of the importance of planning (planned essays are typically more focused on the question and answer it more fully) and set a time limit of five minutes. You might wish to collect the plans and stick them to the board/walls so that students can compare their own with other students' plans. If you do this, encourage students to point out plans which they feel are comprehensive and cover each part of the question fully, and to provide suggestions for improving plans which are weaker.

3 Students work in pairs before you elicit answers from the class. When eliciting ideas for question 2, you may wish to ask students how long they think a plan should take. Students often underestimate planning and tend to say one or two minutes. If they do, it may be worth pointing out that they have around 40 minutes to write their essay of between 140 to 190 words, which is around four words per minute. Therefore, even if they spent ten minutes planning and five minutes checking their completed essay, it would still leave them twenty-five minutes to write their essay, which is around seven words per minute.

Suggested answers
1 No, because you need to show your knowledge of a range of vocabulary and the ability to express your ideas in your own words.
2 Students' own answers
3 Yes; candidates will lose marks if they don't cover all the points in the task as they won't have answered the question completely.

4 As one approach to the group work, you could put students into threes and ask them to read one opening paragraph each before discussing whether they think it is a good or bad example and why. As students read, encourage them to look back at the essay question and check their paragraph/the paragraphs for relevance. At this stage avoid giving feedback to students as this will be covered in Exercise 5.

5 Students work individually before comparing their answers in pairs. You may wish to ask if students were surprised by any of the teacher's comments. If so, they could highlight these and refer back to them when they write their opening paragraph in the next exercise.

Answers
a 3 **b** 2 **c** 1

6 As students have already spent time planning and discussing this question, set a time limit of ten minutes.

Extension activity
After completion, students swap opening paragraphs and, taking the role of the teacher, write three pieces of feedback about their partner's paragraph. Remind them to look at the essay question while they do this and also refer to the feedback in Exercise 5 (although make sure they do not simply copy what is written there).

7 Tell students to read the essay quickly, ignoring the gaps, before they reread it and complete the task. Weaker students can work in pairs. Monitor and support weaker students. Make notes of common errors with any phrases. Elicit the correct answers and teach or concept check the use of any phrases which students are unclear about.

Answers
1 with the result that **2** Also **3** for example
4 These opportunities **5** if **6** A further point is that
7 It **8** For all these reasons **9** do so

8 As this is exam practice and students have practised this type of activity before, tell them they should work individually. Set a time limit of ten minutes for them to read the question and write their plan. Do not elicit ideas or encourage students to compare plans. Instead, move straight on to Exercise 9.

9 Students continue to work on their own with a time limit of 30 minutes to answer the question: 40 minutes less the ten minutes they had for writing their plan in Exercise 8. (Note: exam candidates will have 80 minutes to answer two writing questions in the exam so, although in the exam they may take slightly longer on Writing Part 1 (the essay) than Writing Part 2, it is probably a good idea if students get into the habit of dividing the time equally). For this task, you could give students a five-minute warning after twenty-five minutes, perhaps encouraging any students who you notice have completed their essays and put their pens down to use the extra time to read their essay and check for common errors.

Extension activity
Students swap essays and, using the checklist in the Writing bank on page 203, provide feedback to their partner. As an alternative, or follow-up, you could photocopy the model answer and ask students, still working in pairs, to compare their essays against the sample answer. If you opt to do the latter, encourage students to write down three to five improvements they could make to their essay, then allow them fifteen minutes to make the improvements, or if time is tight, you could set making the improvements as a homework task.

Model answer
In the modern world, it is essential for young people to get experience of other countries and other cultures, not only to learn the language, but also to learn to live with people from other parts of the world. For this reason, I believe it is a good idea to do an international exchange.
Young people who study abroad may have to study in the language of the country they visit, with the result that they gain extra language skills. They also learn to interact with people from other countries and understand their interests and way of life.
Another major advantage of studying abroad is that young people learn independence, because many of them will be living away from home for the first time. This allows them to return home more mature and self-confident than they were when they left.
Finally, I think it is important to build international understanding, and this can be achieved when young people form friendships across borders.
For all these reasons, I am strongly in favour of giving people the chance to study abroad when they are young.

Vocabulary

Education

admission
course requirement
job prospects
learner
mark (verb)
pass (noun)
research (verb)
sit (an exam)
tutor

Phrasal verbs

get away with sth
get over
hand (sth) back
live up to sth
look back
point out
put (sth) off
turn out

Commonly confused words

find out, get to know, know, learn, teach, study
attend, join, take part, assist

Vocabulary activity 1

In groups, students create a poster, like the brochure idea in Exercise 3 (page 54) which outlines the reasons why people should study for the B2 First exam at your school. You could encourage them to be creative, thinking up their own reasons why learners might enjoy studying on their course, or you could provide them with a format to follow. For example, the poster should include:

Purpose of the course
Duration of the course
Expectations of students (attendance, contribution, etc.)
Teaching methods
Reasons to choose your school/course instead of another.

Vocabulary activity 2

This activity is a fun way of practising the 2nd conditional, whilst at the same time recycling phrasal verbs from the unit. You will see there are five example questions below, although you may want to include your own, depending on the students' context. If so, allow yourself time to prepare the questions before class. Tell students you are going to give them questions which involve some sort of moral dilemma. Either write the questions on the board or ask students to write them down as you dictate them. Put the students into groups and ask them to discuss the questions, giving reasons for their responses. Point out that there are no right or wrong answers.

Example questions:
If your friend had a new pair of trousers they loved and which were the last ones in the shop, but you noticed there was a small tear in them, would you point it out?
If you felt you couldn't live up to the expectations of your parents, would you tell them?
If your friend accidently left their secret diary at your house and you knew they'd written about you in it, would you hand it back without reading it?
Would you advise a friend to put off doing something which they didn't enjoy, even if you thought it was good for them?

DIGITAL CLASSROOM

Practice Extra Unit 5
Test Generator Unit 5 test

Test and Train Exam Practice

6 Good job!

Unit objectives

Topic: jobs and careers

Reading and Use of English Part 5 (multiple choice): identifying the locations in the text that relate to each question

Reading and Use of English Part 2 (open cloze): identifying types of words required for each gap

Writing Part 2 (letter or email): describing jobs students do in your country in a letter or email

Listening Part 3 (multiple matching): recognising distractors

Speaking Part 2 (long turn): describing different kinds of work; describing similarities and differences when comparing

Pronunciation: sentence stress (2); contrastive sentence stress

Vocabulary: *work* or *job*; *possibility*, *occasion* or *opportunity*; *fun* or *funny*; collocations with *job* and *work*

Grammar: countable and uncountable nouns; articles

Starting off SB page 62

1 Look at the photos with the students. Elicit the first job (farmer), plus an advantage and disadvantage of doing this job (e.g. advantage: lots of physical exercise, disadvantage: have to work outside in all weathers) before allowing students to do the task.

Suggested answers
Photo 1: farmer
Photo 2: doctor
Photo 3: artist/painter
Photo 4: engineer
Photo 5: programmer / software developer

Listening Part 3 SB page 62

1 This exercise helps students to think about meaning in order to avoid word spotting. Point out that the paraphrases may be positive or negative forms. For example, *I find some aspects of my job boring*, could be paraphrased as, *not all aspects of my job are enjoyable* or *I find some aspects of my job uninteresting*. Encourage pairs to come up with one paraphrase for each option, before asking them to change partner and come up with a second paraphrase. Elicit examples during whole-class feedback.

Suggested answers
B Not all aspects of my job are enjoyable.
C My job isn't what people think it is.
D Working long hours isn't a problem for me.
E It doesn't feel like a job a lot of the time.
F My job makes me feel relaxed.
G I have more opportunities to be with my family.
H I'm thinking about finding a new job.

Exam advice

Read the advice with the students. Draw their attention to the last bullet point and tell them to look at option D from Exercise 1. Ask for an example of what a speaker might say which was connected to this sentence whilst it not being the correct answer (the speaker may mention something about working long hours but not within the context of how they feel about the hours they work).

2 Remind students that the speakers' individual scripts are not connected. Tell them they should think of meaning and avoid word spotting. Play the recording twice. Before eliciting the correct answers, you could ask students to check their answers using the audioscript on page 225 in pairs or individually.

Answers
1 C **2** A **3** E **4** B **5** G

Track 22

1 Flight attendant: Many people imagine that being a flight attendant is a glamorous job and that we take lots of holidays. Neither of these ideas could be further from the truth. We might look elegant, but we have to do a lot of unpleasant tasks, like picking up rubbish and cleaning. We travel to some exotic destinations, but we usually have to get straight back on the plane, so there's no possibility of spending any time there. What I like best about my job is helping families with young children. They're always so excited and often say funny things, which cheers me up when I'm having a difficult day.

2 Tour guide: I work as a tour guide, giving people historical tours of my home city. A lot of my work comes from people reading positive reviews on social media, so it's vital that I keep tourists engaged and happy throughout the tour. I love having the opportunity to share my knowledge with visitors.
I adapt the information that I give depending on my audience, and I'm now thinking about branching out into online tours for people who want to discover new places from the comfort of their own home. I want to make the tours as much fun for everyone as possible. It's a nice way to earn a living, even if the pay isn't that great.

3 Host: My husband and I have an apartment which we rent out to tourists. We've lived here for ten years, so we're in a good position to give our guests plenty of local knowledge. When guests arrive, we welcome them with an information pack and some traditional cakes. Of course, we have to spend quite a lot of time cleaning and getting the apartment ready for the next guests, but it's really no bother, as we live in the same building. We love being hosts so much that we tend to forget that it's a job.

4 Yoga teacher: I've been running yoga holidays for two years, and really love my job. When people first arrive, they often seem a bit anxious, but by the time they leave, they always look so much more relaxed and happy. After working in an office for so many years, I'm glad I changed my job and it's great to have the possibility of working from home. However, it can still be quite hard work. As well as teaching yoga, I have to do a lot of administrative tasks, which can be a bit dull. But it's worth it to be able to spend all day doing what I love!

5 Chef: My husband and I opened our restaurant two years ago. It's right in the centre of the historic old town, so we do good business. We want to give people an authentic dining experience with plenty of traditional home-cooked food. People often come to celebrate special occasions, like birthdays or anniversaries, and we want to make sure that they have an unforgettable experience. Our son and daughter help out during the school holidays, waiting tables and preparing food in the kitchen, so we actually see more of each other than we did with our old jobs.

Extension activity
As with previous listening practice, you could put students into pairs or small groups and ask them to find examples in the audioscript of why the incorrect options are incorrect. The exam advice makes reference to speakers talking about something connected with other sentences, so you may find this activity particularly useful now. You might also want to point out that students should not let their own biases or preconceptions make them choose an incorrect option. They should focus on what they hear, not what they believe to be the case themselves. For example, in script 1, students might assume that the line: *but we have to do a lot of unpleasant tasks, like picking up rubbish and cleaning* refers to *boring* in option B (bias); the line: *We travel to some exotic destinations* refers to *relaxing* in option F (bias/preconception); the line: *so there's no possibility of spending any time there* connects to *long hours* in option D or *time* in option G; and the line: *What I like best about my job is helping families with young children* connects to *family* in option G.

3 Before students do this task and to help them prepare, you could ask them to make a list, using the audioscript, of the speakers' jobs (flight attendant, tour guide, host, yoga teacher, restaurateur) plus things each speaker does (e.g. tour guide: historical tours of city, share knowledge, adapt information, online tours). Additionally, you may want to encourage them to think about the type of personality needed for each job, perhaps recycling adjectives from previous units (e.g. Unit 2: *hard-working*, *sensitive*, *mature*, *reliable*, etc.). Finally, you could, as an alternative or extension, tell students to compare and contrast the jobs using complex language to make comparisons (*By far the most interesting/boring job is …*)

Vocabulary SB page 63

work or *job*; *possibility*, *occasion* or *opportunity*, *fun* or *funny*

Lead in
Say something to students about your job, e.g. *Although it can be hard work at times, teaching is a rewarding job as I get to help students to achieve their language goals.* Elicit the different meanings of *job* and *work* (*job* is the regular and specific activity of your profession; *work* is non-specific, referring to a general activity). Point out that *job* is a countable noun and that *work* is a verb or an uncountable noun (when used in a non-specific sense). If students are still unsure of the difference in meaning, you could elicit examples of compound nouns for *work*, which may help them understand that the general term needs to be modified to give it a specific meaning, e.g. *homework* – activities done to complete school tasks; *housework* – necessary jobs done in the home, such as washing up.

1 Read the rubric with the students. Elicit why the vocabulary in this exercise is important (because it often causes confusion and leads to real errors made by exam candidates). Students work in pairs before checking their answers in the audioscript.

Answers
1 job **2** funny **3** opportunity **4** fun **5** job
6 possibility **7** work **8** occasions

2 Students work on their own before comparing their answers in pairs. If students find this task challenging, put them into pairs. Give one student three words and the other four (to encourage more discussion, try and split the commonly confused words, e.g. A has *opportunity* and B has *possibility*). Allow them five minutes to look their words up in an English to English dictionary and write down the meaning together with an example sentence. Once they have looked up all their words, they must explain the meaning of their words to their partner before completing the task together. Monitor, encouraging students to discuss the differences between the words. Elicit the answers from the whole class.

Answers
1 job **2** funny **3** possibility **4** work **5** occasions
6 fun **7** jobs **8** opportunity

3 If preferred, you could put students into groups and allocate one or two words to each member of the group. Tell them to complete the diagram for their word(s) only. After a minute, tell students to take turns to share their ideas before they complete the diagram together. You could also get students to look up *job* and *work* in the dictionary and check for any additional collocations (e.g. *out of work*, *hold down a job*). During feedback, select students to write the collocations on the board, including those in the Student's Book and those which students have found in the dictionary.

Answers

(well-paid)	(outdoor)	(full-time)	(fascinating)
badly-paid	office	holiday	pleasant
		part-time	responsible
(hard)	(skilled)	permanent	worthwhile
challenging	manual	temporary	
demanding		weekend	
tiring			
tough			

4 If there are not enough jobs to give a different one to each pair, you could add more to the list. As students might waste time choosing a job rather than writing a story, you could tell them that when a job has been chosen by a pair, it is gone. Give students thirty seconds to look at the list of jobs and confer with their partner, before telling them to shout out the job they want. The first pair to say the job gets it (make a note of the jobs taken). Allow students fifteen minutes to write their funny story. Tell them to start with a brief description of the job and what work they were doing before the funny thing happened, next describe the funny thing that happened, and then give a brief description of what happened next, or as a result. You could point out this structure in the example answer and elicit the 'funny thing' (*tripped and threw food over the table*). As students need to include adjectives from Exercise 3, elicit these from the example too (*part-time, demanding, badly paid, permanent, hard*).

Extension activity

Collect the pairs' stories. Put them on the board or walls and ask students to walk around the class and read them. Encourage students to point out adjective collocations as they do this. While they are doing this, read the stories yourself and make notes of common errors with the target language. Once students have read every story, ask them to vote for their favourite story, telling them that they cannot vote for their own. During feedback, draw attention to the common errors you wrote down earlier and elicit corrections from the class.

Reading and Use of English Part 5 SB page 64

Lead in

With books closed, elicit from students five jobs they think are dangerous and write them on the board (e.g. deep-sea diver, roofer, miner, logging worker, oil rig worker, high-rise window cleaner, police officer). In groups, tell students to discuss which jobs they would, or would not do, giving reasons for their answers. Set a time limit of three minutes before eliciting ideas from the class.

1 As an alternative to answering the questions in pairs or small groups, you could turn this into a Speaking Part 2 practice task. Students compare and contrast the photos using complex language to make comparisons, and after they have spoken for one minute each, introduce the question: *Say what skills someone would need to do these jobs*. If you choose this alternative, encourage students to compare and contrast in one of two ways: either they can talk about one similarity followed by one difference, or they can talk about all the similarities before talking about all the differences. This latter point will prepare students for Speaking Part 2, Exercise 1 on page 66 (talking about similarities and differences).

Exam advice

Read the advice with the students. Point to the final bullet point and ask them why this is important (because adverbs may help the reader understand the attitude, purpose and opinion of the writer). Remind students that the questions are presented in the same order as the text. So, for example, they would not find the answer to question 6 in the first paragraph. As students might spend too long on one question and waste time, tell them that it is OK for them to move on and return to a difficult question at the end. Finally, tell students that if they do not know the answer, they should make an educated guess rather than leave a question unanswered: an unanswered question will definitely be incorrect, whereas an educated guess may be correct.

2 Read the rubric and elicit the answer to the first question with the class before allowing students to work in pairs. Tell students to write the paragraph number next to the question so that they can move quickly to the correct part of the text when they answer the questions in Exercise 3. Alternatively, tell students to read the text through quickly once before doing this task, in line with the advice given in Exam advice. When eliciting the answers, remind students that the questions follow the order of the text so they will not, for example, find the answer to the final question in the first paragraph.

Answers

1 first paragraph **2** line 10 / second paragraph
3 third paragraph **4** lines 28–29 / fourth paragraph
5 fifth paragraph **6** sixth paragraph

3 As this is an exam task, tell students to work individually and set a time limit of no more than twenty minutes. Put students into pairs to discuss their answers (you could pair weaker students with stronger ones) before eliciting the correct answers from the class. Students may find Part 5 difficult and it is possible that, even after you have elicited the correct answers, not all students will have fully understood. If this is the case, it may be helpful to put students into groups, and ask students who answered correctly to explain to the group how they made their choices. If you choose to do this, make sure that for each question there is at least one person in the group who answered correctly, and monitor to support the students' explanations where necessary.

Answers
1 D 2 A 3 B 4 C 5 A 6 A

Background information
A storm chaser is a person who follows extreme weather events, such as tornados, in order to study, photograph or experience them.

Speaking Part 2 SB page 66

▶ **Page 206 Speaking bank**

1 You could tell pairs to discuss all the similarities before they discuss the differences, or alternatively, get them to discuss one similarity followed by one difference. Elicit ideas from the class. If you want students to later compare their ideas with those given by the speakers (Exercise 3), you could write the students' ideas on the board.

2 It may help if you quickly elicit one or two common collocations from the class before asking students to tackle this task (e.g. *deal with customers*, *not a well-paid job*). Point out that students could also use *badly paid job* from Exercise 3 page 63 and ask them to consider what adjective collocations from Exercise 3 page 63 they could use when discussing the photos (*unskilled/skilled work*, *tiring job*, *tough job*, etc.). Monitor as students discuss the phrases, noting examples of errors with the language. After five minutes, elicit ideas and error correction.

3 Read the rubric with the students. Make sure they understand that 1 and 2 refer to the photos and not the speakers. Students check their answers using the audioscript on page 226 before you elicit them during feedback.

Answers
a B b B c B d 2 e 1 f 2 g 2 h 1 i 2

Track 23

Examiner: Here are your photographs. They show young people doing different jobs. I'd like you to compare the photographs and say what you think the people are learning from doing these jobs.

Nikolai: Well, OK, so firstly I can say that both photos show young people working. Er, both the jobs in the photos involve working in situations where they need good skills in dealing with people in the correct way. I'm sure neither of them is very well paid. Anyway, the first photo shows a man serving people in a restaurant, whereas in the second photo, a woman is working with children and coaching them to play football. The man's job may be full time, whereas the woman's is probably part time. I think both can learn a lot from these jobs. The man can learn how to keep customers happy, while the woman has to keep children in order. The man has to learn to work efficiently under pressure. On the other hand, the woman has to learn to keep cool. She'll probably learn not just to deal with children, but also their parents.

Examiner: Thank you. Antonia, which of these jobs would you prefer to do?

Antonia: I'd prefer to coach children than work in a restaurant because, really, I enjoy being in the fresh air more than being indoors. And I like kids.

Examiner: Thank you.

4 Ask students to read options a and b before you read the rubric. You may wish to put students into pairs to discuss which strategy they think is better before they listen. Once they have listened and you have elicited the correct answer, ask students if their prediction was correct. Elicit why b is the best strategy (a more successful answer will compare and contrast the photos rather than simply describe them).

Answer
b

5 After students have completed this task and you have elicited the answers from the whole class, point out that the two phrases Nikolai does not use are not incorrect and could be used in the exam.

Answers
See underlining in Track **23** above. Nikolai does not use the phrases:
While the girl in the first photo …
Another thing in the second photo is …

Extension activity
Put students into pairs and refer them to Starting off on page 62. Tell them to take turns and choose two photos to compare and contrast, and to use at least five phrases from Exercise 5, speaking for one minute each. Monitor and write down examples of both correct language use and common errors. During feedback, tell students the correct phrases you heard, then elicit corrections for any errors.

/P/ Pronunciation: sentence stress (2)

6 Before starting this pronunciation section, remind students that the words which are stressed in a sentence are typically 'content words' (words which show meaning). These include nouns, adjectives and main verbs, while 'function words' (auxiliary verbs, pronouns, articles, etc.) are not usually stressed. A way to illustrate this is that if they only heard content words, they would still be able to understand the general meaning of a sentence. If this is a challenging concept for students, do the following: write on the board (or say): The ___ is ___ on ___ because of ___ and ask students if they can work out the context using only the words you have written (or said). (No, because there are no content words.) Then write (or say), ___ *shop* ___*closed* ___*Monday* ___ *employee training* and ask the same question. (Yes, because these are the content words.) Now say the complete sentence, whispering the function words and saying the content words clearly: *the **shop** is **closed** on **Monday** because of **employee training**.*). Point out that if students only heard the content words, they could still understand the meaning, which is why this aspect of sentence stress is important for good pronunciation. Finally, point out that when we use stress to contrast ideas, it is the content words showing contrast which will be stressed, not every content word.

6.1 Tell students to focus on *what* Nikolai is comparing (jobs) to stop them from going into too much detail. Elicit the answer from the class.

Answers
Nikolai compares the job of the man in the first photo with the job of the woman in the second photo.

6.2 As an alternative to listening and underlining, you could put students into pairs and ask them to underline all the content words (first photo shows man serving people restaurant; second photo woman working children). Then tell them to circle only the words which are used to make a comparison. Point out that it may help if they look for pairs of words expressing a comparison (first/second, man/woman, people/children; only restaurant has no pair in this extract).

Track 24

Anyway, the first photo shows a man serving people in a restaurant, whereas in the second photo, a woman is working with children …

6.3 If you chose to do the alternative option in 6.2, you could repeat the process or, if not, introduce it here. During the speaking practice, monitor and, if you hear that students are not stressing the correct words, stop them. Model and drill each sentence with the whole class before putting them back into pairs to practise together.

Answers
See underlining in recording script for Track 25.

Track 25

1 Nikolai: The man's job may be full-time, whereas the woman's is probably part-time.

2 Nikolai: The man can learn how to keep customers happy, while the woman has to keep children in order.

3 Nikolai: She'll probably learn not just to deal with children, but also their parents.

4 Antonia: I'd prefer to coach children than work in a restaurant because, really, I enjoy being in the fresh air more than being indoors.

7 Encourage students to look back through the Student's Book for useful language whilst they are preparing (for example they could recycle words and phrases from page 63, Exercises 1 and 3 and page 66, Exercises 2 and 5). Allow them five minutes to look back through the Student's Book and make notes before completing the task.

8 As an alternative to pairwork, you could put the students into threes, with one student listening for two examples each of correct and incorrect contrastive sentence stress, whilst the other listens for a minimum of four examples of target language. Allow a minute after each speaker for students to provide feedback.

Exam advice

Read the advice with the students. Then allow them a few minutes to re-read the Exam info in Unit 2 on page 24. You could put them into pairs and ask them to briefly discuss which approach they prefer (one photo first or both at the same time) and why. Point out that it is a good idea, once they start speaking, to stick to one approach as it may help them to give a more structured answer and achieve a higher score.

9 You may wish to follow the same approach as in Exercises 7 and 8 if the students require extra support. Alternatively, you could allow students just one minute to read the instructions and look at the photos before they start the task. The second option would more closely reflect the exam. Either way, remind them that they need to discuss the similarities as well as the differences. Monitor and write down examples of correct and incorrect language use, focusing on contrastive sentence stress, making comparisons, commonly confused words and adjective collocations. During whole-class feedback, praise students for the correct examples, then elicit correction of any errors.

Grammar

Countable and uncountable nouns

SB page 68

▶ **Page 169 Grammar reference**

Lead in

With books closed, elicit that *work* from the vocabulary section on page 63 was an uncountable noun used for nonspecific activities (*Although it can be hard work at times, teaching is a rewarding job as I get to help students to achieve their language goals*). Then write on the board: *I saw many works of art when I visited the new gallery.* and elicit that in this example *work* is countable because *work of art* refers to a particular work. Point out that whilst some nouns are countable or uncountable, others can be both countable and uncountable with a different meaning. Once you have done this, tell students to open their Student's Books and read the information on Grammar reference page 169.

1 Point out that students should focus on the article (e.g. *the*) or determiner (e.g. *much*) before the noun if they are unsure (e.g. *much* + uncountable noun). Students work individually. Once they have completed the task, ask them to write their answers on slips of paper (one word on one slip of paper) and then hold them up as you ask for each answer in turn. If a lot of students answered incorrectly, tell them to do practice 1 and/or 2 on Grammar reference page 170 before continuing with Exercise 2.

Answers
1 information **2** some **3** job **4** accommodation was **5** furniture **6** damage **7** much luggage **8** music **9** staff

2 Remind students that some nouns can be both countable and uncountable with a slight change in meaning. Elicit one or two examples (e.g. the material *glass* vs. *glasses* as containers; *time* meaning 'duration' vs. *times* as a number of instances). Before students start this exercise, remind them that the questions contain common errors made by exam candidates. After you have elicited the correct answers, tell students to asterisk (*) the questions they answered incorrectly. Once they have done this, tell them to write the asterisked questions in their notebooks under the heading *common errors I make* and refer to it when they are revising for the exam.

Answers
1 accommodation; luggage **2** advice; information; knowledge; assistance **3** damage; traffic; transport **4** air conditioning; furniture; staff **5** food **6** homework; work **7** equipment; machinery **8** cash; money; wealth **9** sightseeing; scenery **10** music

3 Tell students that because countable and uncountable nouns can be challenging to learn, it may help them to learn them within complete phrases. Point out that some of the phrases in this exercise are common collocations (e.g. *piece/bit of advice*) and that using collocations will help them both to sound more natural when they are speaking in English and achieve a higher score in the speaking exam. When you elicit the answers, encourage students to write the complete phrases in their notebooks.

Answers
1 piece/bit **2** number **3** piece/bit **4** piece/bit **5** deal **6** number; amount

Extension activity
To help students remember the phrases from the last exercise, put them in pairs, dictate the following questions, and tell them to ask and answer them. Set a time limit of five minutes
When did you last give someone a piece/bit of advice? What advice did you give them?
When was the last time you put a great deal of effort into doing something? What was it and why?
What's the most useful piece of equipment you have ever bought or used?
When was the last time you heard a great piece/bit of news? What was it?
Do you feel comfortable being around a large number/amount of people?

Articles SB page 68

▶ **Page 170 Grammar reference**

4 Read the rubric with the students. Tell them to read all the examples quickly to get an idea of how the articles are used in context before completing the exercise on their own. Select individual students to provide an answer to one of each of the questions and elicit error corrections from the class if the selected student answers incorrectly.

Answers
1 d **2** b **3** a **4** c **5** e **6** f

5 Tell students to read the text quickly before they do the exercise as they may naturally identify the correct answer for each gap as they read. Alternatively, students read the text out loud as sometimes it is easier to identify the answer aurally. Students compare their answers in pairs before you elicit them from the class.

Answers
1 the **2** an **3** the **4** – **5** a **6** a **7** – **8** the **9** the **10** – **11** the **12** a

6 Student work individually before checking their answers in pairs. Elicit the correct answers before students ask and answer the questions.

Answers
1 the **2** a **3** – **4** a **5** the **6** an **7** – **8** – **9** a **10** –

Reading and Use of English Part 2 SB page 69

Lead in
Tell students what time you usually get up on Saturday or Sunday (or a day you do not work). Ask them to stand up and, starting with 5 am, tell students to sit down when you say the time they usually get up on (say a day they are not at school/work, e.g. Sunday; if students do not have a specific day off, you could say 'a day you

don't have to get up for school or work'). Students sit down as you say the time they get up. The last student(s) standing is (are) the student(s) who get up the latest. Students briefly discuss in pairs, how many hours of sleep they get, or would prefer to get, every night.

1 Read the rubric and elicit ideas from the class.

2 Set a time limit of one minute to encourage students not to stop reading when they reach a gap. Elicit the correct answer. If students read the answer directly from the text, encourage them to reframe it in their own words as this will help them practise paraphrasing.

Answers
People aged 20 to 45 who do not have allergies and do not smoke.

Exam advice

Read the advice with the students. Alternatively, you could put students in pairs, ask them to read the advice, and briefly discuss which points are the most useful for them and why. This will give students the opportunity to internalise the advice and think about how they could apply it in the exam.

3 As this is an exam task, students work individually. Remind them to read the example, which is there to help them understand how the questions are answered. Set a time limit of fifteen minutes. Do not elicit answers at the end of the task (see Exercise 4).

4 Students work individually. Set a time limit of five minutes. Select individual students to read the sentences from Exercise 3, including the gapped word. Listen but do not correct errors. You may find that the student corrects themselves as they are reading, or that members of the class offer corrections. However, the idea is for you to identify common student errors with the grammatical structures and fixed phrases listed in the exercise. Once each sentence has been read out, you could either elicit error corrections from the whole class, or review the language causing difficulty before eliciting the correct answers.

Answers
1 part **2** what **3** from **4** at **5** be/get **6** to **7** have **8** like

5 Before students start the task, elicit one or two ideas from the class of what they might be asked to do or give up for each experiment. As an alternative to discussing all options, you could put students into fours with two students from each group comparing and contrasting two options. Then, after three minutes, ask groups to discuss all four options together.

Writing Part 2 (an email or letter) SB page 70

▶ **Page 194 Writing bank**

1 As the students have completed this type of task before, tell them to work individually and set a time limit of one minute. Students compare their answers in pairs. When eliciting, you might want to tell students to paraphrase the three points (say them in their own words), which will help you identify what topic vocabulary they know and encourage them not to repeat the words in the question in their answer (e.g. the type of work students could do; any challenges they may face; an effective way of finding work).

Answers
Suggested underlining
jobs students do in your country, problems they have, best way to find a good student job

Exam advice

Read the advice with the students. As students have made a number of plans for writing tasks now, you may want to elicit different planning techniques students have used or could use, e.g. headings and a bulleted list, a mind map, a writing frame (*who are you writing to? why are you writing?* etc.), and ask them to reflect on which they prefer and why. Then put them into groups and tell them to briefly discuss their preferred technique.

2 Before students discuss their ideas, put them into groups. Give each group a large piece of paper and tell them to write down five topic-related words or phrases (e.g. *employment, low-paid, flexible hours, staff, employee*). Tell them to change papers and add another five words. Keep doing this until the paper is back with its original group. Not only will this help students to think of ideas to discuss, but it will also provide them with a list of vocabulary to use when they are planning (Exercise 3). Set a time limit of two minutes for students to discuss their ideas before eliciting examples from the class.

3 Students work individually. Remind them that their plan should cover each of the three points underlined in Exercise 1. In addition, tell students to write down ten topic related words or phrases they could use in their answer. They can select words from Exercise 2 if they wish (the paper should still be on their desk unless you chose to write the words and phrases on the board). Point out that it is a good idea to brainstorm a list of topic related vocabulary (five to ten words) when they are planning, as it easy to forget key vocabulary once they start writing, and that they will get higher marks if they use a range of topic related vocabulary including phrases, phrasal verbs and common collocations.

4 If students find the second question difficult to answer, elicit that each paragraph should contain one topic only. Once you have elicited the answers, you may wish to point out that Pablo is using informal phrases (sometimes students will use language that is too formal when writing an email). You could put students into pairs and ask them to compare Pablo's answer with the plan they made in Exercise 3.

Answers
1 It's good to hear from you; I hope this helps and good luck with your project.
2 The first sentence of each paragraph tells us the subject of the paragraph.

Extension activity
Students work in pairs and underline useful topic related phrases (*find part-time work, not often well paid, take somebody on*). Once they have done this, encourage students to write the phrases in their notebooks.

5 Point out that these are common errors made by students. After students have completed the exercise and you have elicited the answers, ask students to asterisk (*) any words from the list that they typically spell incorrectly. Then tell them to write these words in their notebooks under the heading *common spelling mistakes*, which they should refer to when they are checking their writing and when they are revising for the exam.

Answers

~~restaurans~~ restaurants	~~usefull~~ useful
~~easely~~ easily	~~becaus~~ because
~~studing~~ studying	~~corses~~ courses
~~wich~~ which	~~especialy~~ especially
~~payed~~ paid	~~advertisment~~ advertisement

6 Once students have completed the task and you have elicited the answers, you may wish to put them into groups and ask them to discuss their techniques for remembering the correct spelling of commonly misspelt words (this could be in their first language and in English), e.g. *i before e except after c*: *bel**ie**ve, rec**ei**ve* (note: there are exceptions to this rule, e.g. *forfeit, weird*); mnemomics: **n**ever **e**at **c**ake **e**at **s**alad **s**andwiches **a**nd **r**emain **y**oung (the first letter of each word spells *necessary*); endings with sounds like /ʃəs/ are spelt *-cious* or *-tious*. You may wish to point out that some words are spelt differently in English (US) and English (UK), for example *color* (US) and *colour* (UK). Tell students that they can use either UK or US spellings in the exam. However, they should be consistent (and not go between UK and US spelling).

Answers
comfortable grateful beginning prefer

7 Students work individually. You may prefer to set a time limit of one minute for the first bullet point before eliciting the answers from the class. Then, set a time limit of eight to ten minutes for students to write their plans. Remind students that when planning they could write a list of ten topic related words or phrases. At this stage of the course, you may prefer not to ask students to share their plans until after they have written their answer to Exercise 8.

Answers
Suggested underlining
first jobs, first job you had, what was it like, any problems, what, you learn

8 As this is an exam task, set a time limit of thirty minutes (forty minutes less the ten minutes you allowed for the planning). Give students a five-minute warning before you ask them to put their pens down. Tell students to count the number of words in their answer and write this down (they could do this quickly by counting the number of words they have written in three lines (e.g. 8, 10, 12), averaging it (10) and then multiplying this number by the number of lines they have written 14 (lines) x 10 words per line (average) = 140 words). Point out that it is useful for students to know how much they will need to write in *their* handwriting as they should not waste time continuously counting the number of words they have written during the exam (for example, someone with large handwriting may need to write one full A4 page whereas someone with small writing only half a page). Elicit that they will lose marks if they do not write enough words.

Extension activity
Put the students into pairs, provide each pair with a copy of the model answer and ask them to write a plan for it. If time allows, refer students to Exercise 4 on page 70 and tell them to answer the question for both their writing and the model answer. For example, how did they start and finish their email? Did they include the subject of the paragraph in the first sentence?

Model answer
Hi Stephen,
It's nice to hear from you again.
My first job, which I did for a month during my last summer holidays, was as a part-time assistant at a shoe shop in my town. I used to work every day from 9 a.m. until lunchtime serving customers. Basically, I had to welcome them to the shop and help them to find the shoes they were looking for.
The job was a good experience because I learned how to deal with customers and help them to make up their minds when they were not sure what they wanted. On days when there weren't many customers, I had to tidy the store room, which was quite boring, but I certainly also learned a lot about shoes: which are comfortable, what sort of shoes suit different types of people and so on.

> I didn't have any particular difficulties except when dealing with customers who were rude or in too much of a hurry, but I managed to smile just the same.
> Good luck with your project!
> Louise

Vocabulary

Commonly confused words

work / job
possibility / occasion / opportunity
fun / funny

Collocations with *job* and *work*

badly paid
challenging
demanding
fascinating
full-time
hard
holiday
manual
office
outdoor
part-time
permanent
pleasant
responsible
skilled
temporary
tiring
tough
weekend
well-paid
worthwhile

Spelling

accommodation
beginning
believe
comfortable
communicate
convenient
embarrassing
environment
excellent
experience
forward
grateful
necessary
opportunity
prefer
received
recommend
which

Vocabulary activity 1

In pairs, students role-play a conversation with a friend who wants to find part-time or casual work while they are studying in the student's city or town. This is similar to the writing task Exercise 1 on page 70 but will be a dialogue rather than a reply to an email. You could give students fifteen minutes to write the dialogue, which they then read out, before changing partners and having a unscripted version of a similar dialogue. Students could use the points in the writing task to help them structure their dialogue (jobs in their city/town/country, describing jobs/problems/best way to find a job) if they are struggling for ideas.

Example

Student 1: Hey Marci, you know I'm coming to study in [city/town/country] in the autumn? Well, I was thinking about getting a job to help me pay for my food and accommodation.
Student 2: Cool. Do you want something part-time?
Student 1: Yeah, or casual. You know, maybe weekend or evening work.
Student 2: Right, well I worked in a café last year. It's not very well paid but you don't really need much experience …

Vocabulary activity 2

Divide the list of commonly misspelt words in half. Put students into groups, then into two subgroups. Give each subgroup a different list of words. Tell them to write sentences using the commonly misspelt words. If they find it difficult to think of ideas, they could look their words up in the dictionary and write down the example sentences that are given there. They should spell the words correctly in two sentences, but all the other sentences should include a spelling mistake. The subgroups swap sentences, identify which words are spelt incorrectly, and correct them.

> **DIGITAL CLASSROOM**
> **Practice Extra** Unit 6
> **Test Generator** Unit 6 test
>
> **Test and Train Exam Practice**

Unit 5 Vocabulary and grammar review

1
1 get away with 2 put off; got over 3 live up to 4 look back; turned out 5 handed back; pointed out
2
1 learn 2 study 3 teaching 4 join; get to know 5 attend 6 take part in
3
1 harder, he would / he'd 2 study abroad, you will become / you'll become 3 she would not / wouldn't attend 4 look after my book 5 knew the answer, I would / I'd 6 he wasn't / was not so tired
4
1 preference 2 knowledge 3 behaviour 4 comparison 5 activities 6 assistance 7 measurement 8 ability

Unit 6 Vocabulary and grammar review

1
1 occasion 2 work 3 job 4 occasion 5 fun 6 opportunity 7 funny 8 possibility
2
1 such / so much / a lot of fun 2 have / get / the / an opportunity to speak / take the opportunity to speak 3 have the possibility of studying 4 was much better than 5 with a good / great deal of 6 on one occasion
3
1 deal 2 bit / piece 3 bit / piece 4 bit / piece 5 number
4
1 – 2 a 3 the 4 a 5 – 6 a 7 – 8 a 9 the 10 a 11 a 12 – 13 a 14 an 15 the 16 an 17 –

7 High adventure

Unit objectives

Topic: outdoor sports and activities

Reading and Use of English Part 6 (gapped text): identifying words in the sentences that refer to something specific in the text

Reading and Use of English Part 4 (key word transformation): understanding why an answer is incorrect

Writing Part 2 (an article): structuring an article

Listening Part 2 (sentence completion): identifying the type of information needed for each gap

Listening Part 4 (multiple choice): identifying key words in the questions

Speaking Part 3 (collaborative task): suggesting ideas; asking your partner's opinion; agreeing and disagreeing

Pronunciation: Intonation (2); showing interest and enthusiasm

Vocabulary: verb collocations with activities; *look, see, watch, listen* and *hear*

Grammar: infinitive and verb + *-ing*

Starting off SB page 74

1 Allow students to work on their own for a minute before putting them into pairs. When eliciting the answers from the class, encourage students to use words and phrases that would be suitable for Speaking Part 2, e.g. *the top left photo shows someone rock climbing; in the top middle photograph we can see two people skydiving.*

Answers
1 rock climbing **2** skydiving **3** mountain biking
4 paintballing **5** windsurfing **6** skateboarding

2 As an alternative to working in groups, students could work in pairs if you prefer. Encourage students to give reasons for their answers and use language to agree and disagree with each other.

Extension activity
Use the photos from Exercise 1 for a Speaking Part 2 practice task. First elicit some of the equipment that can be seen in the photos (e.g. *harness, rope, parachute, helmet, rifle, sailboard, skateboard*). Then put students into pairs and ask each pair to select two photos to compare and contrast for one minute before asking: *Why might the people have chosen to do these activities?*

Listening Part 2 SB page 74

Lead in
Ask students if they have ever been, or would like to go, scuba diving. Elicit answers from two or three students. Encourage them to justify their responses.

1 Read the rubric and elicit what is needed for the first gap (a person) before allowing students to complete the task. As an alternative to pairwork, students could work individually before comparing their answers in pairs. When eliciting the answers, you might like to ask students why this is a helpful activity (it helps them to identify the answer by listening for the correct type of word).

Suggested answers
1 a person **2** an object **3** a subject **4** a personal quality
5 an object **6** an activity **7** something experienced subjectively **8** an object, person or event **9** a place
10 a month

Read the exam advice with the students. Elicit or explain that a noun phrase is a group of words which contain a noun and could be replaced by a pronoun. For example, in the sentence: *Do you like the car I bought last week?* 'the car I bought last week' is the noun phrase (and could be replaced by the pronoun *it*). Point out that the second bullet point refers to what was done in the task in Exercise 1 and ask students to look at the gaps in the text again, this time discussing what type of word (rather than type of information) is needed (1 a noun, 2–3 a noun or noun phrase, 4 a noun or adjective, 5–10 a noun or noun phrase).

Exam advice

2 As this is an exam task, play the recording twice. Remind students that phrases will be no more than three words in length and that they do not need to change or re-phrase the words they hear. Encourage students to compare their answers in pairs, before checking them using the audioscript on page 227.

Answers
1 father **2** a visa **3** theory **4** humour **5** mask
6 sign language **7** temperature **8** dolphins **9** mountains
10 May

Track 26
Simon: Hi. My name's Simon Lewis and I'd like to tell you about a scuba-diving course that I took part in last month. It was my uncle who originally forwarded me the email for a one-week scuba diving course in Turkey. I wasn't sure at first because I was planning on working with my father in his shop over the summer holidays, but he convinced me to go as my cousin had already agreed to help him out.

The equipment was included in the price of the course, but I was asked to purchase my own insurance before heading out to Turkey, which I got online. I was so focused on what I'd need during my time at the resort that I hadn't thought about the possibility that I might have to get a visa. Luckily, I was able to arrange this when I arrived at the airport before departure.

We spent the first morning learning the basics of diving from our instructor, Mehmet, including how to put your equipment on correctly as well as using breathing techniques when underwater. We also dedicated some time to going over diving theory, which we'd been told to read up on before the course started. Mehmet was very patient when answering our questions – as beginners, we had a lot! And, thanks to his humour, he did a wonderful job of easing the tension a lot of us felt about diving in open water.

We spent the afternoon of the first day in the swimming pool, learning how to cope with various situations underwater. Mehmet taught us what to do when your mouth-piece slips off, and how to adjust your mask, which I had a few issues with at first as mine didn't fit properly. We then learnt about how to read the gauge attached to the wetsuit, which measures the amount of pressure remaining in the air tank. We finished off the first day by learning how to communicate with other divers underwater, which, to my surprise, I already knew how to do. You see, this is done via a series of hand signals and gestures and is heavily influenced by sign language, which is something I'd studied as part of a first-aid course at school.

On the second day, we were divided up into two groups and headed out on boats for the first of four open-water dives. The boat rocked from side to side, on account of the wind, which made some of us feel a little seasick, myself included. There was also the temperature to contend with, which, with it being the peak of summer, was incredibly hot. I didn't really mind this but the same couldn't be said for a few of the other divers, who were desperately trying to hide in the little shade available on the boat. That was all quickly forgotten, though, as, one by one, we dived into the water.

There were lots of memorable moments during the course, most of which happened during the final dive. We were on our way to see a boat on the seabed when one of the group spotted a baby seal swimming along with its mother. While we were heading over to take a closer look, a pair of dolphins appeared out of nowhere. I couldn't believe my eyes. Mehmet had told us that this was extremely rare, so seeing these two beautiful creatures was definitely the highlight of the course.

On the final evening, Mehmet organised a dinner for us all at a restaurant in town. On the bus ride there, I saw the local fishermen bringing in their catch of the day and even managed to catch a glimpse of the mountains on the horizon. We also drove past the market square, which, despite being late in the evening, was still full of people shopping. It was the perfect way to round off the trip.

I couldn't recommend Turkey highly enough for diving. I went in August, which, as I've mentioned, can get pretty hot. Most people think May is the ideal time to go, as it tends to be a bit cheaper, and I'd personally agree with that. September is also an option but the weather can be a bit hit and miss.

Well, that's all from me …

Extension activity

To help students identify why incorrect answers are wrong, ask them to highlight words or phrases in the audioscript which they might have incorrectly chosen, giving reasons why they are incorrect. For example, students may have thought *uncle* or *cousin* was correct for the first gap; however, neither encouraged Simon: the uncle had just forwarded an email about it and the cousin helping in the father's shop is mentioned only in relation to Simon's ability to change his plans.

3 Read the ideas with the students and elicit one or two examples of why a company may choose to do an activity. If students are unsure, point out that they should focus on the company's criteria for a team building event (e.g. the budget; the time of year the event will take place) before putting students in pairs. Allow students a few minutes to discuss the question before stopping them and telling them they must now reach a decision together. Then say: *Now you have one minute to decide which activity would be the most suitable for team building.* Monitor and listen for examples of language to negotiate, agree, disagree and offer an opinion. Do not provide feedback at this stage as useful language for Speaking Part 3 will be explored on page 81. Once students have completed the activity, hold a class vote on which activity students would prefer to do if they were participating in a team building activity.

Background information

An escape room is a room, or rooms, in a building where teams of people are locked in with no obvious means of escape. The aim of the activity is for the team to find clues, solve puzzles and do tasks in order to find a way out.

Dark dining takes place in a dark restaurant where customers cannot see the food. Instead, the focus is on other senses like smell and taste, which some argue enhances the eating experience.

Geocaching is a real-world adventure game using GPS.

Vocabulary SB page 75
Verb collocations with activities

Lead in

Write on the board or dictate the following question: *Do you enjoy taking part in team sports? Why? Why not?* Put students into pairs and allow them to briefly discuss. Listen for common errors with the target collocation (*take part in*) but do not correct: this collocation is targeted in Exercise 1.

1 Students work individually before comparing their answers in pairs. When eliciting the answers, check that students changed the form of the word where necessary.

Answers
2 go **3** divided up **4** held **5** organised
6 competed; donate

2 Write *do, play, go,* on the board then tell students to work in small groups or pairs and discuss which verb is used for sports ending *-ing*, which is used for sports considered games and which is used for those which do not go with *go* or *play*. Ask students to complete the task in their pairs or groups, then elicit answers in whole-class feedback.

Answers
1 organise/hold; compete/take part/enter
2 go; doing/taking **3** play; do; go

3 As students discuss in pairs, remind them to justify their answers by giving reasons and examples.

Extension activity
In pairs, students use the verb collocations to write five questions (e.g. *How often do you do exercise? What sports did you play when you were at school? Where is the best place to go swimming near here?*). Then in groups of four, students take turns to ask and answer the questions.

Reading and Use of English Part 6 SB page 76

Lead in
Ask students if there are any sports they would not take part in and why. Elicit one or two examples.

Background information
A Tough Mudder is an obstacle course which, as the name suggests, is very muddy. It can be for the general public or for competitive and elite athletes. Tough Mudder races typically start at five kilometres and go up to around sixteen kilometres. Obstacles range from climbing bars, cargo net ladders and barbed wire army crawls.

1 Read the rubric with the students. As exam candidates often ignore the title and subheading, you may wish to ask students why it is important to read them (to understand the general idea of what the text is about). Tell them to look at the picture and remind them that vocabulary they are not expected to know, e.g. *mudder*, are often explained. Once students have discussed the question, elicit three questions the students expect the article to answer, e.g. *What is a Tough Mudder? How does this sport test stamina, skill and endurance? Why did Sam Park want to do a Tough Mudder?* etc. This will help prepare students for Exercise 2.

2 Students work individually and ignore the gaps while they do this task. Remind them that the topic is typically, but not always, introduced in the first sentence of a paragraph. Allow students to compare their answers in pairs before eliciting from the class during feedback.

Suggested answers
Paragraph 2: Sam's preparation for the Tough Mudder
Paragraph 3: Tough Mudder obstacles
Paragraph 4: How to do well in a Tough Mudder
Paragraph 5: Sam's personal challenges during the race
Paragraph 6: Sam's positive feelings about the event
Paragraph 7: Conclusion

Exam advice
Ask students to read the exam advice. Elicit examples of reference words which point backward or forward (e.g. *this, these, those*) and remind students that when they see reference words in the sentences (options) they should make sure they find the thing being referred to in the text.

3 Read the rubric with the students. Point out that the connecting language can take various forms, in addition to reference words such as *this* and *these*. The sentences could be connected to the text by exemplifying (illustrating something by giving an example) or by repetition. Read sentence A with the students and tell them to underline the words or phrases which are likely to be illustrating or repeating something already said in the text. Elicit *training hard* and *pushing myself*. Then, put them into pairs and ask them to do this for sentences B–G. Once students have done this, elicit the words before telling them to read the text and find the thing being referred to by the words they underlined. Remind them to use the knowledge gained in Exercise 2 to help them locate the correct part of the text quickly. For example, the topic of paragraph 2 is *Sam's preparation for the event*, which connects to the words *training hard* in sentence A. Monitor as students complete the task and support weaker students.

Possible answers
A *training hard* refers to *preparation*
B *being so out of breath* refers to *wasn't fit enough*
D *these obstacles* refers to *live electrical wires*
E *try something new* refers to *Tough Mudder*
F *teamwork* refers to *joining forces with other competitors*
G *so drained* refers to *exhausting experiences*

4 Point out that students should use their knowledge of the text structure, gained from Exercise 2, to help them choose the correct answer. For example, as G mentions Sam being drained and covered in mud it is likely that this sentence, if it is used, would come towards the end of the text. That is, once Sam had completed the event. As this is an exam task, students work individually. Set a time limit of twenty minutes before allowing students to compare their answers in pairs.

Answers
1 E **2** A **3** D **4** F **5** B **6** G

5 Allow students a minute to look at the questions and consider their answers before putting them into pairs, or small groups. If any of your students have taken part in a Tough Mudder, you could ask them to share their experiences with the class.

6 Tell students that their company, or employer, is going to hold a Tough Mudder, or alternatively, if your students are younger, the organiser could be their school. To get them started, elicit a few ideas about where a Tough Mudder could take place, e.g. a local park, forest or other outside space, the employer's car park; for younger students, the classroom, the school playing field or outside playground. Then, elicit a few obstacles, e.g. climbing ropes attached to trees, crawling under tables. Once groups have discussed their course for five minutes, give them large pieces of paper and ask them to draw their course design. Afterwards, collect the papers and display them on the walls or board while students walk round and discuss which course they would most, or least, like to take part in and why.

Grammar SB page 77

Infinitive and verb + *-ing*

▶ **Page 171 Grammar reference**

Lead in

Write the beginning of a selection of *-ing* and *to* + infinitive sentences on the board. For example,

I've started swimming …

I went on the internet …

My employer allowed me …

Last year, my friend celebrated …

I improved my English by …

Working individually, tell students to write the sentence beginnings in their notebooks and then complete them with an appropriate *to* + infinitive or verb + *-ing* ending. Monitor and elicit error corrections. Select students to provide an example ending for each sentence beginning, eliciting corrections from the class.

1 Encourage students to work individually before comparing their answers in pairs. As students can find verb patterns challenging, you may wish to refer them to the Grammar reference on page 171 before continuing to Exercise 2.

Answers
1 d **2** a **3** e **4** c, g **5** g **6** f **7** h **8** j **9** i **10** b

2 Read the rubric with the students. Draw their attention to the example (sentence 1) to ensure that they understand the form of the verb may need to change. Point out that changing the form includes adding *to* before the infinitive of the verb. Students work individually. Encourage them to refer to Exercise 1 and the Grammar reference on page 171 if they are unsure about any questions, before comparing their answers with a partner.

Answers
2 to go **3** to hold **4** Training **5** to get **6** getting up
7 running **8** pushing

3 Students work individually before comparing their answers in pairs.

Answers
1 to do **2** to learn **3** doing **4** taking part in

Fast finishers

Using three verb patterns from the Grammar reference on page 171, students work in pairs and write three more questions, e.g. (*regret* + *-ing*) *Have you ever regretted taking part in a race? Why? Why not?*, (*force* + somebody + *to* infinitive). *Do you think schools should force students to do exercise? Why? Why not?*

4 If you chose to do the *fast finishers* task, the questions students wrote could be included here. As an alternative to pairwork, ask students to walk around the class taking turns to ask and answer the questions, which would provide them with additional speaking practice.

5 Point out that these are examples of real candidate errors. Once students have completed the activity and you have elicited the answers, tell them to asterisk (*) any questions they answered incorrectly then write correct examples in their notebooks under the heading *common errors*, and to refer to their notes when they are revising for the exam.

Answers
1 ~~running~~ to run **2** ~~spending~~ to spend **3** ~~to live~~ living **4** ~~to run~~ running **5** correct **6** ~~take~~ taking **7** ~~to win~~ in winning **8** ~~to sit and read~~ (by/of/with) sitting and reading **9** correct **10** ~~for ride~~ to ride / for riding

Reading and Use of English Part 4 SB page 78

Lead in

As Reading and Use of English Part 4 was introduced in Unit 2, you may like to ask students to close their books and, in pairs, briefly discuss a) what the exam task is (key word transformation) and b) what they need to do (complete six sentences with between two and five words so that they mean the same as the sentence printed before them). After a minute, stop the students and tell them to check their ideas by referring to the exam advice on page 23.

Exam advice

With books open, read the exam advice with the students and briefly elicit any new advice (e.g. contractions). Point out that even if the correct words are included within their answer, they will not be awarded the marks if it includes more than five words. Point out that although most contractions, such as *don't*, are two words (*do not*), *can't* and its full form *cannot* both count as one word.

1 Read the rubric with the students. You may wish to work through the first question with them. Once you have elicited the correct answer (B), elicit why the other options are incorrect (A has six words, C *suggest* + *to* infinitive is an incorrect verb pattern, D doesn't use *taking*) before allowing students to discuss question 2 together.

Answers
1 B (A uses six words; C/D don't use *taking*)
2 A (B uses six words; C/D don't use *easy*)

2 Put students into groups. Tell them to discuss the clues before deciding the answer. Encourage them to reach a decision together. Elicit the answers from the class.

Answers
1 to get ready **2** couldn't help laughing / couldn't help but laugh **3** can't use / aren't allowed to use / mustn't use

3 As this is an exam task, set a time limit of twenty minutes and tell students to work individually. Remind students that this exam task also tests their knowledge of common collocations and phrases. When the time is up, move to Exercise 4 before eliciting the correct answers.

Answers
1 taking part in **2** more expensive to hire **3** to give her a call **4** succeeded in winning **5** to lose his temper with **6** had no/little difficulty (in) learning

4 Encourage students to work through this exercise, making any necessary changes to their answers in Exercise 3 before finally eliciting the correct answers from the class (see Exercise 3 above).

Listening Part 4 SB page 80

Lead in
Ask students to quickly look at the photograph on page 80 and the one on page 79 and decide which they think is the riskiest (most dangerous).

Read the exam advice with the students and elicit what they should do in the one minute they have before the listening starts (underline the main ideas in the question stem but not waste time reading all the possible options as only one option will be correct).

Exam advice

1 Before students complete this task, you may wish to read them the background information. When discussing the second point, tell students to consider skills which could be transferred to another type of industry (e.g. entertainment or engineering). During whole-class feedback, remind students they should justify their ideas by giving reasons and examples and encourage them to agree and disagree with others' ideas where appropriate (e.g. whether or not wing walking is risky).

Background information
Wing walking is when a person moves or walks on the wings of an aeroplane whilst it is flying. It originally started in the early twentieth century at air shows. Early wing walkers carried out in-the-air mechanical adjustments and many became famous for their daring stunts. These days, people often wing walk for charity events, or to celebrate a once in a lifetime occasion, for example a 50th birthday.

2 Before completing the task, tell students to paraphrase the main ideas, e.g. *1 Why did Karen do a wingwalk?*, or consider how they might answer the question, e.g. *2 I'd feel really nervous but at the same time excited.* This will help prepare them to listen and hear the correct answers. Students work individually before comparing their answers in pairs.

Answers
Suggested underlining
1 what made; try wing walking
2 how feel; morning of the wing walk
3 when talking about; doing during the wing walk; Karen suggests
4 during, first part of wing walk; Karen; aware of
5 what; Karen say about; 360-degree turn
6 when; plane landed
7 what; Karen's plans; future

3 Play the recording twice. Once students have completed the activity, allow them to check their answers using the audioscript on page 228 before eliciting the correct answers.

Answers
1 C **2** B **3** C **4** A **5** C **6** B **7** A

Track 27

Interviewer: I'm here today with Karen Bradley, who's going to talk to us about her experience of wing walking. Welcome, Karen. Firstly, why did you decide to try wing walking?

Karen: Well, my best friend, Richard, is always going on about how I should take more risks in life. He'd done it a few months back and kept telling me how I should try it, too. He even joked that he would pay for me to do it as a birthday present, thinking that I wouldn't be brave enough to organise it myself. Well, I wasn't going to let him get away with that, was I? So, a few days later, I was booked in to go wing walking.

Interviewer: Great. So how did you feel when the day finally arrived?

Karen: Well, the forecast had predicted heavy rain, which would have meant postponing the wing walk. But thankfully, the skies were clear. I made breakfast and looked over all the notes I'd written in preparation. For the first time, I was nervous – so much so that I wondered if I could even do it! That feeling passed, though, and then I just felt excited.

Interviewer: So what exactly would you be doing during the wing walk?

Karen: Well, in air shows, people climb out of the cockpit and onto the wing mid-air. As an amateur, though, I would be strapped against an upright frame before take-off. I wouldn't be able to walk up and down the wing throughout the flight – and I wasn't complaining about that, to be honest! Instead, it was about enjoying the magnificent views as the plane reaches heights of 150 metres … and trying not to be sick as it drops down again!

Interviewer: So how did you feel during the first part of the wing walk?

Karen: Well, it took me about 15 seconds to pluck up the courage to open my eyes as the plane flew up into the sky. I struggled to see properly at first. I could feel my cheeks flapping in the 80 mph wind, as tears poured out of my eyes and my nose started running. Finally, I managed to settle in and look around at the amazing scenery. I tried to wave to the pilot, to show him that everything was alright, but my arm felt too heavy to move. All I could manage was a single thumbs up. Good enough, I thought.

Interviewer: And did you do any particularly memorable turns or manoeuvres?

Karen: Of course! One in particular stands out. Towards the end of the flight, the pilot signalled that we were about to perform a 360-degree turn. This was the manoeuvre I'd been dreading. As the plane pulled up, I watched as the fields changed to sky and back to fields again. It was over in a matter of seconds and all I could feel was my stomach churning under the pressure. The pilot turned to me and gestured to ask if I was okay. A little disoriented, I shouted, 'Fine,' forgetting he probably couldn't hear me – though I was feeling anything but! Fortunately, soon after that, we began our descent.

Interviewer: And how did you feel when the plane touched down again?

Karen: So, we were in the air for a little over ten minutes – although it had felt like an eternity to me. It wasn't so much a feeling of happiness to be back on solid ground again, rather a sense of accomplishment, you know, as if I'd just achieved something I never thought I would.

Interviewer: That's great. So what does the future hold for you, Karen?

Karen: Well, the funny thing is that I'm actually going up again next week! This time, now I know what to expect, I want to record everything that happens and write about it online. I've become a little obsessed with wing walking, if I'm honest – I follow loads of the pros on social media, watching them practise and perform, and listening to their interviews. I've even considered starting my own wing walking business, although that's only a dream at the moment. It's fair to say, though, that wing walking has completely transformed my life!

Interviewer: That's amazing! Thanks very much for speaking to us today, Karen.

Extension activity
Students asterisk (*) the questions they answered incorrectly and discuss the reasons for their choices in small groups. They should use the audioscript on page 228 when doing this activity. The aim is for students to better understand why they chose an incorrect option, which may discourage them from making the same mistake in the future.

Vocabulary SB page 80

look, see and *watch*; *listen* and *hear*

Lead in
Write or dictate this sentence: *I looked out of the window to see if it was raining* and elicit the difference in meaning between *look* and *see* (*look*: directing eyes in a particular direction; *see*: notice or become aware of).

1 Remind students to think about verb patterns, e.g. *to* + infinitive (Q1) when completing this exercise. Allow weaker students to work in pairs. Elicit the correct answers from the class. As these are real candidate errors, encourage students to asterisk (*) any questions they answered incorrectly (these will be compared with errors made in Exercise 2 later).

Answers
1 to see **2** look **3** hear **4** watched **5** listening

2 As these are real candidate errors, once students have completed this exercise and you have elicited the correct answers, ask them to asterisk (*) any questions they answered incorrectly. Then tell them to compare questions asterisked in this exercise with those they asterisked in Exercise 1 and identify any common errors that they are making. If the class are making the same errors, this may indicate additional teaching of these errors is required.

Answers
1 watching **2** listening to **3** look at **4** watching
5 see **6** watching **7** hear **8** watch

3 As an alternative to pairwork, students could answer the questions in small groups. Set a time limit of five minutes. Monitor and write down examples of correct language use. Elicit answers from the students during feedback, encouraging them to use the target language when responding. Then tell students the correct examples you heard.

Speaking Part 3 SB page 81

▶ **Page 209 Speaking bank**

Lead in
Briefly elicit what skill Speaking Part 3 tests (the ability to engage in a discussion and work towards a negotiated outcome) before moving to Exercise 1.

1 Encourage students to read the exam advice again on page 37, before looking back through the exercises. Alternatively, you could put students into pairs with one re-reading the exam advice, whilst the other looks for useful language to discuss and negotiate an outcome (e.g. *I think we should*, *I think you're right but …*). After two minutes, tell students to close their books and share what they read.

2 Read the rubric with the students then select a student to read the examiner's instructions to the class. You could elicit one or two ideas from the students before they do this task, or alternatively, once they have completed the task, ask students for any additional ideas they may have.

Answers
improving health and fitness, d
socialising with other people, a
cost of playing sports, b
developing important skills, e
having enough time and energy, c

3 Point out that using a wider range of language will help them to get a higher score in the Speaking exam. Students work individually before comparing their answers in pairs. When eliciting the answers, elicit further examples to write on the board and encourage students to write them in their notebooks. These could include both synonyms (*regularly, on the plus side*, etc.) and antonyms (*irregularly, on an irregular basis*; *a drawback*, etc.).

Answers
1 on a regular basis (b) **2** a great way (a) **3** lack (c)
4 opportunity (e) **5** put off (b) **6** well-being (d)

4 Ask students to predict what they think Simon and Maria will and will not do, giving reasons to support their ideas, before they listen. Allow students to compare their answers before eliciting them from the class. Point out that whilst Simon and Maria talked about all the points, candidates are not expected to do this in the exam. They should, however, ensure that they have answered the question fully, which they can only do by exploring a number of the prompts.

Answers
1 yes **2** yes **3** yes **4** no **5** no

Track 28

Examiner: Now, I'd like you to talk about something together for about two minutes. Some people think that everyone should spend more of their free time playing sports, and other people disagree. Here are some things they think about and a question for you to discuss. First you have some time to look at the task. Now, talk to each other about whether everyone should spend more of their free time playing sports.

Maria: Shall I start? Well, in my view, I think people should play more sports in their spare time because most sports involve a lot of exercise, which improves both your physical and mental well-being. What are your thoughts on this?

Simon: I couldn't agree more. It's a great way to keep fit, too, and if you consider the point about socialising with other people, playing sport is a great way to meet up with friends and teammates. I know a lot of people who met their best friends through sport.

Maria: That's a really good point. OK, let's move on to cost. To be honest, I think a lot of sports are relatively cheap to do these days, like going for a run or playing football, so I'm not sure this would be a reason for people not to spend more time playing sport.

Simon: I suppose so, but some people might be put off by how expensive it can be to play sport on a regular basis. Being a member of a tennis club, for example, can be pretty costly when you consider membership and equipment costs.

Maria: I guess you're right. And there's also the issue that people may lack the motivation to go out and play sports, particularly after a long day at school or at work. Speaking from my own experience, I always find it difficult to motivate myself to go out and be active after I come home.

Simon: And me! I actually think this is one of the main reasons why people don't do enough exercise. The temptation to chill out at home after a busy day is just too high. OK, so what do you think about the idea that playing sport helps you to develop important skills?

Maria: I think that's a really important point. It's a good opportunitytolearnnewskillswhichyoucanuseinotherareas oflife,suchasatschooloratwork.Thingsliketeamworkand leadershipskillsareabigpartofsportandthesecaneasilybe transferred to our everyday lives. Don't you agree?

Simon: Absolutely! What's more, it can really improve your confidence and decision-making under pressure.

Maria: That's not always the case, though, is it? If you lose, for example, you might not feel too good about yourself and perhaps won't want to continue playing.

Examiner: Thank you.

5 You may wish to refer students to the audioscript on page 229 so that they can see the phrases in context before asking them to complete the task. When eliciting the answers, write the functions as headings on the board and select students to come to the front of the class and write the phrases under the correct heading. Finally, refer students to pages 37 and 38, and add phrases from Unit 3 to those already on the board. (*In my opinion, the best choice is … because …, I think we should choose … because …*, etc.)

Answers
A suggesting ideas: In my view …; To be honest; I think…
B asking your partner's opinion: Don't you agree?; What do you think about …?; What are your thoughts on this?
C agreeing: Absolutely!; I couldn't agree more.; I guess you're right.; That's a really good point.
D disagreeing: I suppose so, but …; That's not always the case …

/P/ Pronunciation: intonation (2)

6 Read the information with the students. To make the point more obvious, you could read the information in a disinterested tone of voice. Alternatively, you could select a student to read the information in a bored-sounding voice, followed by another who should read it sounding enthusiastic.

6.1 Before students listen, you could put them into pairs and tell them to read the extract and predict how they think the voices will rise and fall.

Track 29
See page 82 of Student's Book for audioscript.

6.2 Students may feel they sound unnatural if the intonation is different from their first language. Remind them that this is not unusual. You could play the recording again, stopping it after each phrase or chunk so students can repeat what they heard, mimicking the intonation, e.g. *and me* (stop), *I actually think* (stop) *this is one of the biggest reasons* (stop), etc.

Extension activity
After students have read the extract, tell them to work with a new partner, but this time they should stand up as they read. Tell them they should use their hands and facial expressions in addition to rising and falling intonation. Whilst they will not be stood up in the exam, standing may encourage students to sound more enthusiastic.

Exam advice
Read the exam advice and refer students to the Speaking bank on page 210 where they can find examples of useful language to reach agreement. (*So, what do you think would be the best …, I'd suggest either … or …. So shall we choose …*).

7 Set a time limit of one minute. Remind students that, in the exam, they do not need to reach agreement, as long as they have attempted to do so.

8 As an alternative to working in pairs, you could put students into threes (A, B, C), telling the third student (C) to listen for examples of language from Exercise 5 on page 81. This could include additional phrases from pages 37 and 38 if you choose to include them. Remind Students A and B that when discussing the prompts, they should make positive attempts to move the conversation forward as well as respond to each other's contributions.

9 If you decided to put students into threes, the third student (C) could read the instructions to Students A and B. After one minute, encourage Student C to give feedback to Students A and B, perhaps by telling them the phrases they heard from pages 37, 38 and 81, before asking students to change roles and repeat Exercises 8 and 9.

Writing Part 2 (an article) SB page 82

▶ **Page 196 Writing bank**

Lead in
With books closed, put students into pairs. Tell them to imagine a new student has joined the class and they need to give them four tips about how to get a good mark for writing an article. Allow students three minutes to discuss their ideas before turning to Writing bank page 196 and comparing their ideas with the tips given in Exercise 4.

1 Students work individually before comparing their answers in pairs. When eliciting the answers, elicit what students might include in a 'description' (what the exercise is, where they do the exercise, what equipment they need to do the exercise, etc.). You could also elicit language to make recommendations with a focus on verb patterns from this unit. (*You could try* + *-ing*, *You might want to* + infinitive, *If you enjoy* + *-ing, you could…*, etc.)

Answers
Suggested underlining
college magazine, great way to keep fit, describe sporting activity, form of exercise you enjoy, how you started, why, recommend it to other people, article

2 Elicit how ideas can be expressed (by giving and justifying an opinion, making a recommendation, etc.). If you chose to elicit language to make recommendations in Exercise 1, remind students of one of these (e.g. *You could try* + *-ing*) before eliciting one or two examples of language to give and justify opinions (e.g., *It's a good idea to …*, *If you want to …*, *You'd need to …*). Before students complete the exercise, remind them that unlike an essay, which should be written in a formal or neutral register, an article can be written using language which is less formal. This means that (subjective) phrases such as *You'll need to* are acceptable when writing an article.

3 Tell the students to read the article once quickly before reading it again and underlining where it answers the question. Students compare their answers before you elicit them from the class. Concept check new language, e.g. *opponent* (someone who competes with, or opposes, another person in a contest or competition).

Answers
running past opponents, scoring points, playing in a team, it's a ball game. You run a lot and keep fit.

4 Once students have completed the task, elicit that the article is structured in the same order as the question. Point out that, as the question is typically structured logically, it makes sense for their answer to follow the same pattern.

Answers
1 Paragraph 2 **2** Paragraph 1 **3** Paragraph 3

5 Point out that students should look at the sentence structure as well as the meaning of the underlined word. For example, *despite* is a preposition and is therefore followed by a noun or gerund, whilst *although* is a conjunction and should be followed by a subject and verb. Point out that *in spite of* is used in the same way as *despite* (e.g., *In spite of not having much money, I bought the new dress. Despite not having much time, I helped Mum in the garden.*). It is also worth noting the alternative form *despite the fact that*, which is followed by a subject and verb and is used similarly to *although* (compare: *Despite the fact that the pool isn't close, I go there weekly* with *Despite the pool being a long way away, I go there weekly*). As students often find exercises with linking language challenging, you may prefer to pair weaker students with stronger ones.

Answers
1 Although **2** Despite **3** Although **4** despite **5** However
6 although **7** Despite **8** However

6 Before students complete the gap fill, tell them to find the words in the article and underline them. Then tell them to read the whole sentence and, in pairs, guess (if they do not know) the meaning of the word using the context. For example, when the writer mentions being *athletic*, they go on to say they could *run past others*. This indicates that *athletic* means they could *run fast* or *are fit*. Once students have guessed the meaning using the context, you could either tell them to complete the exercise or ask them to look the words up in the dictionary before completing it.

Answers
1 competitive **2** rough **3** athletic **4** opponents **5** coach
6 spectators **7** trophy

7 Remind students of the importance of making a plan (their answer will be more focused and answer the question more fully) and allow them five minutes to do this. If your students need more practice with linking language, tell them to include *although, despite* and *however* each at least once in their article. You may wish to read the exam advice before students complete the task, or alternatively, you could tell them to read the advice afterwards and use it as a checklist. For example: *Did I organise my ideas into paragraphs? Did I use linking language? Did I consider who would be reading my article?* etc.).

Vocabulary

Collocations

Verb	Sport
hold / organise / compete in / enter / take part in	a race / a competition / a tournament / a championship
do / take	exercise
go	jogging / cycling / skiing / swimming / hiking / mountain biking
play	football / golf / basketball
do	athletics / gymnastics / judo / weightlifting

Commonly confused words

look / see / watch
listen / hear

Vocabulary activity 1

Put students into pairs. Refer back to the photos on pages 79 and 80 and ask them to take turns to compare and contrast them. In addition to using complex language to make comparisons, you could tell students to use sports verb collocations, commonly confused words and verb patterns, e.g. *In both photographs we can* ***see*** *people who* ***like to do/enjoy doing*** *risky sports. In the first, we can see someone* ***enjoying rock-climbing*** *whilst in the other …*

Vocabulary activity 2

Put students into pairs. Tell them to choose two sports from the list and brainstorm both the equipment needed to do the sport and where you do the sport (e.g. golf equipment: clubs – drivers, woods, irons; a tee, golf ball, gloves; where: golf course). Then, ask them to compare and contrast the sports and say what type of person (i.e. age, personality, skills, interests, etc.) would like to do each one.

DIGITAL CLASSROOM

Practice Extra Unit 7

Test Generator Unit 7 test

Test and Train Exam Practice

8 Dream of the stars

Unit objectives

Topic: entertainment, celebrities

Reading and Use of English Part 7 (multiple matching): distinguishing between similar texts

Reading and Use of English Part 1 (multiple-choice cloze): understanding why an answer is incorrect

Writing Part 1 (essay): writing a balanced essay

Listening Part 2 (sentence completion): avoiding distractors of the same information-type

Speaking Part 4 (discussion): discussing different aspects of entertainment; giving balanced answers

Pronunciation: grouping words and pausing (2)

Vocabulary: describing entertainment; *play, performance* and *acting; audience, (the) public* and *spectators; scene* and *stage*

Grammar: *at, in* and *on* to express location; reported speech

Starting off SB page 84

1 Look at the photos with the students and elicit the celebrity types – chef (Gordon Ramsay), actress (Olivia Colman), singer (Taylor Swift), footballer (Kylian Mbappé) – before putting them into groups. Encourage students to justify their responses, particularly when making comparisons. As an alternative to group work, students could work in pairs and choose two photos to compare and contrast as they would in Speaking Part 2 (*In this photo we can see a celebrity chef …*). Set a time limit of five minutes before inviting ideas from the class.

2 Elicit examples of other types of celebrity from the students (e.g. news reader, author, game show host, reality TV star). Put them into pairs. Encourage students to make notes about what their partner says, then during feedback, select students to report their partner's ideas rather than their own. (*Soraya said she'd like to be a singer because …*). This may help you to identify whether students are naturally using reported speech, which is covered on page 88 of this unit.

Reading and Use of English Part 7 SB page 84

Lead in

Write *film genres* on the board and ask students to call out all the film genres they know. Write them on the board as students call them out, e.g. horror, rom-com (romantic-comedy), documentary, thriller, comedy, drama, etc.). Once you have between five and ten, students discuss in pairs which genres they like and dislike and why. You may like to point out that in British English *film* and *cinema* are commonly used, whereas US English uses *movies* and *movie theatre*.

Exam advice

Read the exam advice with the students and remind them that Part 7 tests their ability to find specific pieces of information and detail, in addition to recognising opinion or attitude.

1 Start by asking students to raise their hands if they have seen a documentary recently and/or have ever been to a concert. If, for example, they have never been to a concert, you could tell them to talk about whether they would like to go to one or not. Remind students to justify their ideas. As with Starting off, Exercise 2, ask students to report what their partner said rather than their own ideas during whole-class feedback. If you do this, do not correct errors made with reported speech, as they may be covered on page 88.

2 Students work individually before comparing their answers in pairs. When you elicit the correct answers, encourage students to paraphrase. For example, for Q1 students could say: *prefers to vary the type of film they watch* or, using the negative: *doesn't like watching the same type of film all the time*. Doing this helps encourage students not to word spot when they are answering the questions.

Answers
1 tends to alternate between different genres
2 understands the limitations of certain types of film
3 was hesitant about their preferred form of film at first
4 prefers films that help them to relax
5 explains how their taste in films has changed over time
6 describes the steps they take before watching a film to avoid disappointment
7 says that the films they watch help them to socialise with other people
8 is often disappointed by their choice of films
9 feels that their taste in films is shared by the general public
10 believes that the element of surprise is what makes their choice of films appealing

3 Ask students to skim read the thread in order to prepare them for the task before they start answering the questions. Point out that it is important that they do not waste time on one question: if they are stuck on a question, they can move on and return to it later. As this is an exam task, tell students they must work individually and set a time limit of twenty minutes. When eliciting the answers, encourage students to say why a particular part of the text matches a question as this will help them to check their choices.

Answers
1 D 2 C 3 D 4 A 5 E 6 B 7 D 8 C 9 A 10 B

Extension activity
Remind students that word spotting may cause them to choose an incorrect option and ask them to find and underline examples of word spotting in the questions and text, e.g. *mix*, in text A might have been incorrectly matched with *alternate between different* in Q1. Allow students five minutes to do this before putting them into groups to discuss the word spots they found. Elicit examples from the class.

Vocabulary SB page 86

Describing entertainment

Lead in
Briefly tell students about a film you watched recently using the adjectives in Exercise 1, e.g. *I watched a really gripping thriller recently. I tried to guess the ending, but it was completely unexpected.* Elicit that *gripping* means exciting and that *unexpected* means surprising.

1 You may wish to ask students to find the adjectives in the texts (Exercise 3 page 85) so that they can see the words in context, before getting them to complete the task on their own or in pairs. Before you elicit the answers, allow students to check the meaning of new words in an English to English dictionary. Once you have elicited the answers, you could elicit antonyms for the words given, e.g. *heavy going – lighthearted; complex – straightforward; confusing – clear; gripping – dull; predictable – unexpected; impressive – unimpressive; hilarious – unfunny.* Some of these pairs of opposites can be formed from the items in the box.

Suggested answers
positive: gripping, hilarious, impressive, light-hearted, stunning
negative: confusing, heavy-going, predictable, unappealing
both (depending on taste): complex, unexpected

2 Allow students a few minutes to think about their ideas, and make notes if they wish, before putting them into pairs to discuss. During feedback, ask students to report what their partner told them.

3 As an alternative to matching straightaway, students cover the definitions then read the text and, in pairs, discuss what they think the words in bold mean. Once they have done this, allow them to check their ideas by looking at the definitions and matching them.

Answers
1 c 2 f 3 a 4 g 5 d 6 i 7 e 8 b 9 h

4 Put students into pairs and tell them that they are going to interview their partner. They must take turns to ask all of the questions and make notes of the answers their partner gives them. Once both students have asked and answered the questions, put them into different pairs. Students must now use their notes to tell their new partner what their previous partner said.

Lead in
Ask students if they have ever acted in a play (or school play) or if they would like to. Elicit examples from the class.

5 Read the rubric with the students. As these are real candidate errors, you may wish to tell students to work individually before eliciting the correct answers. Once you have done this, ask students to asterisk (*) any questions they answered incorrectly. You could then poll students (*Raise your hand if you answered question 1 incorrectly …*) to identify common errors. Encourage students to look problem words up in an English dictionary before eliciting the meaning.

Answers
1 scene 2 plays 3 audience; stage 4 spectator 5 acting

6 Read the rubric with the students, pointing out that each word is only used once and that the form of the word does not change. Encourage students to read the sentences quickly, ignoring the gaps, to help them understand the context before they tackle the task. Allow weaker students to work in pairs. Monitor and support pairs who are struggling.

Answers
1 the public 2 play 3 acting 4 performance 5 audience
6 scene 7 stage 8 spectators

7 Remind students that they should compare both similarities and differences. Encourage them to speak for one minute each before they answer the second part of the question (*… and say what the people are enjoying about performing in these locations*). As an alternative to pairwork, you could put students into threes with the third student listening for examples of phrases using the target language (*play, performance, acting, the public, spectators, scene* and *stage*), or into groups of four, with the fourth student listening for examples of complex language to make comparisons (*by far the most* … etc.). If you choose one of the alternatives, the listener(s) should provide feedback about what they heard, including examples of correct language use and at least one thing the speaker could improve.

Extension activity
Write or type the definitions (Exercise 3) on slips of paper – enough sets for every group of three or four students. Put students into groups of three or four, write the target words on the board and ask them to match the definition to the correct word. Once completed, ask students to write one sentence for each word. The sentences should be true for them. Monitor and elicit error corrections.

Grammar SB page 87

at, *in* and *on* to express location

▶ **Page 172 Grammar reference**

Lead in
Use photos or artwork for the following: a person stood outside a building, e.g. a cinema, or a photo of someone sat in a theatre and say: *I'll meet you at the cinema. / I'll meet you in the theatre.* Point out the slight difference in meaning between these prepositions. For example, *at* expresses the idea of being somewhere unspecified at a location whereas *in* specifically expresses the idea of being inside the location. Be prepared to explain exceptions, e.g. if students query the use of *in school* and *at school*, tell them that *at school* means at the location, and *in school* means enrolled in an institution or a specific class. Therefore, if a child's parent were visiting a teacher you would say *Mum is at school* not *Mum is in school*. You may also wish to remind students that for public transport *on* is used rather than *in* (*on the bus*, *on a plane*, etc.).

1 Students work individually before comparing their answers in pairs. When eliciting the answers, refer students to the ideas you explored in the Lead in. For example, the answer to Q3 is *in* because it refers specifically to watching a film as opposed to being somewhere unspecified at the location of the cinema.

Answers
1 at **2** on **3** in

2 As these are real errors made by exam candidates, encourage students to work individually before eliciting the correct answers. Ask students to asterisk (*) any questions they answered incorrectly before putting them into groups (where possible, ensure that one student in each group answered at least one question correctly) and encourage students to explain their decisions.

Answers
1 in **2** on **3** at **4** in **5** at; at; at **6** on **7** in; on
8 at **9** on **10** in; in

Listening Part 2 SB page 88

Lead in
Ask students who the best and worst cook in their family is. Select two or three students to respond, encouraging them to support their ideas with reasons. Next, elicit the difference between *cook* (someone who prepares and cooks food) and *chef* (someone who is a skilled and trained cook and typically works in a restaurant or hotel). Do not ask students if they would like to be a chef at this stage as they will discuss this in Exercise 3.

Exam advice
Tell students to read the exam advice and highlight the most important advice for them before putting them into pairs to briefly discuss their reasons. Considering the advice from a personal perspective will help students to internalise the advice and make it more meaningful and useful.

1 Remind students that they need to consider what type of information is needed as well as the form of the word. As an alternative to pairwork, and as students have completed this type of activity before, you could encourage them to work individually before comparing their ideas in pairs. Once you have elicited the answers, encourage students to make brief notes in the margin (e.g. *job/noun* in the margin next to Q1) to use as prompts to help them hear the correct answer.

Answers
1 a type of job (noun)
2 a person (noun)
3 something associated with people (plural noun)
4 a word that describes working with someone (adjective)
5 an object / objects (noun)
6 a benefit of a job (noun)
7 a word that describes an emotion (adjective)
8 a personal characteristic needed to do a job (adjective)
9 something that happened to him (verb – past participle)
10 something that can be written (a noun)

2 Play the recording twice. After the listening, encourage students to check their answers in pairs, using the audioscript on page 230. When eliciting the answers from the class, encourage students to give reasons for their decisions and invite corrections from the class if a student's answer is incorrect, rather than providing the answer yourself. This will encourage more autonomous learning through peer correction.

Answers
1 analyst **2** grandma **3** names **4** tough
5 (special) ingredients **6** flexibility **7** shocked
8 invisible **9** fired **10** recipe books

Track 30

Mark: Hi. My name's Mark King. I've been working as a personal chef for a number of celebrities around the world for over fifteen years and I'm here today to tell you about my work.

It seems like a lifetime ago now that I was just a fresh-faced computer graduate, firing off CVs to every tech company in the country in the hope of landing my dream job as a software engineer. I kept getting knocked back, so I ended up becoming an analyst for a local firm. The role didn't suit me, so to counter the boredom, I took up cooking in my free time. Needless to say, my parents were extremely happy with this decision, as I would cook for them most nights. I actually have my grandma to thank for this skill as she spent hours teaching me the basics when I stayed with her and my grandad at weekends. I loved it so much that I knew I had to make a career out of it.

Fast forward three years to the time I got my first job as a personal chef for a renowned pop star. Sorry, I can't give any names! I received a set of instructions from his agent, which gave me more details about his dietary requirements. They were short and to the point. 'He eats nothing,' it read. 'He's a vegetarian and hates almost all vegetables.' I'd be lying if I said it was an easy first assignment. In reality, it was tough and involved a lot of careful preparation to get the menu just right.

People often ask me what the most bizarre request I've ever received is. Well, that occurred a few years later when I was working for an actor in the States. While out filming, he texted me to say that he wanted an Alice in Wonderland-style tea party, complete with decorations, costumes and special ingredients, the latter of which I found very hard to get hold of. Nevertheless, I did it and I was tipped 5,000 dollars for my troubles.

That, I must say, is a definite perk of the job. Celebrities are happy to hand over extraordinary amounts of money to personal chefs to create the perfect dishes. The salary is what drives most personal chefs I know, along with the travel. For me, it's the flexibility. I can pick and choose how and when I work, which is ideal for someone with three kids.

My biggest achievement was when I was offered the chance to cook for the royal family at a state banquet. I refused to believe it was a genuine offer at first but then I received a phone call from one of their advisors. I told her I was worried I'd get too nervous and be unable to do it justice. With a casual smile, she told me not to worry and that I had been hand-picked by the princess herself. I was shocked! The thought that a member of the royal family knew who I was was one thing, but the fact that she had asked for me personally was just incredible.

So what makes a good personal chef besides being a good cook? Well, above all, you need to be invisible. Of course, it helps if you're a talented chef who can create fantastic dishes at short notice but it's vital that you remain out of the public eye. I remember hearing about one personal chef who did a 'tell-all' interview with a gossip magazine. He was subsequently fired, having revealed personal information about the celebrity's private life. He managed to avoid being sued, which is another risk in this line of work.

I don't plan on working in the shadows for very much longer. As mentioned, it wouldn't be right for me to write articles about the private lives of my clients, but I have received a number of interesting offers to author recipe books, and I must admit I'm seriously tempted by this. I've been writing a blog for years and it would be good to publish a printed version of this.

Well, that's all from me. Does anyone have any questions?

3 Before students answer these questions, refer them to the audioscript on page 230 and ask them to underline examples of useful topic-related phrases (including phrases to talk about jobs and work), e.g. (*landing*) *my dream job*, *getting knocked back*, *make a career out of something*. Once you have elicited examples of language and concept checked the meaning of new phrases, encourage students to use some of them when answering the questions, e.g. *being a personal chef is/isn't my idea of a dream job because …* Monitor and listen for examples of phrases used correctly in context and praise students during whole-class feedback.

4 Read the rubric with the students. Elicit the meaning of any new vocabulary, such as *lactose-intolerant* (unable to digest lactose, the main carbohydrate in dairy products) and that students need to create three courses: starter, main course and dessert. If students have access to the internet, you may wish to allow them to use their smartphones to research menu ideas; alternatively, put students into larger groups to brainstorm ideas before putting them into pairs to design their menus. Set a time limit of fifteen minutes for students to do this task.

5 As an alternative to comparing menus with another pair, you could collect the menus (from Exercise 4) and display them on the walls or board. Students could then walk round the class, reading each menu, before voting for their favourite (or least favourite).

Grammar SB page 88

Reported speech

▶ **Page 174 Grammar reference**

Lead in

Refer back to the notes you made in Starting off and Reading and Use of English Part 7 on page 84 and Exercise 2 on page 86, when students reported what their partner had said. Identify examples where the students had not changed the tense and write them on the board, e.g. original sentence: Student A: *I saw a good thriller at the cinema.* Student B: *Peyton said she saw a good thriller at the cinema* (incorrect tense change). If you made a note of any correct examples of reported speech, where the tense had been changed, you could write these on the board too, e.g. Student B: *Peyton said she had seen a good thriller at the cinema recently.* (correct tense change). Elicit that we change tenses in reported speech; that if the reporting verb is in the past, *said, told* (*me*), etc. that the original verb typically changes to the past as well (e.g. present simple to past simple). Depending on the students' level, you may wish to refer them to Grammar reference on page 174 to review how verbs change.

1 Allow students to work in pairs and refer to the Grammar reference if they find this task challenging.

Answers
1 a **2** b

2 Ask students to complete practice activity 1 (Grammar reference page 175) first if they need more support. When students are ready to complete this exercise, read the rubric and elicit that answers including six words would be marked as incorrect. Remind students that contractions (other than *can't*) count as two words. Finally remind students that in the real exam a range of forms rather than one focus (reported speech in this question) will be tested. Tell students to work individually. Set a time limit of twenty minutes before allowing students to compare their answers in pairs.

Answers
1 he didn't intend to **2** she would get back
3 would arrive on **4** wasn't allowed to borrow
5 had made several mistakes **6** had found the play

3 Allow weaker students to work in pairs or groups. Encourage students to discuss their choices. Monitor and make notes of common errors. Elicit the correct answers from the class followed by correction of any common errors.

Answers
1 to cook **2** to believe **3** hearing

4 Before doing this activity, concept-check the meaning of the reporting verbs (*admit, accuse, agree, apologise, invite, persuade, promise, recommend, remind, warn*). Once you have done this, you could elicit any reporting verb pairs which have the opposite meanings (e.g. to *deny* doing something is the opposite of *admitting* it). If students remain unsure, you could allow them five minutes to look up any new vocabulary in an English to English dictionary. When completing the task, allow students to work in pairs before changing pairs to compare their answers.

Answers
1 stealing/to stealing **2** lying **3** to buy **4** breaking
5 to visit **6** to lend **7** to phone **8** installing **9** to send
10 not to use

Fast finishers
Write questions, using reporting verbs, on the board and ask students to discuss them in pairs or small groups, e.g. *When was the last time you admitted to doing something wrong? What was it? Have you ever been accused of something you didn't do? What? What was the last thing you agreed to do for someone? When did you last persuade someone to do something for you? What was it?*

5 Read the rubric with the students. As this is an exam style task, tell students to work individually and set a time limit of twenty minutes. Elicit the answers, without allowing students to compare them. This will help you to identify whether students need additional practice or teaching. If so, refer them to the exercises in Grammar reference page 175.

Answers
1 advised him to see **2** suggested going swimming that
3 told me to switch off **4** reminded Natasha to post
5 of not taking any **6** to do her best

Reading and Use of English Part 1 SB page 90

Lead in
Elicit from the class different music genres (e.g. hip-hop, country, RnB, disco, classical). Put students into pairs and ask them to take turns to briefly talk about the types of music they prefer, along with any genres they particularly dislike and why. Tell students to make notes as they listen because they will need to report what their partner told them using reported speech afterwards. Allow students to talk for one minute each before stopping them and putting them into different pairs. Then, tell them to use their notes to tell their new partner in reported speech what their first partner told them. Monitor and listen for common errors with the target language. Once students have finished, select stronger students to report what their partner said and elicit error corrections for the common errors that you heard from the whole class.

Background information
Bedroom producers are independent artists who work in their own home studios, often with less equipment than a traditional studio. They might play instruments in addition to writing their own songs and recording their own music.

Tell the students to read the exam advice and underline the pieces of advice that are the most useful for them. After one minute, ask students to tell a partner what they underlined and why.

Exam advice

1 Read the rubric with the class and elicit one or two ideas from stronger students before putting the students into pairs. As an alternative, divide the class in half with half of the students (As) discussing the first question while the other half (Bs) discuss the second. After one minute, change partners so that each student is with someone who discussed a different question (AB) and tell students to share their ideas.

2 Ask students to predict what they think a bedroom producer is before they read the article so that they are reading to check if their ideas were correct. Remind them that they are skim-reading. Set a time limit of thirty seconds before eliciting the answer from the class.

Answers
A musician who writes and creates music at home, usually in their bedroom.

3 Read the rubric with the students and then read the first sentence and the example. Tell students it is important that they read the example as this will help them understand how to complete the task. Before students answer the question, you could put them into pairs and ask them to discuss why answers A, B and D (in the example) are incorrect. Remind them to think about how each word is used in context (e.g. *propose* is usually used when talking about a plan or action: *The government proposed building a new road*; *recommend* is used to give advice: *She recommends studying in the UK.*). As this is an exam task, students should answer questions 1–8 individually. Set a time limit of twenty minutes before putting students into groups to compare their answers. Tell students that they must discuss the reasons for their choices, especially if they disagree. Encourage them to reach an agreement over which option is correct where possible. Do not elicit the answers from the class until after the students have completed the next exercise.

Answers
1 B **2** A **3** B **4** D **5** B **6** C **7** D **8** A

4 Still working in the same groups from Exercise 3, tell students to check their choices using the clues. As students have already discussed their choices in Exercise 3, you could ask them to asterisk (*) any answers they change after reading the clues. Elicit the correct answers from the class, with reasons why they made any changes.

5 Encourage students to consider their favourite music genre, as discussed in the Lead in, or alternatively a genre of music they think would be most suitable for this type of production. Remind students that they must justify their ideas with reasons and examples. After four minutes, stop students and select groups to share ideas with the class.

Speaking Part 4 SB page 91

▶ **Page 211 Speaking bank**

Lead in
Ask students if they play, have ever played, or would like to play a musical instrument. Elicit some examples from the class.

Exam advice
Read the exam advice with the students. Tell them that in this part of the exam, candidates are expected to broaden, and discuss further, topics which were introduced in Part 3. Point out that Part 4 differs from Part 1 in that the questions ask for evaluation, as opposed to information. Finally, tell them that in Part 4 they have the opportunity to show the examiner that they are capable of discussing issues in more depth than in previous parts of the exam.

1 Read the rubric with the students. Point out how the examiner asks Antonia a question and then goes on to ask Peter whether he agrees. Ensure students understand that this means it is important for them to listen to each other as they will be expected to respond to the other candidate's opinion in addition to giving their own. Allow students to compare their answers before eliciting from the class. You may like to point out that they could also say 'in general' when referring to things in general.

Answers
generally speaking, generally, they tend to have, on the whole

Track 31

Examiner:	Do you think schools should teach subjects such as dance, drama or music?
Antonia:	Well, I think, generally speaking, schools should teach these subjects to small children so that they can find out if they like them. I think these subjects help children to learn how to express themselves. But I don't think, generally, that it's so important for older children or teenagers to do these subjects because they tend to have lots of other things to study. So, on the whole, I guess these subjects should be voluntary, not compulsory, as children get older.
Examiner:	Peter, do you agree with Antonia?
Peter:	Generally, yes, but I feel it's a pity when students don't have time for the subjects they enjoy.

2 Students work individually and then compare their answers in pairs. Monitor as students complete the activity and support weaker students. Elicit the answers during whole-class feedback.

Answers
1 She talks about teaching small children these subjects and then balances it with *but* and her views on older children and teenagers. **2** For young children – to discover if they like the subjects and to learn to express themselves. For older children and teenagers – because they have so many other subjects to study. **3** b

3 Elicit phrases that students can use to offer a balanced view (*but, however, yet, even so*, etc.) along with those used to speak in general (*generally, generally speaking,*

in general, tend to have, on the whole). If students are struggling with ideas, you could put them into groups to brainstorm advantages (e.g. develops creative problem-solving skills; connects pupils with their culture) and disadvantages (e.g. insufficient focus on key skills, like maths; not all pupils enjoy the activities) of schools teaching painting and photography, before pairing them to answer the questions. Monitor and listen for correct use of the target language for giving a balanced answer. After two minutes, stop the students and select two of the stronger pairs to answer the question in front of the class.

/P/ Pronunciation: grouping words and pausing (2)

4 Read the title and the information to the students, ensuring that you pause where marked (/).

4.1 Encourage students to read the conversation aloud while they are doing this task as hearing it may help them mark (/) in the correct place.

Answers
Well, / I think, / generally speaking, / schools should teach these subjects to small children / so that they can find out / if they like them. / I think these subjects / help children to learn / how to express themselves. But I don't think, generally, that it's so important for older children / or teenagers / to do these subjects / because they tend to have lots of other things to study. / So, / on the whole, / I guess these subjects should be / voluntary, not compulsory, / as children get older.

4.2 If students find this task challenging, play the recording a second time. During whole-class feedback, if you discover that students have marked the conversation incorrectly, you might like to draw their attention to the fact that groups of words will typically include both content and function words. This is because content words (nouns, adjectives, main verbs, adverbs) are words that have meaning whereas function words (pronouns, articles, auxiliary verbs, etc.) are structural.

Track 32
Antonia: Well, / I think, / generally speaking, / schools should teach these subjects to small children / so that they can find out / if they like them. / I think these subjects / help children to learn / how to express themselves. But I don't think, generally, that it's so important for older children / or teenagers / to do these subjects / because they tend to have lots of other things to study. / So, / on the whole, / I guess these subjects should be / voluntary, not compulsory, / as children get older.

4.3 First, select two stronger students to read the conversation with you, so that the class can hear the correct pronunciation. Depending on the level of the students, you could take the part of Antonia, Peter or the examiner. As students are speaking, monitor and listen for examples of correct or incorrect pausing. After the students have taken each role, drill examples of incorrect pausing that you heard during whole-class feedback.

4.4 As an alternative to writing down ideas to the question in Exercise 1, you could ask students to use their ideas from Exercise 3. Students then work in pairs and write a conversation between themselves and the examiner, then mark (/) the pauses before they read the conversation to each other. Once they have done this, tell them to put their scripts away before putting them into new pairs so they can take turns to answer the question more authentically.

5 Read the rubric with the students. Before students complete the task, you may like to ask them to read the phrases in the box and look up any unknown words or phrases in an English to English dictionary before you concept-check the meaning.

Suggested answers
1 a compulsory/voluntary activity, develop their musical abilities, develop their artistic expression, develop their musical knowledge
2 work in a team, develop their acting abilities, develop their artistic expression
3 interrupt a film with advertisements, when the film is released
4 a celebrity, avoid/cause a scandal, the media, a tabloid (newspaper), disturb/protect someone's privacy
5 help society develop, make people aware of problems

6 Encourage students to look back at Exercise 1 on page 91 if they need reminding of the phrases to speak about something generally.

Extension activity
Put students into threes: two candidates and one examiner. Tell them to choose one of the questions in Exercise 5 and write a conversation similar to the one in Exercise 1 between Antonia, Peter and the examiner. Remind students that candidates' answers should be balanced and include phrases to speak in general. Allow students fifteen minutes to write their conversation, before getting them to mark the pauses as shown in Exercise 4. Then, select students to read their conversations to the class.

Writing Part 1 (an essay) SB page 92

▶ **Page 192 Writing bank**

Lead in
Point to the photograph on page 92 and ask students what is happening (a famous person is getting into a car whilst being photographed by paparazzi). Put students into pairs to briefly discuss if they would like to live this way, giving reasons to justify their responses.

Exam advice

Read the exam advice with the students. Highlight that in order to write a balanced essay, students must include points both in favour and against the argument.

1 Students work individually before comparing their answers in pairs. Point out that their own idea must be a distinct idea and is in addition to any conclusion.

Answers
being famous; film star; both advantages and disadvantages; media attention; lifestyle; your own idea

2 As an alternative to working in groups, you could divide the class in half, with one half discussing the advantages and the other disadvantages (large classes could be divided into subgroups). Give groups a large piece of paper each and ask them to brainstorm (note down) their ideas, using a spider diagram. After five minutes, ask the groups to swap papers, adding their own ideas to those already noted.

3 If you chose to do the alternative suggested for Exercise 2, you could display the spider diagrams on the walls or board and allow students to look at them as they consider which ideas they are going to use. Remind students that each main body paragraph should address only one point from the task question (in this case either advantages or disadvantages), and which is typically introduced in the first sentence.

4 You may prefer to do this task with books closed so that students are not influenced by the opening paragraph shown in Exercise 5. Before students do this task, elicit that the opening paragraph is the introduction and its purpose is to tell the reader how they are going to answer the question.

5 Allow students a minute to compare their own paragraph individually before discussing in pairs.

6 Allow students five minutes to read the essay and answer the questions individually before discussing them in pairs or small groups.

Answers
1 Students' own answers
2 He gives the advantages, then the disadvantages, and then decides whether or not the advantages outweigh the disadvantages.
3 They introduce the paragraph.
4 They show the main ideas of each paragraph.
5 paragraph a: However
paragraph b: Firstly, Also, There is no doubt that, Finally
paragraph c: On the other hand, First, Next, Finally
paragraph d: To conclude, I think,
6 paragraph d
7 Because the exam task asks you to say if you agree with the statement.

7 Encourage students to use the plan they wrote in Exercise 3. You may wish to remind them that each main body paragraph should logically follow the outline in the opening paragraph (introduction) they wrote in Exercise 4. For example, if the student's opening paragraph says: *In this essay I will discuss the drawbacks and benefits …* then their second paragraph should discuss *disadvantages* and the third the *advantages*. Allow students twenty minutes to complete this task.

Extension activity

As students have written the first three paragraphs of their essay, you could ask them to write a concluding paragraph which should include their opinion. Allow students ten minutes to do this. Then, put them into groups and encourage them to read their classmates' essays, finding and underlining the main idea in each paragraph, together with examples of linking language (*on the other hand*, etc.).

8 Before students read the rubric, you may like to elicit phrases to write about advantages and disadvantages so that they can use a wider range of language (*drawback*, *negative aspect*, *downside*, *benefit*, *positive aspect*, etc.). As students have had several opportunities throughout the course to practise answering exam questions, you may now prefer not to provide them with additional support. Instead, tell the students to read the rubric and allow them two minutes to do this. Then, stop the students and tell them they have forty minutes to answer the question. After thirty minutes, give students a ten-minute warning. When the time is up, tell students to put their pens down (even if they have not finished). Once they have completed the task, refer students to the essay checklist in the Writing bank, page 203, telling them to read their answer whilst completing the checklist. Then put them into pairs or small groups so they can discuss their checklist answers together. Encourage them to use their answers to the checklist to identify two things they did well and two things they could improve.

Model answer
Nowadays, more and more people are choosing to pursue a career as a social media influencer. It is a job that has both advantages and disadvantages. Influencers need to produce content quickly and regularly. It can be difficult to produce something that's both entertaining and original on a regular basis. However, if an influencer can achieve this, they can become very successful.
When influencers become well-known, they open themselves up to a lot of new opportunities. For example, they might choose to receive money from companies in return for advertising certain products. However, they are also open to a lot more online criticism, which they aren't used to and can cause them a lot of emotional distress.
Finally, not every social media influencer is destined for success. It's important to remember that while some people become very successful influencers, others cannot make a living from it.

> Overall, I believe a career as a social media influencer can be rewarding but it's important for people not to think that they are guaranteed to be successful without working hard.

Vocabulary

Entertainment

binge-watch
catch up on
cliff-hanger
complex
confusing
gripping
heavy-going
hilarious
hooked
impressive
light-hearted
on the edge of your seat
predictable
rerun
stunning
switch off
twist
unappealing
unexpected

Commonly confused words

play / performance / acting
audience / (the) public / spectators
scene / stage

Reporting verbs

accuse
admit
agree
apologise for
invite
persuade
promise
recommend
remind
warn

Vocabulary activity 1

Refer students to page 85 and tell them they are going to write a paragraph which describes their taste in films. First, put students into groups and allocate one text to each student. Then, tell them to find and highlight phrases which could be used to describe their taste in films, e.g. *spend time in front of the TV*, *I enjoy a good blockbuster*, *a happy ending*, etc. Allow students two minutes to do this before asking them to share the phrases they found. Next, tell the groups to brainstorm film genres and write them on the board. Finally, tell students to look at the entertainment and commonly confused words in the vocabulary list and, working individually, choose ten words or phrases that they would like to use. Give students 15 minutes to write their paragraph. At the end of the task, you could collect the paragraphs, stick them on the walls or board, and ask the students to walk around the class and read them.

Vocabulary activity 2

Write the following statements on separate slips of paper (one set for each pair of students), or if you prefer, dictate them to the class.

You'd better not go there. It's dangerous.
I'll do it as soon as I get home.
Don't forget to feed the dog before you go out.
Yes, it was me. I took the money.
You can go to the party, as long as you are back before midnight.
I'm sorry. I broke the saddle on your bike when I borrowed it last week.
Will you make dinner, please? I'm busy at the moment.

Put the students into pairs. Divide the statements in half (one half for each student in the pair). Tell them that these statements were said to them, or by them, and now they must use the reporting verbs to tell their partner what was said. They can make up who was speaking (if it wasn't them) or who they were speaking to (e.g. a parent/friend). You could do the first one with the students before getting them to do the activity.

Example answers:

She warned me not to go there because it was dangerous.
I promised I'd do it as soon as I got home.
Mum reminded me to feed the dog before I went out.
The bank robber admitted it was him who had taken the money.
Mum agreed I could go to the party as long as I was back before midnight.
She apologised for breaking the saddle on my bike when she had borrowed it the week before.
I persuaded him to make dinner because I was busy at that time.

> **DIGITAL CLASSROOM**
>
> **Practice Extra** Unit 8
>
> **Test Generator** Unit 8 test
>
> **Test and Train Exam Practice**

Unit 7 Vocabulary and grammar review

1
1 unpredictable 2 patience 3 preparations 4 inexperienced 5 simply 6 unwilling 7 realistic 8 valuable

2
1 taking 2 to get 3 to invite 4 changing 5 to have 6 stealing 7 to finish 8 to become 9 working 10 asking 11 working 12 spending

3
1 aren't allowed/are not allowed to go 2 to avoid getting 3 can't bear windsurfing 4 you mind turning 5 you (may) risk having 6 no/little point (in) going

Unit 8 Vocabulary and grammar review

1
1 C 2 B 3 A 4 C 5 A 6 D 7 B 8 D 9 A 10 B

2
1 in 2 on 3 in 4 in 5 at 6 on 7 on 8 on 9 at 10 at

3
1 refused to lend 2 apologised for being late 3 accused him of forgetting 4 to arrive (at the cinema) 5 us/them to bring our/their jackets 6 to drive everyone/all of us

9 The power of the mind

Unit objectives

Topic: psychology

Reading and Use of English Part 5 (multiple choice): understanding questions that ask what a specific word refers to

Reading and Use of English Part 4 (key word transformation): understanding the language forms needed for the transformation, e.g. changing from active to passive; identifying when a fixed expression or phrasal verb is required

Writing Part 2 (report): making recommendations and suggestions in a report

Listening Part 1 (multiple choice): listening for the general idea; deciding which answers are wrong before listening a second time

Speaking Part 2 (long turn): speculating about photos using modals and *look*, *seem* and *appear*

Pronunciation: sentence stress (3); using stress for emphasis

Vocabulary: *achieve, carry out* and *devote*; *stay, spend* and *pass*; *make, cause* and *have*

Grammar: modal verbs to express certainty and possibility

Starting off SB page 96

1 Look at the photos with the students and briefly elicit what is happening in each (a person graduating; a family opening a box in a new home; people on a fairground/theme park ride; women at a keep fit/dance class) before putting them into pairs to complete the exercise. Once you have elicited the correct answers during whole-class feedback, put students into different pairs and ask them to discuss which phrases could be used to discuss each photo (e.g. phrase 1 could be used to talk about photos C and D; phrase 4 could be used to talk about photos A and B). This will help prepare students for the task in Exercise 3. Elicit a few ideas from the whole class.

Answers
1 c 2 a 3 h 4 d 5 b 6 g 7 e 8 f

2 First ask students to work individually and order the phrases from one to eight with one being the most important for happiness and eight being the least important. Remind them that, along with giving reasons to support their ideas, they should agree and disagree with the opinions of others. Point out that useful phrases to agree and disagree can be found in Unit 7, page 81, exercise 5 and Speaking bank page 210 and that phrases to support opinions with reasons and examples can be found in Speaking pages 211 and 212. If you do this, allow students five minutes to refer to these units and make notes of the phrases they could use. Then, put students into pairs or groups of three to discuss the questions. Monitor and listen for examples of error free language to agree, disagree and give opinions and reasons in order to praise students during whole-class feedback.

3 Point out that students should use phrases from Exercise 1 and elicit that they should compare the differences between the photos, as well as the similarities. As an alternative to pairwork, put students into threes and ask the third student (C) to act as the examiner. Student C reads the task instructions (*The photos show …*) and then, as they listen to students A and B, they write down two examples of phrases from Exercise 1 along with two examples of complex language to make comparisons. Once students A and B have spoken for one minute, ask student C to provide feedback before the students swap roles.

Reading and Use of English Part 5 SB page 96

Lead in

Ask students to think of something they do which makes them happy, together with a reason why. Point out that this can be anything from spending time with family to taking part in a sporting event or finishing a project at work. After a few minutes' thinking time, put students into threes (A, B, C) and tell them that in addition to talking about an activity that makes them happy, and why, they are going to practise using reported speech for revision of Unit 8. Explain that A should tell B what they do that makes them happy and why. B must then report to C what A told them, using reported speech, before telling C what they do that makes them happy. C then reports to A what B told them, and so on. Monitor and support students with reported speech tense changes as needed.

Exam advice

Read the exam advice with the students before telling them they are going to read a text with the title *The secret of happiness*. Put them into pairs and ask them to write two or three questions they think a text with this title will answer, e.g. *What is the definition of happiness? How does a person know they are happy? Which countries are the happiest?* Elicit ideas from the class during whole-class feedback.

1 Remind students they are reading quickly to find specific information and, as the topic of each paragraph is typically found in the first sentence (topic sentence), they could move to the next paragraph if the topic sentence indicates the information they are looking for will not be in there. For example, the first sentence of the first paragraph introduces the topic of the *World Happiness Report*. Point out (or elicit) that from this we could predict the first paragraph might provide information about what the World Happiness Report is, how countries are ranked, and which countries are ranked high (or low). It is unlikely to include Lesley's thoughts about conditions for happiness as there is no connection between this and the topic being introduced. Students work individually for one minute before comparing their answers in pairs. When eliciting the correct answer, draw attention to the first (topic) sentence in the last paragraph and elicit its connection to the information they were looking for. At the end of the activity, put students into pairs and ask them to briefly discuss how they can use this skill in the exam (using the topic sentence to make predictions about a text helps students improve their reading speed and comprehension).

Answers
According to Lesley Lavender, maintaining strong relationships is the most important condition for being happy (final paragraph).

Extension activity
Students work individually and read the first sentence of each paragraph again, using it to predict two or three questions they think the paragraph will answer. Point out that as you did this for paragraph one (in Exercise 1) they should look at paragraphs 2, 3, 4 and 5 only. Once they have written their questions, tell them to read the remainder of each paragraph and see if their predictions were correct.

2 Students work individually. Remind them to use the knowledge gained from the first exercise (and the extension activity if you chose to do it) to help them quickly locate where they will find an answer. For example, Q5 mentions *Lesley's view of money and happiness* and in the topic sentence of paragraph 4 the writer asks if Lesley believes that *having more money makes us happier*, which tells us the answer to question 5 is likely to be in paragraph 4. As this is an exam task, set a time limit of no more than twenty minutes before comparing their answers in pairs.

Answers
1 A **2** C **3** A **4** B **5** B **6** D

3 Elicit the meaning of *fixated* (obsessive attachment) and ask students to highlight the Einstein quotation (line 24) before they do this task. Tell students to give reasons to support their ideas and agree and disagree with the opinions of others.

4 Set a word limit of ten words, or alternatively a time limit of thirty seconds (or both) before students compare. As an alternative, get students to write their definitions on blank pieces of paper for you to collect and display on the walls or board. Then, ask students to walk round the class, read each definition and vote on which they think is the best definition.

Vocabulary SB page 98

achieve, carry out and devote

Lead in
Ask students to think about an ambition they have, e.g. gaining a promotion, passing Cambridge First or, for younger students, passing their driving test. After students have thought for a moment, tell them to think about how they intend to achieve their ambition before putting them into pairs to discuss. When you elicit examples from the class, you could further practise reported speech by selecting students to report what their partner told them.

1 Students work in pairs. If they are unsure, allow them to look the target words up in an English dictionary as they answer the questions. Alternatively, you could ask students to work individually and then check their answers using an English dictionary before comparing them with a partner.

Answers
1 devoted **2** achieve **3** carried out

2 Students work individually before comparing their answers in pairs. Remind them that as errors with these collocations are often made by exam candidates, they should write them in their notebooks under the heading *common errors I make*, and refer to them when they are revising for the exam.

Answers
1 achieve: an aim, an ambition, an objective, success
2 carry out: an improvement, an instruction, an order, research, a test, a threat
3 devote: energy, one's life, time

3 Point out that students should be careful of making errors with articles and singular/plural forms. Students work individually before comparing their answers in groups of three.

Answers
1 achieved; ambition **2** carrying out research/tests
3 devote; time **4** devoted; energy **5** carry out; threat
6 carry out orders/instructions

> **Fast finishers**
> Students work in pairs and take turns to ask and answer the following questions: *How much time do you devote to studying after class? Why? What will you do after you have achieved success in the Cambridge First exam?* Monitor and support students if they make errors with the target language.

stay, spend and *pass; make, cause* and *have*

4 Read the rubric with the students. Tell them to work individually and, after you have elicited the correct answers, tell students to asterisk (*) the questions they answered incorrectly. Once they have done this, tell them to write the asterisked questions in their notebooks under the heading *common errors I make*, and refer to them when they are revising for the exam. Note: You may find that students' first language can influence errors made with these words, e.g. *spend* and *pass* might be confused by Spanish and Italian first language speakers (*I will pass time in London next year*). If this is the case for your students, you could ask them to translate the sentences they answered incorrectly into their own language, then discuss in small groups which words are problematic perhaps due to directly translating them into English as they write. This can help raise students' awareness of common errors and why they are making them.

> **Answers**
> **1** have **2** caused **3** spent **4** spent **5** stay **6** made

5 Students work individually before comparing their answers in pairs. Elicit the answers from the class. As with Exercise 5, tell students to asterisk (*) the questions they answered incorrectly. Once they have done this, tell them to write the asterisked questions in their notebooks under the heading *common errors I make*, and refer to them when they are revising for the exam.

> **Answers**
> **1** spend **2** pass **3** stay **4** had/made **5** spend **6** spent
> **7** causing **8** makes/made **9** have **10** spent

6 Write *cause*, *have* and *make* on the board. Put students into groups of three and tell them to close their Student's Book. Next, give them one minute to write down as many nouns as they can which collocate with the verbs. Invite students to come to the front of the class and write the nouns on the board. Do not correct errors at this stage. Next, tell the groups to open their Student's Books and complete the task. Finally, get them to look up the words (*cause*, *have* and *make*) in an English to English dictionary and use the examples given to correct their errors. Then elicit the answers to the exercise and write any error corrections for the collocations on the board.

> **Answers**
> cause: an accident, a problem, trouble
> have: an effect, an impact, an impression, a problem
> make: a change, an effort, an impact, an impression, trouble

7 Students work individually. Monitor and support weaker students. Once students finish the task, tell them to compare their answers in pairs or small groups. Elicit the answers during whole-class feedback.

> **Answers**
> **1** caused an accident **2** made; impression **3** caused; (any) trouble / a problem **4** have the impression **5** makes / made / has made; change **6** have; impact/effect

Listening Part 1 SB page 99

> Read the exam advice with the students. Tell students they should put a line through answers they think are wrong as they listen the first time as this will give them fewer options to consider the second time they listen.
> **Exam advice**

1 Point out that students should justify their responses with examples and remind them to agree and disagree with the ideas of others, particularly when discussing the final two questions, which are opinion based. Set a time limit of five minutes. During whole-class feedback, select students to share their ideas and encourage others to agree and disagree with the ideas given.

2 As students have done this type of task before, you may prefer them to work individually before comparing their answers in pairs. When you elicit the answers, encourage students to paraphrase by using synonyms, which will help them avoid word spotting as they are listening.

> **Suggested answers**
> **1** You hear a woman talking about a number that has a special meaning in her life. Why is this number important to her?
> **2** You hear a man and a woman discovering something that they have in common. What is it?

3 Play the recording twice. Tell students to check their answers using the audioscript on page 232 before you elicit them in whole-class feedback.

> **Answers**
> **1** B **2** C

Extension activity
In groups, students underline the part of the audioscript on page 232 where they heard the correct answer and discuss reasons why the other options are incorrect. For example, in question 1, the woman says, *it was the number of the house I grew up in, the date I married my husband and the number of the first house we bought,* which indicates the correct option, B. The distractor for option A is the whole of the woman's second line, which may be incorrectly matched with important events; for option C, the distractor is *When I told my husband about this, though, he didn't see the significance: husband* is a distractor for *somebody she's close to* and *significance* is a word spot for *significant.*

Track 33

Narrator: One. You hear a woman talking about a number that has a special meaning in her life.
Man: Do you have a lucky number?
Woman: Yes, the number 18. It's not really a lucky number as such, rather one that's associated with a lot of my happiest memories.
Man: Such as?
Woman: Well, it was the number of the house I grew up in, the date I married my husband and the number of the first house we bought.
Man: Wow!
Woman: When I told my husband about this, though, he didn't see the significance and put it down to nothing more than a coincidence.

Narrator: Two. You hear a man and a woman discovering something that they have in common.
Man: Are you going to David's party?
Woman: No, I'm not a big fan of parties. They make me nervous.
Man: Really? You seem very sociable. Not like me.
Woman: It's because I can't stand dancing.
Man: Me neither. My parents forced me to do ballroom as a kid and I hated it.
Woman: I have an actual fear of it. If I see dancing, my heart beats faster and I start sweating.
Man: That sounds terrible. Where do you think it came from?
Woman: Well, like you, my parents made me do ballet when I was younger. I hated it and fell over in the middle of a performance. It might have started after that.
Man: Really? What a strange coincidence!

4 Play the recording twice. Once students have answered the questions, tell them to work individually and check their answers using the audioscript on page 232. Encourage students to explain their choices when you elicit the answers during whole-class feedback.

Answers
3 A **4** C **5** B **6** A **7** A **8** C

Track 34

Narrator: Three. You hear a man talking to his friend about a relaxation class he attended.
Woman: Hi, Michael. What did you get up to last night?
Man I went along to a relaxation class.
Woman: What was it like?
Man: We had to sit quietly with our eyes closed and focus on something that made us happy. I had difficulty staying awake, to be honest – it can't have been more than two minutes before I started dropping off! But that was to be expected, I suppose, as I'd had a really stressful day at work, worrying about the various projects I'm working on. The floor was quite hard but, luckily, I'd remembered to bring a cushion with me, which helped me get through it.

Narrator: Four. You hear a sports coach talking about problems faced by professional athletes.
Sports Coach: We all feel the pressure when we really want to succeed, and professional sportspeople are no exception. We can probably think of many examples of times when teams or individuals suddenly seem to lose focus in the final match. So why might this be? Well, it has very little to do with their ability, even if they are playing against somebody equally skilled. Evidence suggests that athletes who come second in a final often find it difficult to stop thinking about other times when they have lost, which could result in a loss of both confidence and the desire to win.

Narrator: Five. You overhear a man and a woman talking about a television series.
Man: Have you been watching that new crime drama on TV?
Woman: Yes, I love it. I couldn't believe what happened in the last episode. The main character … what's his name … Lars … is truly bad.
Man: I know … I often feel angry after watching it. I know it's not real, but I still think, 'how could you do that'?
Woman: He's obviously really intelligent, though. It's a shame that he uses his brain for such negative purposes. He'd probably be a genius if his life had worked out differently.
Man: It sounds as if you like him.
Woman: It's not that I like him, but I do feel a bit of sympathy for him sometimes. He must have had a really unhappy childhood.

Narrator: Six. You hear a woman talking about a past fear of heights.
Woman: I used to be terrified of heights. I remember the day when my company announced that they were moving our offices to the top floor of the building. I ended up seeking professional help because I just couldn't get over the thought of being that high up. My therapist taught me a few breathing techniques that I could use when I started to feel uncomfortable. Amazingly, they worked, much more effectively than any of the advice I'd read online about forcing myself to climb to the top of

a tall building to face my fears. In the end, it meant that I didn't have to quit my job, which was great!

Narrator: Seven. You hear a man talking about the happiest countries in the world.

Man: For many years now, the Scandinavian countries Denmark, Iceland and Finland have featured in the top five happiest countries in the world. But why is this, and what could other countries learn from them? Well, these countries have some of the lowest crime rates in the world, which helps make people feel more at ease. The public are also well provided for with excellent education, healthcare and housing. However, it's the attitude to life, and the idea that time with friends and family is as significant as your job, that has the greatest impact on their positivity.

Narrator: Eight. You hear a woman talking about a study she carried out into leisure activities.

Woman: In our latest study, we looked at leisure activities that people reported to have had the most positive impact on their mood. Three groups of people were asked to take up different activities – gardening, reading and cooking – and to do them regularly for four weeks. The reading group reported feeling more relaxed as a result of reading regularly, and feeling slightly more positive. The gardening group reported that they felt both more relaxed and significantly more cheerful than they did before, while the cooking group reported no real difference in mood before and after the experiment. It would be interesting to repeat this study with larger groups of people.

5 Allow students a few minutes to consider their responses before putting them into pairs to discuss.

Grammar SB page 100

Modal verbs to express certainty and possibility

▶ **Page 176 Grammar reference**

1 Read the rubric with the students. Tell them to work individually. Monitor and support weaker students before allowing them to compare their answers in pairs. If students are struggling, refer them to the Grammar reference on page 176 and tell them to read the information section. If you have referred students to the Grammar reference, draw their attention to *may*, *might* or *could*, and point out that *could* is being used to refer to a possible present or future event and not as a past form of *can*. If students ask if there is any difference between *may* and *might*, tell them they have an interchangeable meaning in the context of possibility.

Answers
1
a must **b** can't **c** might, could; may
2
Present: could
Past: must have, might have and can't have

2 Point out that these are real errors made by exam candidates. Tell students to work individually before you elicit the answers. Then tell them to asterisk (*) the questions they answered incorrectly. Once they have done this, tell them to write the asterisked questions in their notebooks under the heading *common errors I make*, and refer to them when they are revising for the exam.

Answers
1 ~~may have~~ must have **2** ~~mustn't be~~ can't be
3 ~~can have~~ may/might/could **4** ~~can~~ must **5** correct

3 Allow weaker students to work in pairs and refer to the Grammar reference on page 176 as they complete their answers. Monitor and support students who are struggling. Elicit the answers during whole-class feedback.

Answers
1 must have worked **2** must be **3** must have had / must have been having **4** may/might/could have had to; may/might/could have stopped **5** can't be **6** may/might/could rain

4 Look at the photos with the students and elicit a few ideas from the class. Next, tell them to work individually, choose one photo and write down two example sentences using the target language *may*, *might*, *must*, *could* and *can't*, e.g. *In the first picture the women might be celebrating together …* Allow them five minutes to do this. As students work, monitor and elicit error corrections so that the sentences produced are accurate. Once they have done this, put them into pairs and ask them to take turns saying their sentences, then tell them to discuss the remaining two photos whilst continuing to use the target language. Monitor and write down examples of common errors. After up to five minutes, stop the students and elicit error correction for the common errors you heard.

5 Put students into pairs to discuss the questions. Alternatively, students could talk about someone they know who has experienced the situations, predicting why the situations might have happened and how the person must have felt.

Extension activity
This would be an opportunity to recycle modal verbs to express certainty and possibility in a Speaking Part 2 task which will prepare students for *speculating about photos* on page 103. Put students into pairs and tell them to choose two of the photos each (they may choose the same pair of photos). Tell them to take turns to compare their photos and then say what the people are looking at and what they might be thinking about doing next. Remind students they must speak individually for one minute before answering the question. Monitor and listen for examples of the correct use of modal verbs for expressing certainty and possibility and complex language to make comparisons.

Reading and Use of English Part 4 SB page 101

Read the exam advice with the students. Remind them that as they may be tested on their knowledge of common expressions, it is important that they record new language at phrase level in their notebooks. Point out that this includes common collocations, e.g. *achieve an aim*.

Exam advice

1 Read the rubric with the students before eliciting the answer to question 1 from the class. Then draw students' attention to incorrect answer b and remind them that even if the correct words are included within their answer, it will be awarded no marks if they go over the five-word maximum. Tell students to work individually and answer questions 2–6 before comparing their answers in pairs. When eliciting answers, make a note of any common errors so that you can provide additional targeted support.

Answers
1
a correct **b** this is more than five words **c** *lend* should be *borrow* in this sentence
2
a this is more than five words **b** incorrect verb form used with *despite* **c** correct
3
a incorrect phrasal verb **b** correct **c** incorrect phrasal verb
4
a incorrect use of second conditional **b** incorrect tense with *until* **c** correct
5
a incorrect use of double modal **b** the second sentence doesn't have a similar meaning to the first sentence
c correct
6
a correct **b** incorrect use of the gerund form **c** this is more than five words

2 As this is an exam task, set a time limit of twenty minutes and tell students to work individually. Then elicit the correct answers from the class.

Answers
1 will stop me (from) sleeping **2** keep (on) playing loud music **3** had been decorated **4** reminded him to water **5** did you spend reading **6** take responsibility for

Extension activity
If students have already completed the Grammar reference page 175, Exercise 4 (reported speech), ask them to create their own Reading and Use of English Part 4 practice questions. First, put students into pairs. Tell half the pairs they will be creating five Reading and Use of English Part 4 questions using sentences from the Grammar reference page 174 and the other half from the Grammar reference page 175 (Exercise 4). Next, write an example on the board to show them what they need to do. (Taken from the bottom left column of Grammar reference page 174.):

'You mustn't open the files relating to the new product launch.'

TOLD

Her boss ______ open the files relating to the new product launch.

Elicit the answer: *told her she mustn't*. Once you are happy students understand the task, give them 20 minutes to write their five questions. After they have done this, tell the whole class to close their Student's Books, swap questions and answer them before referring to the Grammar reference to check their answers.

Speaking Part 2 SB page 102

▶ **Page 206 Speaking bank**

Lead in
Put students into pairs. Ask them to look at the photos and briefly discuss what activities the people are doing. Elicit ideas from the class (mountain climbing; welding) before asking them if they have already done, or would do, these activities. Note: at this stage of the course, you may find that students naturally start to compare the photographs as they would in a Speaking Part 2 activity. If they do so, allow extra time without interrupting. Monitor and listen for examples of modal verbs to express certainty and possibility and complex language to make comparisons. Praise them for the correct examples you heard during whole-class feedback before eliciting error correction.

Read the exam advice with the students. Tell them to look at the photos again and, if students did not do this in the Lead in, elicit a few example sentences using modal verbs to speculate about what is happening in each (e.g. … *might be tied together with rope*; … *could be fixing a lamp* …).

Exam advice

1 Students work individually before comparing their answers in pairs. If students find the task challenging, remind them to look at the words directly before and after the gaps and make sure the gapped word or phrase fits grammatically. Elicit that the subject *they* before gap (1) and *to be* after, indicates the pattern verb + *to be* is required. There are only two options which follow this pattern (*may have decided*; *seem*), so this will help students to narrow down their choices.

2 Play the recording twice before eliciting the answers from the class.

> **Answers**
> **1** seem **2** might **3** perhaps **4** very different
> **5** exactly what **6** could be **7** who appears
> **8** may have decided **9** looks as if **10** unlike

Track 35

Examiner: Here are your photographs. They show young people doing difficult activities. I'd like you to compare the photographs and say why you think the people have decided to do these activities. All right?

Peter: The first photo shows young people walking up a mountain. They seem to be tied together with ropes and they might be resting, or perhaps they've been waiting for one of the group to catch them up. They may be part of an adventure activity which they're doing from their school or college and they may have been climbing for quite a long time. The second photo shows a very different situation. The girl seems to be working with equipment in a factory. I'm not sure exactly what she's doing, but she could be building a machine or something. There's a man who appears to be supervising her. The people in the first photo may have decided to climb the mountain because they want a new experience, or perhaps they just enjoy being in the mountains, even though they look a bit tired. The girl in the second photo looks as if she's starting a new job and learning to do something. It's clear that she's working indoors, unlike the people in the first photo, who are outdoors.

3 Read the rubric with the students and point to the sentences underneath the photos so that students are clear which phrases are being referred to. Elicit one example for the first sentence from the class, encouraging the student you select to say the sentence in full before putting students into pairs to complete the activity. Tell them to write the sentences in full in their notebooks, explaining that writing the complete sentence may help them to remember the target language. Monitor and elicit error corrections. Once students have completed the task, put them into new pairs and ask them to take it in turns to read their sentences.

> **Suggested answers**
> **1** … they are celebrating the older man's birthday. **2** … very happy. **3** … sing 'Happy Birthday' to him. **4** … at the end of a race. **5** … feeling very tired. **6** … the people in this photo are all active. **7** … really happy.

/P/ Pronunciation: sentence stress (3)

4 Read the information with the students. Elicit that we typically stress content words, i.e. nouns, and then point out that while auxiliary verbs are not normally stressed, they can be stressed for emphasis. (For example, in the sentence: *I **may** come to the party*, the speaker stresses the modal verb *may* to emphasise that they are uncertain.)

4.1 Play the recording once before allowing students to compare their ideas in pairs. Once they have done this, tell them to look at the words they have underlined and consider why the speaker might want to change the emphasis (in version 1 the speaker may be less certain than in version 2 and so has emphasised the verb *seem*, the adverb *exactly* and the modal *could*). To elicit the answers from the whole class, select two stronger students to read one version each, copying the stress patterns they heard.

> **Answers**
> See Track 36 recording script for answers
> In version 1, Peter emphasises the fact that he's speculating, while in version 2, he emphasises the different possible activities she could be doing.

Track 36

Version 1

Peter: The girl <u>seems</u> to be working with equipment in a factory. I'm not sure <u>exactly</u> what she's doing, but she <u>could</u> be building a machine or something.

Version 2

Peter: The girl seems to be working with <u>equipment</u> in a <u>factory</u>. I'm not sure exactly what she's doing, but she could be building a <u>machine</u> or something.

4.2 As students may become dependent on familiarity with the way their usual partner speaks, pair them with someone they do not normally work with. Tell each student to choose a version to read to their partner without telling them which version they have chosen. If their partner guesses the incorrect version, tell them they should read their version again, this time with more emphasis on the stressed words (say the stressed words more loudly and slightly more slowly).

4.3 For weaker students, play the recording twice before asking them to compare their answers in pairs.

> **Answers**
> See Track 37 recording script for answers.

Track 37

Peter: The people in the first photo <u>may</u> have decided to climb the mountain because they want a new experience, or <u>perhaps</u> they just enjoy being in the mountains, <u>even though</u> they look a bit tired. The girl in the second photo <u>looks as if</u> she's starting a new job and learning to do something.

5 Students work individually. Before they start, tell them to consider the words and phrases they would stress to emphasise that they are speculating and, once they start the activity, allow them to refer to the audioscript on page 234 (version 1) and the words they underlined in Exercise 4.1 if they need support. Monitor as students complete the task, eliciting self-corrections for errors where necessary. Put students into pairs to compare their ideas before they take turns to say their sentences. Monitor and identify stronger students who can model the correct sentence stress during whole-class feedback.

6 Refer students to the examiner instructions on page 102 to remind them of the task before putting them into pairs to complete the activity.

7 Allow students a few minutes to read the bullet points and the speaking task before putting them into pairs. Assign each student one pair of photos and tell them to read their instructions. Before students start speaking, remind them to use language to speculate covered in this unit. The students should be comfortable giving and receiving feedback by this stage of the course. However, you could elicit the target language and sentence stress that they will be listening for and remind them to praise three correct examples and offer two suggestions for improvement so that the feedback stage is a positive experience.

Writing Part 2 (a report) SB page 104

▶ **Page 198 Writing bank**

Lead in

With Student's Books closed, tell students you are going to write the following three statements on the board (or dictate them) and they must decide if the statements are true or false. If false, they must say why.

A report should have a title (true); *If the report is divided into sections, sections do not need headings* (false: sections need headings); *A report must always make suggestions and recommendations* (false: only true when required by the task).

Once students have briefly discussed their ideas, tell them to open their Student's Books and refer to the exam advice on page 39 to check their answers.

1 As students have completed this type of activity before, ask them to underline individually before comparing their answers in pairs and discussing the question.

Answers
Suggested underlining
money to spend, improving the classrooms, students' social activities, director of your college, report, explain the benefits of both ideas, which idea, chosen, why

2 Students work individually before comparing their answers. Alternatively, if your students are stronger, elicit the answers from the class without prior discussion.

Answers
1 the director of your college **2** formal or neutral-formal
3 benefits of both ideas; which idea should be chosen and why

3 Allow weaker students to work in pairs. Encourage them to read the answer through quickly, ignoring the gaps initially, in order to get an idea of how the report is structured and also to practise their skimming skills (reading quickly to get an overview) before they read it again and fill in the gaps.

Answers
1 discuss **2** spent **3** put forward **4** contains **5** find
6 benefit **7** improve **8** participate **9** reduce
10 recommend

Fast finishers

Ask students to read the answer in Exercise 3 again and find a more formal word or phrase with a similar meaning to these less formal words or phrases: *reason for* (purpose of), *if* (whether), *include* (contain), *but* (however), *also* (furthermore).

4 Encourage students to read all the questions individually and spend five minutes noting their answers before they discuss them in pairs for a further five minutes. Before eliciting the answers, ask student to find and underline the parts in the answer which address the points in the task. When eliciting the answer to question 5, draw students' attention to the writer's use of the second conditional to hypothesise, and elicit that the situation they describe is unreal (the writer does not know if his/her recommendations will be carried out).

Suggested answers
1 The writer recommends new furniture and an air-conditioning system.
2 They can look at the section headings.
3 Yes
4
Introduction: states the purpose of the report
The classrooms: talks about the need for improvements
Social activities: talks about the effect of the money on these
Recommendation: makes a recommendation for spending the money and gives a reason.
5 The present tense to talk about the present situation and the second conditional to talk about the effects if the money were spent in the ways suggested.
6 No – it uses a formal style, as appropriate in a report.

5 If students need support, refer them to the Grammar reference on page 171, infinitive and verb + *-ing*, and tell them to read the information and examples before completing the task.

Answers
1 installing **2** spending **3** buy **4** to equip

6 Allow students five minutes to consider their own ideas before working in pairs to complete the task. Put students into groups of four or six and ask them to share their ideas. Tell them to agree and disagree with the opinions of others before deciding their group's top three recommendations or suggestions and why their institution should adopt them. Instead of whole-class feedback, you could ask the students to select one member of their group to come to the front of the class and present their group's ideas, before the whole class vote on the idea they think is the most important.

7 Encourage students to underline the main points in the question before they discuss their ideas.

8 As this is an exam task and students have now had significant writing practice, hand them two or three sheets of blank paper each, then tell them to close their notebooks and write their answer on the paper, including their plans. Doing this will discourage students from checking language or grammar points in their notebooks, if they have done so previously, and replicate exam conditions more authentically. Allow forty minutes to complete the task. Once the time is up, tell the students to put down their pens and collect the plans and answers.

Extension activity
If you chose to collect the students' plans and writing, return the plans to the students. Put them into groups and ask them to share their plans. When comparing plans, they should discuss whether they are divided into sections with headings that deal with each of the main points in the question. Once students have done this, put them into different groups, return their reports and ask them to compare their reports with their plans. They should identify and discuss whether their report covers the points outlined in their plan. Then, ask students to work individually and check their writing against the Report checklist on page 203 of the Writing bank, noting points they did well and what could be improved. Finally, provide students with a copy of the model answer to compare their report against, underlining useful phrases in the sample answer (e.g. *the aim of this report*), which they should record in their notebooks and use in their future report writing.

Model answer
Improvements to the Palmar District
Introduction
The aim of this report is to suggest how the town can spend the money which it has available for improving this district.

The streets
The Palmar District is an old part of the city with narrow streets and pavements. Because the pavements are so narrow, it is difficult for pedestrians to walk together or pass each other without stepping into the road, which can be dangerous. Also, many of the streets are badly lit at night, which means that it can be quite frightening to walk there.

The traffic
Unfortunately, the district has a lot of traffic, which makes it very noisy and polluted. Also there is very little space available for residents to park their cars.

Recommendations
It would be a good idea to make some of the main streets for pedestrians only, with wider pavements. I also suggest that the council should provide good street lights and build a car park for residents. Finally, I recommend that the town council should build a ring road so that traffic does not have to enter the neighbourhood.

Vocabulary

Commonly confused words

achieve: an aim, an ambition, an objective, success
carry out: an improvement, an instruction, an order, research, a test, a threat
devote: energy, one's life, time
stay: awake, like this
spend: one's life, an hour, an afternoon, the weekend, the whole lecture
pass: the time
make: a change, an impact, an impression, trouble
cause: an accident, a problem, trouble
have: an effect, an impact, an impression, a problem

Vocabulary activity 1

Put students into groups. Give each group a different colour board pen and tell them to close their Student's Books and notebooks. Write *achieve, carry out* and *devote* on the board, then divide the board into as many sections as there are groups. Tell students they have three minutes to write as many nouns as they can remember which collocate with each verb. The winning team is the group that has remembered the most noun-verb collocations correctly from the vocabulary list.

Vocabulary activity 2

This is the reverse of Activity one. Put the students into groups and give each group a blank piece of paper. Tell them to close their Student's Books and notebooks. Write on the board *an accident, a change, an effect, an impact, an instruction, an impression, a problem, trouble, an improvement*. Tell students they have five minutes to write as many sentences as they can using the correct verb, *cause, have, make* or *carry out*. If students need help with a topic, suggest they write sentences connected to their work or home life. Tell them that they should use each of the nouns once only and should aim to write full and complex sentences, e.g. *I decided to catch the train to work as it would make a change from sitting in traffic*, rather than, e.g. *I made a change at work*. After five minutes, collect the papers and display them around the class. Invite the students to walk round and read the sentences. Elicit error corrections as necessary. The winning team is the group which has written the highest number of complex, error-free sentences.

DIGITAL CLASSROOM

Practice Extra Unit 9

Test Generator Unit 9 test

Test and Train Exam Practice

10 Spend, spend, spend

Unit objectives

Topic: money, shopping and business

Reading and Use of English Part 2 (open cloze): checking the type of word required and whether an answer makes sense with the surrounding text

Reading and Use of English Part 5 (multiple choice): understanding how the order of questions relates to the text

Writing Part 2 (a review): building complex sentences

Listening Part 4 (multiple choice): appropriately dividing focus between the main question and the answer options

Speaking Part 1 (interview): talking about spending money; strategies for answering Part 1 questions

Pronunciation: linking (1)

Vocabulary: *arrive, get* and *reach*; phrasal verbs connected with shopping

Grammar: *as* and *like*; modal verbs to express ability

Starting off SB page 106

Lead in

Ask students to close their Student's Books. Write on the board the advantages and disadvantages of online shopping. Elicit four or five examples for each and write them on the board. Then hold a brief open discussion on whether online shopping has more advantages than disadvantages.

1 Put students into groups. Tell them they should agree and disagree with the opinions of others before giving their own opinion. Elicit ideas from the class and encourage students to justify their ideas.

2 Before students complete the task, tell them to write next to each belief A (for *advantage*) or D (for *disadvantage*). Set a time limit of one or two minutes for students to match the reasons before putting them into pairs to compare their ideas. As you elicit the answers, ask students to say why someone might have this belief (e.g. not being able to touch or try a product may result in buying something which is of poor quality and/or does not fit).

3 Put students into pairs to discuss. Alternatively, as students have discussed this topic at some length already, you may prefer to elicit one or two ideas from the whole class.

Answers

Advantages of shopping online

32% = 2 29% = 5 22% = 6 17% = 8

Disadvantages of shopping online

51% = 1 24% = 4 11% = 7 10% = 9 4% = 3

Reading and Use of English Part 2 SB page 106

1 Before students start the activity, elicit the meaning of unknown vocabulary, e.g. *influencer* (a person who presents products on social media so that people are persuaded to buy them). Remind them to use words and phrases for giving examples, which were introduced in Unit 4 page 46 (e.g. *for instance, like*). You may wish to provide students with additional phrases to give examples (*to give you an idea …, imagine that …, suppose that …*) and encourage them to write them in their notebooks. Allow students five minutes to discuss the questions before eliciting ideas in whole-class feedback.

Exam advice

Put students into threes (ABC). Tell As to re-read the Reading and Use of English Part 2 exam advice from Unit 1 on page 13, Bs from Unit 6 on page 69 and Cs from this unit on this page (107). Once they have done this, tell them to discuss all the advice given before each team member evaluates their own performance in this part of the exam and decides which pieces of advice might address any specific weaknesses they have.

2 If your students are likely to start reading immediately, you could instruct the whole class to read the title and look at the picture, then elicit two or three ideas from the class. As students give their ideas, encourage them to use language to speculate from Unit 9 (*It looks as if, They must be*, etc.), before putting them into pairs to complete the task.

3 Remind students to consider the exam advice they decided would address their individual weaknesses as they are answering the questions. Tell them to work individually. As this is an exam task, set a time limit of fifteen minutes. Once the time is up, tell students to compare their answers in pairs before eliciting them in whole-class feedback.

Answers

1 been **2** as **3** in **4** take **5** up **6** rather **7** whether **8** one

4 Allow students a few minutes to consider their ideas before putting them into pairs. Select students to offer opinions during whole-class feedback, encouraging them to agree and disagree with the opinions of others before offering and justifying their own.

Grammar SB page 107

as and *like*

▶ **Page 177 Grammar reference**

Lead in
Dictate the following questions: *Who in your family do you most look like? Who in your family are you most like?* Elicit that *look like* refers to physical appearance and *like* refers to personality. Then put students into pairs to briefly ask and answer the questions before eliciting examples from the class.

1 Read the rubric and ask the students to find and underline the examples of *as* and *like* before they begin. Students work individually before comparing their answers in pairs. After you have elicited the answers, point out that *like* and the phrase *such as* are also used to give examples, (*I enjoy playing team sports* ***like*** *football and rugby; I enjoy playing team sports* ***such as*** *football and rugby*).

Answers
1 as **2** like

2 Weaker students can work in pairs. Allow students to check their answers using the Grammar reference on page 177 before eliciting in whole-class feedback.

Answers
1 as **2** as **3** as **4** like **5** as **6** as, as **7** as **8** like **9** as, as, like **10** as

Fast finishers
Tell students to turn to the Grammar reference on page 177 and read the information. Put them into pairs and ask them to decide which phrases are useful in the Speaking exam and why (e.g. *as far as I am concerned*: offering an opinion in Speaking Parts 3 and 4; *as far as I can see/tell*: speculating about photos in Speaking Part 2; *the same … as*: comparing how photos are similar in Speaking Part 2). Encourage students to write down the phrases in their notebooks so they can refer to them when they are practising. Finally, ask the students to write the phrases on the board so they can be reviewed when the rest of the class have finished Exercise 2.

Reading and Use of English Part 5 SB page 108

Lead in
Ask students if they would ever like to write a book and, if so, what they would write about. Elicit ideas from the class.

Exam advice
Read the exam advice with the students. Then tell them to re-read the exam advice on pages 20, 64 and 96, making notes of the points they believe are the most useful for helping them to address their individual weaknesses. Once they have done this, put them into pairs to discuss their decisions. Encourage students to give reasons to support their ideas (e.g. by explaining how a specific piece of advice will help them personally).

1 Before students start the task, write *A Journey of Self-Discovery* on the board and ask students what they think a book with this title will be about, before eliciting one or two ideas from the class (e.g. lifestyle changes or travel experiences). For each question, encourage students to think of one example to support their opinion.

2 As an alternative to pairwork, students could work in small groups. Select students to offer opinions during whole-class feedback, encouraging them to agree and disagree with the opinions of others before offering and justifying their own.

3 Students have practised this exam task a number of times, so in order to help students identify if they are using the techniques they learnt in Units 2, 5 and 9, do not provide additional support. Simply remind them to use the techniques they have practised, and tell them they have twenty minutes to answer the question. Elicit the answers during whole-class feedback.

Answers
1 A **2** C **3** A **4** D **5** C **6** C

Extension activity
Put students into small groups. Ask them to refer to the exam advice notes they made for this section, then discuss what pieces of advice they found most helpful when they were completing Exercise 3, what pieces of advice they found difficult to follow, and how their technique has changed since the beginning of the course. Encourage students to justify their responses.

4 Read the rubric with the students and refer them to the words highlighted in yellow in the text. Point out that as the thing being referred to is not always in the same sentence as the pronoun or determiner (*it, that, them,* etc.), they should also read the sentence before, and sometimes the one after.

Answers
1 b **2** a **3** a **4** a **5** b **6** b **7** a

5 Encourage students to agree and disagree with the opinions of others before offering their own and remind them to justify their ideas with reasons and examples. Allow students five minutes to discuss the questions before selecting one or two from each group to come to the front and report their group's ideas, using reported speech where appropriate. Listen and make notes of correct and incorrect language use. Once representatives from every group have spoken, elicit error correction for the incorrect examples and praise the correct examples you heard.

Vocabulary SB page 110

arrive, get and reach

Lead in
Write *arrive, get* and *reach* on the board. Then elicit the answers to the following questions: *Which word can be followed by 'to'?* (get); *Which word means to arrive at a place or decision often after some difficulty?* (reach) and *Which word is intransitive?* (arrive).

1 Before students start the activity, point out that when making their choices, they should look at the words immediately before and after and check that their choice fits grammatically. For example, as *reach* is followed by a noun or noun phrase, it cannot be the correct answer to question 1 (*The easiest way to reach ~~to~~ the coast*). Point out that these are examples of real candidate errors. Once students have completed the activity and you have elicited the answers, tell students to asterisk (*) any questions they answered incorrectly. They could then write correct examples in their notebooks under the heading *common errors* and refer to their notes when they are revising for the exam.

Answers
1 get **2** arrived **3** reached

2 Students work individually. Monitor and support weaker students. Allow students to compare their answers in pairs before eliciting the correct answers.

Answers
1 reached **2** got **3** arrives **4** get **5** arrived **6** reach

3 Point out that adverbs of manner, place and time typically come after the main verb (*I **left shortly** after 10 pm.*); however, this can be reversed when there are multiple auxiliary verbs with the adverb positioned between the auxiliaries (e.g. *They **will be** leaving **shortly**. → They **will shortly be** leaving.*) Allow students to work in pairs. Monitor and support weaker students.

Answers
1 arrived; safe and sound **2** arrived in time
3 arriving on time **4** shortly; arriving
5 arrived unannounced **6** finally arrived

Listening Part 4

Lead in
Select a student to read the exam advice to the class. As it is important that students know how long one minute feels like in the exam when they are under pressure, give them one minute to read the question stems in Exercise 3, encouraging them to make notes in the margin or underline the main points as they do so. For example, for question one they might underline *why, decide, call, Tailor.*) When the time is up, put the students into pairs, telling them to briefly discuss whether they were able to read and understand all of the question stems. Point out that they should not waste time re-reading a question stem several times, or stop reading every time they come to a word they do not understand.

1 Read the rubric with the students, then put them into small groups to complete the activity. If students are struggling with ideas, you could give them points to consider, e.g. attracting readers or social media marketing. Give each group a board pen and invite them to write their lists on the board before asking them to discuss briefly if their ideas are the same as, or different from, the other groups'.

2 To discourage students from reading the questions, tell them to close their Student's Books and read the rubric for them. Encourage students to make notes as they are listening and refer to them when they are comparing ideas.

Track 38

Interviewer: Today I'm joined by Cathy Ko who runs the fashion magazine *Tailor*. Welcome, Cathy. Let's start with the name *Tailor* – what made you choose that name?

Cathy: It's actually harder than you think to come up with a name for a magazine. I was so stuck at one point that I even considered selecting a random word from the dictionary. If the magazine was to do well internationally, it had to be something that people wouldn't struggle to pronounce, so I settled on *Tailor*. It also happens to be the surname of my best friend, though that was completely coincidental.

Interviewer: How do you cope with the tight deadlines of editing a magazine?

Cathy: It's probably the toughest part of the job, to be honest. I've lost count of the number of times I've had to cancel arrangements with friends to work late in the office. Part of my role as editor is to monitor the well-being of my team and watch out for signs of stress and fatigue. If you're able to pick up on these in the early stages, you can avoid any potential conflicts in the office that may occur as a result.

Interviewer: Tell us more about the writers at the magazine. What are they like to work with?

Cathy: I really couldn't ask for a better team. They're passionate about what they do and all go about their work with big smiles on their faces. The publishing industry can be quite cruel at times and nobody likes to hear that their work isn't up to standard, but what impresses me above everything else is how they take all the feedback on board and learn from it to become the best writers they can be.

Interviewer: I read that you were almost sued a few years ago over an article you published. Can you tell us more about that?

Cathy: Sure. This centred around a piece we'd written about London Fashion Week. It's a huge fixture on the fashion calendar, so, understandably, there are hundreds of writers there to cover it, making it tricky to come up with something unique. The article was about the fur-free theme at the fashion show that year. I spent so much time ensuring all the facts were correct in the article that I forgot to check whether we were allowed to use the image that accompanied it – a week later we received a letter asking us to pay for the rights or we'd be sued.

Interviewer: That must have been an unpleasant surprise! What's your opinion of fashion blogs?

Cathy: When I first started out in the magazine industry, fashion blogs were just beginning to take off and some editors felt threatened that they'd one day put print magazines out of business. There's no denying the influence they have on the hundreds and thousands of readers they pull in, many of whom subscribe to our magazine as well. So I figured, why not embrace that? They're home to some really talented writers and we work closely with them to promote each other's businesses, so everyone's a winner.

Interviewer: How did you feel about winning the award for 'magazine of the year'?

Cathy: I couldn't believe it when they read my name out. People were coming up to me all night to congratulate me, including icons of the fashion industry who I'd looked up to my entire life ... it was all a bit too much if I'm honest. That being said, I was thrilled to win. It led to a number of high-profile interviews, of course, and it meant that we could put 'magazine of the year' on the front cover, which was great for business.

Interviewer: Finally, what are your thoughts on the fashion industry in general?

Cathy: Well, one hot topic at the moment is 'fast fashion', where people buy cheap items of clothing with the intention of wearing them only once or twice before throwing them away. What people don't realise is that this is having a huge impact, not just on the quality of the clothing but also on the working environment for the people making the clothes. Clothing brands must prioritise safety over quick profits and introduce more measures to protect those working in the manufacturing plants.

3 Tell students to work individually and use the knowledge they gained from the first listening. Encourage them to put a line through any options which they know are definitely incorrect, as this will narrow their choices when they listen the second time. To avoid the possibility of students confusing each other, do not ask them to compare their answers until after the second listening (Exercise 4).

4 Students work individually before comparing their answers in pairs. Alternatively, students use the audioscript on page 235 to check their answers.

Answers
1 C **2** B **3** A **4** B **5** C **6** C **7** A

Extension activity
To help students identify why incorrect answers are wrong, ask them to highlight words or phrases in the audioscript on page 235 which they might have incorrectly chosen, giving reasons why they are incorrect.

5 If students are struggling with ideas, you could ask the groups to spend a few minutes brainstorming their ideas for the second question before discussing the first.

Vocabulary SB page 111

Phrasal verbs

Lead in
With Student's Books closed, write on the board: *We've almost run out of milk, so I'm just popping out to get some.* Put students into pairs and ask them to identify the phrasal verbs (*run out; pop out*), decide if they think they are separable or inseparable (both are inseparable) and think of a verb which has a similar meaning for each (e.g. *finished; leave*).

1 Students work in pairs. As an alternative to eliciting the answers, pairs divide the phrasal verbs in half and look up six each in an English dictionary. They should also note down whether their phrasal verbs are separable or inseparable. If the dictionary entries are not explicit, point out that this will often be clear from how the entry is recorded. For example, if *sb/sth* is written after the phrasal verb, (e.g. *cater for sb/sth*), then it is inseparable whereas if *sb/sth* is written between the verb and the particle (e.g. *turn sb/sth off*) it is separable. Once they have done this, students tell their partner if their phrasal verbs are separable or inseparable and correct any errors they made when answering the questions.

Answers
1 j **2** a **3** g **4** h **5** l **6** k **7** d **8** f **9** c **10** e **11** i **12** b

2 Students work in pairs. Monitor and support weaker students.

Answers
1 came up with **2** cut down on **3** pop into **4** caters for **5** hanging around with **6** wore, out **7** pulling in **8** took over **9** come up against **10** pick up **11** been up to **12** chill out

3 It is better to break this task into two parts so that students do not discuss the questions using an incorrect option. First, ask students to work individually and choose the correct options before putting them into pairs to compare their answers. Once they have done this, elicit the correct options before putting the students into different pairs to discuss the questions.

Answers
1 cut down on **2** come up against **3** worn out **4** picked up

Grammar SB page 112

Modal verbs to express ability

▶ **Page 177 Grammar reference**

Lead in
Put students into fours (ABCD). Tell As to read the advice about *can/able to* in the Grammar reference, page 177, Bs to read *could/were able to* on pages 177 and 178, Cs to read *be able to* on page 178, and Ds to read *manage* towards the bottom of the same page. As they read, encourage the students to make notes, telling them that they will need to explain to their group how their words are used. Monitor as students do this and support weaker students with their explanations, eliciting examples from the group as you do so. If you think students have not fully understood, you could refer them back to the Grammar reference, giving them time to check the uses or rules they are unsure about.

1 To help students avoid getting confused, tell them to read the first sentence (a), then read options 1–4, deciding which option is correct before reading the second sentence. Monitor and support weaker students. Once they have done this for each sentence, put them into pairs to compare their answers before eliciting the correct answers from the class.

Answers
1 d; f **2** c; g **3** a; e **4** b; h

2 Elicit the answer to the first question with the students before putting them into pairs to complete the activity. If students are struggling, allow them to refer to the Grammar reference on pages 177 and 178.

Answers
1 were able to **2** couldn't sleep **3** could **4** Can you **5** could have bought **6** were able to

3 Before students answer the question, point out that *managed to* has a similar meaning to *was able to*, although *managed to* is typically used when we achieved something difficult (e.g. *The test was hard but I managed to answer all the questions*).

Answers
Sentences 1, 6

4 Read the rubric with the students. If your students find this Reading and Use of English task challenging, unpick the first question with them. First, read the first and second sentence for question 1 slowly. Then elicit the words in the first sentence that must be transformed in the second (*succeeded in reducing*). Point out that there are two parts that need to be transformed (*not*) *succeeded* and *in reducing*. Point to the words before the gap in the second sentence (*not been*) and elicit what verb can follow that has a similar meaning to *succeeded* (*able to*). Next point to CUT and elicit the phrasal verb which has a similar meaning to *in reducing* (*cut down on*). Finally, elicit the correct answer before telling students to work individually to answer the remaining questions.

Answers
1 able to cut down **2** you could have had **3** you able to pick up **4** cannot/can't cater for such

5 As these are real candidate mistakes and your students are likely to make similar ones, you may prefer them to work individually so that their choices are not influenced or corrected by other (stronger) students. Once they have completed the activity and you have elicited the answers, tell them to asterisk (*) any questions they answered incorrectly. They can then write correct examples in their note books under the heading *common errors*, and refer to their notes when they are revising for the exam.

Answers
1 ~~can't~~ couldn't **2** ~~could~~ was able to or ~~that I could~~ to be able to **3** ~~can~~ could **4** ~~could~~ can **5** ~~can~~ could **6** ~~could~~ were able to **7** correct **8** ~~could~~ can

Speaking Part 1 SB page 113

▶ **Page 204 Speaking bank**

Lead in
Ask students to close their Student's Books. Write the word *money* on the board. Tell them they are going to try to think of five phrases they could use to talk about money and give them the example *spend money on something*. Next, put students into pairs and give them a few minutes to think of their phrases before eliciting

examples from the class and writing them on the board (examples: *cost a fortune, couldn't / wasn't able to afford, managed to save up, be broke, waste of money*). As an alternative, you could ask students to think of as many words or phrases as they can which collocate with *money*, e.g. *waste of money, save money up for, throw money at something, money is tight/short*). Leave the phrases on the board so students can use them when they tackle Exercises 1, 2 and 3.

Exam advice

Read the exam advice with the students. Tell them that they should try and make eye contact with the examiner when they are talking as this is important during good communication, and remind them to follow the examiner's instructions properly.

1 Point to the phrases on the board (from the Lead in) as you read the rubric with the students and encourage them to use some of them when they are considering ideas. Point out that students should not answer the questions at this stage as they will have the opportunity to do this in Exercise 3.

2 Allow students a few minutes to read the descriptions before playing the recording once. Put them into pairs to compare their ideas before playing the recording a second time. Once you have elicited the answers, put students into different pairs, ask them to turn to the audioscript on page 235 and underline the parts of Peter and Irene's two responses which refer specifically to each strategy. For example, we know Peter's second response refers to strategy one because he uses the phrase *I'd have to think because …*. Then tell students to discuss when they think each strategy would be useful in the exam, giving reasons to support their ideas. For example, strategy 1 could be useful if they need time to think about their response as they are speaking, strategies 2 and 3 could be useful to describe their personal life, strategy 4 might be useful if they are asked to speculate about the views of others or if they do not have a strong opinion about a topic.

Answers
1 P **2** B **3** P **4** I

Track 39

Examiner: Peter, what things do you enjoy spending money on?

Peter: Well, like many young people in my country, I'm a big football fan. I support Bayern Munich and I try to go to all their home matches and a few away matches when I don't have too much school work. So that's what I really like spending money on: my season ticket to Bayern.

Examiner: And Irene, what do teenagers in your country typically spend their money on?

Irene: I think it really depends on each individual and what they're into. I know people used to say girls spend more money on clothes, while boys spend more on technology, but this isn't the case in reality. I actually think both boys and girls often spend money on going out to places and having a good time with friends.

Examiner: Peter, do you have a favourite shop?

Peter: Hmm, I'd have to think because I'm not too keen on shopping actually. Um, there is one shop I really enjoy going to. It's one of a chain of sports shops and what I really like about it is just to wander round and see all the clothes and equipment they sell. I see things for sports I don't do but I'd like to try, and that gives me the idea that one day I could try the sport, when I can afford the clothes and equipment, I mean.

Examiner: Irene. Is there anything you'd like to buy that you can't afford?

Irene: Of course! Lots of things! I mean, I don't have a lot of money. My parents give me an allowance, and other people in my family give me money for my birthday and at other times. At the moment, I'm saving up for a better computer – I'd like to study IT when I go to university.

Extension activity

Ask students to refer to the audioscript on page 235 and either underline useful phrases to talk about money, or if appropriate, look in the audioscript for any phrases they came up with in the Lead in exercise so they can see how they are used in context (*My parents give me an allowance, I can afford …, I'm saving up for …*).

3 Ask students to re-read the notes they made in Exercise 2 and consider which strategies would be suitable and why. As students prepare, monitor and ask weaker students to tell you why they intend to use a particular strategy. Elicit ideas from the class before putting students into pairs to answer the questions.

Extension activity

Put students into small groups. Give each group a blank piece of paper and ask them to brainstorm (write down) five possible Speaking Part 1 topics, e.g. *hobbies*. Remind them, or elicit, that the topics will be related to their personal life and interests. Allow students a minute or so to do this before checking they have the right types of topic by eliciting examples from the class (topics would include their hobbies, their work or education, things they like or don't like, their friends and family, their home town, holidays, sports, future plans, how they save or spend money, music, etc.). Next, tell students they must write down one or two useful phrases / vocabulary items they could use for each topic. You may wish to point to the second bullet point in the exam advice as you say this and elicit an example (e.g. hobbies: *I'm (particularly) interested* in …) before allowing students to complete the task. Monitor to support weaker students and correct language errors. After five minutes, ask students to swap papers and add another two phrases for each topic. Continue until each topic has around six useful phrases or students have run out of ideas. Collect the papers and stick them on the board or walls. Ask students to walk round with their notebooks, select three phrases for each topic and write them in their notebooks under the heading *Speaking Part 1 topics and useful phrases.*

/P/ Pronunciation: linking (1)

4 Read the information with the students and allow them time to re-read and consider it. You may then wish to elicit an example for the third bullet point to check students have understood (e.g. *My parents give me an allowance*).

4.1 Play the recording once. Then play it a second time but this time stop the recording after each sentence and ask the students to repeat it. As they do so, they should try to mimic the speaker's pronunciation.

Track 40

See page 113 of Student's Book for audioscript.

4.2 Allow students a minute to read Irene's answer and practise the linked and deleted words and phrases individually (*depends on*, etc.) before they listen and check if Irene's pronunciation is the same.

Track 41

See page 113 of Student's Book for audioscript.

4.3 Play the recording from Exercise 4.2 again, telling them to read Irene's answer as they listen. Then put the students into pairs to complete the activity.

4.4 Students work individually. Encourage them to look back at Irene's answer (Exercise 4.2) and the information shown in 4 if they need help as they complete the task. Monitor and support weaker students. Once the students have marked Peter's answer, put them into pairs and tell them to take turns reading their answer out loud. As hearing themselves may help them to link the words correctly, allow students time to discuss and make changes to their answer before playing the recording twice for them to check.

Track 42

Peter: Hmm, I'd have to think, because I'm not too keen on shopping actually. Um, there is one shop I really enjoy going to. It's one of a chain of sports shops and what I really like about it is just to wander round and see all the clothes and equipment they sell. I see things for sports I don't do but I'd like to try, and that gives me the idea that one day I could try the sport, when I can afford the clothes and equipment, I mean.

5 Tell students to re-read the strategies in Exercise 2 before you play the recording twice. Put them into pairs to discuss their answers. Monitor and support weaker students. Elicit the answers from the class.

Answers

Peter: description 1; Irene: description 3.

Track 43

Examiner: Peter, what's shopping like in the area where you live?

Peter: I'm not sure, because I don't do a lot of shopping, at least not where I live. There's a place where they sell snacks and takeaways that I quite like and I've been there a few times with my mates and I guess the shopping must be pretty good, because my mum and dad do all the shopping locally and they never complain!

Examiner: And Irene, what's shopping like in the area where you live?

Irene: I think it's really good. My dad and I love cooking together at weekends and making these really exotic dishes, and there are plenty of shops in the area which sell good vegetables, food from different parts of the world, and spices and things, so we can find all our ingredients locally. My dad's a brilliant cook. I'm learning a lot from him and we have a great time together!

6 Allow students to look up unknown vocabulary in an English dictionary before they complete the task.

7 Put students into pairs to complete the task. As an alternative, put students into threes (ABC) with A asking a question and B answering it. As B answers, A should listen for two examples of the words or phrases from Exercise 6, and C for two examples of correct linking pronunciation and one example that is incorrect (Exercise 4). If you choose to do the alternative, you may wish to point out that Student B should also use appropriate linking when they ask their question (e.g. in question 1: *What is … like in …*). After one question has been asked, answered and feedback from the two listeners given, tell students to swap roles until each student has answered at least three questions. Monitor and listen for correct linking pronunciation. During whole-class feedback select stronger students to answer one or two questions.

Writing Part 2 (a review) SB page 114

▶ **Page 200 Writing bank**

Lead in
Tell students something you enjoy doing in your town or city and why you enjoy doing it. Then put students into pairs and ask them to briefly discuss what they enjoy doing in their town or city and why. Elicit examples from the class and write them on the board: these examples may be helpful when students complete Exercise 2.

Exam advice
Read the exam advice with the students. Point to the third bullet point and elicit examples of language to make a recommendation.

1 Students work individually before comparing their answers in pairs. Once you have elicited the answers, elicit who the readers of the website are (visitors). Refer to the first bullet point in the exam advice on this page and tell students it may help them to answer a question like this if they consider what information they would like to know if they were visiting a different town. For example, the task asks for a description of *how to find it*: for a visitor who was not familiar with the town, this might include information about public transport.

Answers
Suggested underlining
website for visitors, visitors to our town, enjoy, place in or near our town, people your age, meeting up, having a good time, review, type of place, what, do there, how to find, why, recommend

2 Allow students time to read the options, choose which is appropriate for their context and consider their ideas. If students are struggling for ideas, encourage them to consider the ideas they or their classmates came up with in the Lead in activity, referring them to the examples you wrote on the board.

3 Elicit why writing a plan is important (they will write a more thorough answer and get higher marks). Set a time limit of between five and ten minutes for students to write their plans before they compare them.

4 Allow weaker students to work in pairs. Tell them to use no more than five words in the notes for each paragraph: this will encourage them not to write long sentences, which is an ineffective use of their planning time. If you encouraged students to write down topic-specific vocabulary when planning in Unit 4 page 49, you may wish to ask them to find and highlight five topic words or phrases that Eva may have added to her plan, e.g. *entertainment complex, screen(s), bowling alley, range of films, tastes, karaoke bar.*

Answers
Suggested plan
Paragraph 1: Place – Cinecity – activities available
Paragraph 2: Most popular activities – (mention karaoke)
Paragraph 3: Location + how to get there
Paragraph 4: Why I recommend it

5 Read the rubric with the students, then ask them to work individually. Monitor and support weaker students. As some students will be quicker than others, stop them after five minutes, put them into pairs and ask them to either complete any unanswered questions together or, if they have finished, compare their answers.

Answers
2 Apart from three roller coasters, there is a tunnel of horrors, a terror swing and many other rides.
3 Although the theme park is quite expensive, it's well worth the entrance fee, which includes all the attractions.
4 If you bring your swimsuit, one of the best attractions is a waterslide, where you slide more than 100 metres into a bubbling pool.
5 Funtime is about ten kilometres from the town centre, but don't worry if you don't have a car because you can get there by bus.
6 In fact, taking the bus is probably the best way to avoid parking problems.
7 I would recommend Funtime because there is such a huge variety of attractions that everyone who goes there will be entertained.
8 Furthermore, you can get a weekend pass, which is an entrance ticket for the whole weekend, so you will have time to visit every attraction.

6 In addition to referring to Eva's answer, you may wish to tell students to re-read their answers to Exercise 5 as this will provide more examples of how to use the highlighted words in context. Tell students to refer to the plan they wrote in Exercise 3 and give them an additional five minutes to make changes or improve it, now that they have completed Exercises 4 and 5. For example, they may wish to add between five to ten topic specific words or phrases that they intend to use. Set a time limit of thirty minutes for students to complete the task itself (forty minutes less the ten minutes students have spent planning).

Extension activity
In this activity, students will explore how well they are using their plans. First, put students into pairs, making sure they are paired with someone who they did not compare plans with in Exercise 3. Tell students to read their partner's answer and write a plan for it (as they did for Eva's answer in Exercise 4). Once they have done this, ask them to compare both sets of plans and discuss if the original plans are similar to the original plans written by each partner; if not, ask students to discuss why. For example, the student may have

changed direction once they started writing their answer or written without referring to their plan. Finally, ask students to discuss any differences in approaches to writing the plan and how they might develop their approach the next time they write an essay plan.

Vocabulary

Commonly confused words

arrive / get / reach

Phrasal verbs

be up to	hang around with
cater for	pick up
chill out	pop into
come up against	pull in
come up with	take over
cut down (on)	wear out

Vocabulary activity 1

Tell the students that you are going to ask them five questions. Once you have asked each question, they will have one minute to write down an answer. Tell them that although there are no right or wrong answers, each answer must answer the question fully and use one of the phrasal verbs in the vocabulary list. If students are unsure, you could use the first question and the sample answer as an example.

Q1: How do young people like to relax in your town or city?
Example answer: Some young people like to **chill out** by going to the local park with friends, while others prefer to play sports, like football.
Q2: When was the last time you suggested a good idea at your workplace (or school)?
Example answer: I **came up with** an idea to make ordering new products more efficient by creating a new spreadsheet.
Q3: If I wanted to lose weight, what would you suggest I do?
Example answer: I'd recommend you **cut down on** sugary treats like sweets and cakes.
Q4: Who was the last person you visited briefly and why?
Example answer: I **popped into** my mum's last Sunday because I wanted to give her some flowers from my garden.
Q5: What was the most tiring thing you have done recently?
Example answer: I was really **worn out** after walking around the museum all day with my friends last weekend.
Once you have asked all the questions and students have written down their answers, put them into pairs and give them a few minutes to take turns reading their answers. As they do so, they should help each other with error corrections. Monitor and support weaker students. During whole-class feedback, ask each question again and select two or three students to answer it before moving to the next question. Elicit error corrections from the class as you go.

Vocabulary activity 2

Tell students you are going to dictate something to them. They must write down what you say and as you say 'blank' they must write either *get*, *arrive* or *reach* in the correct tense. Remind them to listen carefully to the words you say after 'blank' as this may help them chose the correct option. Then dictate twice: *Because the train never blank on time, I blank my destination late and was the last person to blank to the party.* (arrived, reached, get). Once you have elicited the answers, put students into pairs (AB), making sure that B students are stronger as they will be creating their own sentences. Tell A to go to page 110 and find three sentences using *arrive*, *get*, *reach* while student B writes down three sentences of their own. Then tell them to take turns reading one sentence at a time, replacing *get*, *reach* or *arrive* with the word 'blank'. Once they have read their sentence, their partner must say it back to them, replacing 'blank' with the correct word in the correct form. As these words can sometime be used interchangeably (*I got home late*, *I arrived home late*) monitor and be prepared to step in if students disagree on the correct option and point out when more than one option is possible.

DIGITAL CLASSROOM

Practice Extra Unit 10

Test Generator Unit 10 test

Test and Train Exam Practice

Unit 9 Vocabulary and grammar review

1
1 spent 2 have 3 causes 4 pass 5 had 6 made 7 spent
2
1 may be 2 could just 3 might be doing it 4 very different 5 look 6 appear to 7 look as if 8 perhaps 9 both
3
1 must have switched 2 can't have turned 3 may not have heard 4 could have left 5 might answer 6 might have forgotten 7 can't have forgotten

Unit 10 Vocabulary and grammar review

1
1 C 2 B 3 D 4 A 5 C 6 B 7 B 8 A
2
1 was not / wasn't able to finish
2 down (on) the amount of
3 was/felt so worn out by
4 could not / couldn't come up with
5 able to pick Paz up
6 get to the cinema until
3
1 as 2 as 3 as 4 as 5 like 6 as 7 as 8 Like 9 like 10 like

11 Medical matters

Unit objectives

Topic: health and medical issues

Reading and Use of English Part 6 (gapped text): identifying words in the sentences that refer to something specific in the text

Reading and Use of English Part 3 (word formation): understanding how to use prefixes

Writing Part 1 (essay): writing concluding paragraphs

Listening Part 3 (multiple matching): focusing on the meaning of each option

Speaking Part 2 (long turn): describing situations related to health; expressions when you need time to think, can't think of a word or have made a mistake

Pronunciation: Intonation (3)

Vocabulary: health vocabulary; idiomatic expressions

Grammar: relative pronouns and relative clauses

Starting off SB page 118

1 Put students into pairs and ask them to read the sentences. Draw their attention to the words and phrases in **bold** and tell them to discuss what they think the words and phrases mean. Once they have done this, put them into new pairs and ask them to share their ideas before checking them using an English dictionary. Encourage the students to write the phrases, the meanings and example sentences in their notebooks so they can refer to them when they answer Exercises 4 and 5.

2 Look at the photos with the students and read the rubric. Elicit one or two examples from the class before allowing students to discuss the question. Point out that they should use language to speculate what they can see (*could be*, *may have*, *seems to*, *appears to*, etc.), referring them to page 102 if they need to review the language.

3 Encourage students to write notes as they listen and allow them to compare their ideas in pairs, or alternatively check their ideas with the audioscript on page 236 before you elicit them from the class.

Suggested answers
1 Speaker 3 **2** Speaker 4 **3** Speaker 2 **4** Speaker 1
5 Speaker 5

Track 44

Narrator: 1

Woman: I backpacked around the world a lot when I was younger, so with all the markets and street food, not always cooked in the cleanest of conditions, I thought I'd be immune to food poisoning by now. So when I started feeling queasy, and then properly nauseous, I thought it was a stomach bug. Well, after throwing up for hours, when I started feeling a bit better, I double checked the expiry date of the yogurt I'd had for breakfast. Surprise surprise, it had gone off. I called in sick that day but I think my boss thought I was pulling a sickie – making up an excuse, that is. It wasn't, though. I wish it had been!

Narrator: 2

Woman: Like many people in spring, I suffer from hay fever. Pollen is not my friend, but I take antihistamine every day and I cope. What I can't cope with is nuts. I'm severely allergic to them, and you'd think my friends would know by now. Well, we were playing volleyball and after the match our friend Georgia offered us cookies. Unfortunately, they had nuts in them. I started getting a rash on my neck and was struggling to breathe. Nothing happened of course – I had my EpiPen with me and one quick jab solved the problem. Still, if I hadn't had it with me, an allergic reaction like that could have put me in the hospital!

Narrator: 3

Woman: When you get bitten by a mosquito you don't really feel it happening. It gets itchy after a while and it's annoying trying not to scratch it, but that's it. When you get stung by a wasp, that's worse. You feel a stabbing pain straightaway, and you have to apply cream to make sure it doesn't get infected. It's definitely irritating. But it turns out that spider bites are just agony. I screamed as soon as one bit me, and I knew it was bad because it kept on hurting for hours, a sort of throbbing pain that just wouldn't go away. The bite got swollen and black, and itchy, too, though it was too painful to scratch. Thankfully the spider wasn't venomous, or I'd have had to go to hospital for an antidote!

Narrator: 4

Man: So I was at the gym, and someone had left a pair of shoes in the middle of the changing room. First I tripped on those and bumped my toes, and then with my next step I slipped because of how wet the floor was from the showers. From the stabbing pain, I knew I was badly injured and I was really scared I had broken my ankle. It had already happened to me a few years back and I didn't want to be in a plaster cast for weeks again. My ankle turned purple and swollen really quickly, despite the fact that I'd applied ice to it straightaway. At the hospital, an X-ray showed that thankfully it was only a sprain. They bandaged it and gave me crutches to use for a couple of days, because it still hurts when I put pressure on it.

Narrator: 5

Woman: I think I'm coming down with the flu again. It's my fault, really, I should have gone to get a flu jab like every year, but I got so busy I didn't bother in the end. It's bad news, though, because last time I got the flu I was bedridden for a whole week, feeling dizzy, sneezing and coughing with a fever and a runny nose. I know it's my fault, but I wish people would wash their hands more frequently this time of year. That way maybe the germs wouldn't spread as much, and I wouldn't have caught this bug!

4 If you feel students need to listen to the recording more than once, first play it as students listen for topic related words and phrases and then a second time as they write the words and phrases in their notebooks. Once they have compared their ideas in pairs, allow students to check them using the audioscript on page 236 and allow them to look up any unknown words or phrases in an English dictionary. Then ask them to close their books and retell the stories using their notes from this exercise and Exercise 1.

5 As an alternative to pairwork, you could put the students into small groups. Encourage students to use the words and phrases they wrote down from Exercise 4 in addition to the vocabulary in Exercise 1. Monitor and listen for examples of correct and incorrect language use.

Reading and Use of English Part 6 SB page 118

Lead in

Ask students if they think it is a good idea to check medical conditions by searching for symptoms online or on social media. Put students into pairs to discuss briefly, telling them to justify their responses with reasons and examples before eliciting ideas from the class. As students will discuss advantages and disadvantages in Exercise 1, write ideas on the board so that students will be able to refer to them.

Exam advice

To help you understand how much of the advice in previous units students have assimilated, write *Reading and Use of English Part 6* on the board and ask them to close their Student's Books. Put them into small groups and ask them to make a list of the advice they would give a student who was answering this question for the first time. Once groups have done this, elicit ideas from the class before telling students to review the advice given on this page and from Units 1, 4 and 7, checking if they want to add anything to their lists.

1 Read the rubric with the students. Refer to the students' ideas on the board from the Lead in before allowing them to discuss the questions.

2 Read the rubric. As students practised this technique in Unit 7, (page 76, Exercise 2) do not to provide additional support to the class; however, monitor and support weaker students. Put students into pairs to compare their notes before eliciting from the class.

Answers
para 2 why people look for health advice online; para 3 apps; para 4 misinformation; para 5 unclear motives of medical professionals; para 6 false advertising of qualifications; para 7 the #VerfiyHealthcare initiative

3 Read the rubric. As students practised this technique in Unit 7 (page 77, Exercise 3), do not provide additional support for the whole class; however, monitor and support weaker students. Set a time limit of around five minutes for students to work individually before putting them into pairs to discuss their ideas. When you elicit answers from the class, make sure students say what might be referred to in addition to what they underlined. If the selected student gets stuck, ask if other students can help before you step in.

Answers
Suggested underlining
A them / reasons B from this point of view C such people's D The latter E Some / doing so F Examples G Nevertheless / these

4 Before students answer the question, put them into pairs and ask them to tell their partner what strategies they are going to adopt as they complete the task, referring them to the exam advice list they made at the start of this section. Set a time limit of twenty minutes. Elicit the answers from the class.

Answers
1 E **2** D **3** F **4** G **5** C **6** A

Extension activity

Put students into groups and tell them to justify why each answer is correct or incorrect. This works well if students have come up with different answers to the same question.

5 Allow students time to re-read the text and consider their ideas. As students discuss, encourage them to justify their responses. If they try to quote sections of the text, e.g. *I agree with the text that physicians simply may not know how to approach social media*, encourage them to paraphrase, e.g. *I agree with the text that it's possible doctors may not know how to use social media effectively …*

Grammar SB page 120

Relative pronouns and relative clauses

▶ **Page 178 Grammar reference**

Lead in

Elicit from the class the list of relative pronouns (*who, which, that, whose, where, when, why*). Then write the following two sentences on the board: *A: The students who had completed their assignment went home early; B: The students, who had completed their assignment, went home early.* Put students into pairs. Tell them to discuss how and why the two sentences differ. Depending on the students' level, elicit or tell them that sentence A is a defining relative clause which gives essential information: only the students who had completed their assignment left early (the others did not). Sentence B is non-defining and provides additional (non-essential) information: all the students went home early.

1 Allow weaker students to work in pairs. Monitor and, if students are struggling, refer them to Grammar reference pages 178 and 179, where they can find additional support.

Answers
1 that (or which); **2** who (or that); **3** who; whose; **4** where

2 Tell students to think back to the example given in the Lead in, then put them into pairs to complete the task.

Answers
1 A, **2** A, **3** defining = A; non-defining = B

3 Students work individually. Monitor and support weaker students. Allow students to compare their answers in pairs before you elicit them from the class.

Answers
1 where D **2** who ND **3** that D **4** that D **5** who ND **6** that D

4 Point out that the relative pronoun can only be omitted when it is the object of the clause. For example, in the sentence *The woman that/who spoke to the students was from England*, the relative pronoun *that* or *who* cannot be omitted as it is the subject of the clause; however, in the sentence *The teacher that/who the students loved was taking them to England*, the relative pronoun is the object of the clause (the students are the subject) and can be removed: *The teacher the students loved was taking them to England.* Students complete the task in pairs. If they are unsure, encourage them to find and underline both the subject and the object of the clause.

Answers
3 and **4**

5 As these are real candidate errors, you may prefer students to work individually before asking them to compare their answers. Once students have completed the activity and you have elicited the answers, tell them to asterisk (*) any questions they answered incorrectly and write correct examples in their note books under the heading *common errors*, and to refer to their notes when they are revising for the exam.

Suggested answers
1 ~~it's~~ which is **2** ~~his~~ whose **3** ~~that~~ which **4** ~~you wrote it last week~~ you wrote last week **5** ~~who you met them this morning~~ who you met this morning **6** ~~that~~ what **7** ~~which it has a view~~ which has a view **8** ~~which it won~~ which won

6 Students work in pairs or small groups. Point out that for questions 2 and 3, more than one option is possible. As students sometimes duplicate the object of the clause in error, tell them they may find this task easier if they underline the object of the two sentences before they begin and then delete duplications as necessary. For example, in question 1, *film* is the object of the first sentence and *it* the object of the second; however, in the combined sentence there is one object (*film*).

Answers
2 He studied hard for his maths exam, which he found quite easy. / He found the maths exam, which he studied hard for, quite easy.
3 The man (who/that) they sold the car to is a taxi driver. / They sold the car to a man who is a taxi driver.
4 Could you give me the newspaper (which/that) you were reading earlier?
5 That white house over there is the house where he was born.
6 Where's the envelope (which/that) I put the money in?
7 Every morning I go running in the park with Holly, whose brother you know.
8 Katelyn and Faiza, whose dog we're looking after, are on holiday in the Caribbean at the moment.

Listening Part 3 SB page 121

1 Put students into pairs. Point out that they should compare the photos, saying what is similar and different, before answering the question, and encourage them to speak for one minute each. Remind students to focus on both photos equally and make it clear which photo they are referring to. Monitor and write down examples of language to select one or both of the photos (e.g. *both pictures show …*; *in the first/other photo …*), and prompt them if they are not giving equal attention to both photos. After around two minutes stop the students. Select a couple of stronger pairs to discuss the photos in front of the class before praising the class for the correct examples you heard and eliciting error correction.

Exam advice

Read the exam advice with the students. Point to the first point and remind them that they should use the time they are given before they listen to read through the options so that they know what they are listening for. Remind them that if they are unsure about an answer after the speaker finishes, they should wait for the second listening before they make their final decision.

2 Students work individually before comparing their answers in pairs. After you have elicited possible answers, put students into pairs again and ask them to come up with paraphrases for the main ideas by considering what the speaker might say. For example, for option B, you could ask students how the speaker might describe *big social events* and elicit *birthdays*, *celebrations*, *weddings*, etc.; and that for option G *stress-related illnesses* might be described as *anxiety, headaches, depression*. Remind them that it is important they consider what words or phrases they might hear before they listen as this will help them to avoid word spotting as they listen.

Answers
Suggested underlining
A – get, a lot of respect B – miss out on, big social events C – pay, working hours, not, most important aspects D – enjoy, working under pressure E – typically, work more hours, I'm supposed to F – good salary G – suffer from, stress-related illnesses H – speak, medical conferences

3 Read the rubric with the students before playing the recording twice. When eliciting the answers, encourage students to justify their choices as this will help you find out if students are word spotting. If a student gives an incorrect answer, ask the class if anyone chose a different option until the correct option has been provided with justification given. If no one chose the correct option, tell the students to refer to the audioscript on page 237.

Answers
1 B **2** D **3** F **4** G **5** C

Track 45

Speaker 1: I love being a doctor and that hasn't changed after ten years in the profession. I regularly attend talks, often in countries that I would otherwise never have visited if I didn't practise medicine. I get to rub shoulders with leading professionals in my field and hear them discuss the latest developments in healthcare. The travelling does interfere with my personal life and I don't always get to attend celebrations with friends and family, but I guess that's one of the sacrifices us doctors have to make.

Speaker 2: Working as a newly qualified doctor in the accident and emergency department can be quite demanding at times. We're often thrown in at the deep end, trying to help huge numbers of patients as quickly as possible without compromising on the quality of care. I really like this aspect of the role, though. I know a lot of my colleagues find it very stressful and don't always feel like they get enough respect for working such long hours in what can be, at times, very difficult circumstances. For me, however, the sense of achievement in being able to do my job well under tough conditions makes it worthwhile.

Speaker 3: As doctors, we have the opportunity to work in public or private healthcare. I work in the private sector simply because I can earn so much more. Those who work in the public sector are often taken aback when I tell them this, but we all have bills to pay. In my eyes, it's a reward for constantly being rushed off my feet and giving up large amounts of my free time to help others. Don't get me wrong; patient well-being is still my number one priority and I will always ensure that they receive the best care possible.

Speaker 4: I deal with a wide range of issues as a doctor, from patients who are a little under the weather to those suffering from serious diseases. Because you devote so much of your time to helping others, it's easy to forget to look after yourself. I often go through periods where I feel anxious and depressed. I spoke to a well-respected doctor specialising in this area at a conference last year and described the problem I was facing. He was able to give me some really useful advice on how to cope with it. I'm so glad I reached out to him.

Speaker 5: I've been working as a doctor for a medical charity for just over a year now. There were a few teething problems at the beginning: getting the equipment set up, ensuring we had enough personnel on site, that sort of thing. Now, though, we're in full swing. I know I'm not as well paid as I would be elsewhere and I don't always get as much time off as I'd like, but ultimately it's the feeling that I'm doing something of great value and benefit that motivates me most and that's why I've just agreed to stay on for another year.

Extension activity
Put students into groups and ask them to find examples in the audioscript on page 237 of why the incorrect options are incorrect. Refer to the exam advice and remind students that the speakers may talk about something connected with other sentences, so doing this activity now will help to consolidate that point. During whole-class feedback, encourage students to give examples of when speakers talked about something connected to another sentence and why it is incorrect. For example, Speaker 1 says, *I regularly attend talks …*, which could be connected to *medical conferences* in option H. However, option H is incorrect as Speaker 1 only says he is an attendee at these events without mentioning whether he speaks at them or not.

4 Allow students a few minutes to read the questions and consider their ideas before putting them into pairs. Encourage students to give reasons and examples to support their opinion.

Extension activity
Put students into new pairs. Tell them they are going to practise a Speaking Part 2 task and that they are going to compare photos 4 and 5 on page 118. Remind them they should talk about the similarities and differences and speculate where appropriate (*it looks as if; it might/could be that …*) Then say, *These photos show people who are feeling unwell. I'd like you to compare the photographs and say what help these people need.* Monitor and listen for examples of correct and incorrect use of complex language to make comparisons and language to speculate.

Vocabulary SB page 122

Idiomatic expressions

Lead in
Elicit that an idiomatic expression is a fixed group of words that have a specific meaning which is different from the meaning of the words on their own. Then

dictate the following sentence: *She studied the documents over the weekend so she could hit the ground running when the project started the following week.* Put students into pairs. Tell them to underline the idiomatic expression (hit the ground running) and use the context to discuss what they think it means. After a few minutes, elicit ideas before allowing students to look up the expression in an English dictionary. Point out that whilst the grammatical form of an idiomatic expression can be changed (e.g. *He always hits the ground running when he starts a new job*) the word order and words themselves cannot change without changing the meaning. For example, in the sentence, *I was running when I hit the ground* the meaning is literal.

1 Put students into pairs. Tell them to cover the definitions and use the context to guess the meaning before checking their ideas using the definitions. Elicit the answers during whole-class feedback.

Answers
1 c **2** f **3** a **4** g **5** b **6** e **7** d

Fast finishers
Students look up the expressions in an English dictionary and write down one additional example sentence for each in their notebooks. Once they have done this, tell them to choose three expressions and include them in sentences which are true for them, e.g. *I was thrown in at the deep end when my boss gave me an important project to lead.* Monitor and support students.

2 Read the rubric with the students. Tell them to read the text through once to get an idea of the context before reading it again and completing the gaps. Students work individually before comparing their answers in small groups.

Answers
1 teething problems; **2** thrown in at the deep end; **3** rushed off our feet; **4** under the weather; **5** taken aback; **6** In their eyes

3 Put students into pairs. Tell them to make a list of five things someone at work may be stressed about. If your students are younger, ask them to think about things that make them stressed as a student. Once they have written their lists, tell them they are going to take part in a role-play activity: one student feels stressed at work (or school) and, using the list they produced earlier, tells their partner how they feel and why. The other student is a colleague (classmate) who must listen and then give advice. Before students start, remind them to use the idiomatic expressions from this section where possible. Set a time limit of five minutes. Monitor and listen for examples of correct and incorrect use of the idiomatic expressions. During feedback, offer praise for the correct examples before eliciting error corrections.

Reading and Use of English Part 3 SB page 122

Exam advice

As students have covered similar exam advice in Units 3 and 5, it is good idea do a true/false activity based on all the exam advice. With books closed, tell students you are going to make six statements about Part 3 and they must decide if the statements are true or false. If false, they must discuss why. Then dictate the following:
There are ten gaps in Reading and Use of English Part 3; The text is between 150 and 160 words long; Candidates are tested on nouns and adjectives; The word in capitals cannot be changed; Mistakes with singular and plural noun forms are not acceptable; It is OK to make minor errors with spelling. After a few minutes, refer students to the exam advice on this page and pages 33 and 58 to check their answers. (F there are eight gaps; T; F adverbs and verbs may also be tested; F the word must be changed to its correct form; T; F words should be spelt correctly).

1 Put students into pairs to complete this task. If they are struggling, tell them to consider the meaning of other words which have the same prefix (*misheard*, *misbehave*, *misspell*, etc.)

Answers
1 a

2 Allow weaker students to work in pairs. As with Exercise 1, it may help students if they think of other words with the same prefix as they make their choices.

Answers
1 b **2** b

3 Students work individually before comparing their answers in pairs. Encourage them to refer to Exercises 1 and 2 before making their choice.

Answers
un-

4 Read the rubric with the students. Elicit the answer to the first question before allowing them to answer the remaining questions in pairs. Spelling is important in this part of the exam, so before students complete the task, remind them that prefixes do not typically change the spelling of the root word. For example, when students add *un-* to the root word *necessary*, they may delete an *n* and incorrectly spell *unnecessary* as *unecessary*.

Answers
1 undoes **2** disappoint **3** misuse **4** untied **5** misspell **6** disappeared **7** undressed **8** misinformed

5 Read the rubric with the students and point out that where more than one answer is possible, the meaning of the words will differ. Students work individually before comparing their answers in pairs or small groups. Once you have elicited the correct answers, encourage students to check the meaning of any unknown words in an English dictionary. This is particularly important when more than one answer is possible.

Answers
inability/disability, disagreement, disappear, unaware, uncertain, inexperienced, informal, unhappiness, unhelpful, dishonest, dislike/unlike, unlikely, impatient, unpredictable, unreliable, dissatisfied/unsatisfied, misunderstand

6 As this is an exam task, tell students to work individually and set a time limit of ten minutes. When eliciting the answers, ask students to spell the word after they have said it. This will help you establish if students are making errors with common prefix or suffix spellings and need additional support. For example, for question 3 students may have spelt *unsuccessful* incorrectly with two ls (*unsuccessfull*).

Answers
1 action 2 consciousness 3 unsuccessful 4 assistance
5 educational 6 reliable 7 inexperienced 8 understanding

Speaking Part 2 SB page 124

▶ **Page 206 Speaking bank**

Lead in
Ask students to briefly consider what activities they do, or would like to do, in order to stay healthy. Elicit ideas from the class.

Read the exam advice with the students and ask them why the first point is important (so they don't waste time trying to remember one word).

Exam advice

1 Ask students to close their Student's Books and put them into pairs or small groups. Dictate functions A–C and ask them to write down any phrases they already know. Once students have run out of ideas, stop them and elicit examples from the class, correcting errors at the same time. Then tell them to open their books and complete the exercise, adding any additional phrases they came up with to the list as they do so. Remind students that the phrases are used naturally in spoken English, so they will not lose marks for using them. Point out that if they know they have made a mistake, correcting it is better than saying nothing in the hope that the examiner did not hear it.

Answers
A When you need time to think: Let me think …
B When you can't think of the word: I can't think of the word, but it's a type of …; I'm not sure how to say it, but it's used for …; What's the word?
C When you've made a mistake: I'm sorry, what I meant was …; No, I mean …; What I want to say is that …; Sorry, I mean …

2 Allow students time to read the checklist before playing the recording twice. You may find it helps to tell the students to listen with their pens down the first time, so they get an idea of what Antonia says before they complete the checklist during the second listening. Once you have elicited the answers, you may wish to follow up by playing the recording a third time and asking the students to tick the phrases from Exercise 1 that Antonia uses. (8, 7, 6, 1)

Answers
Antonia did all the things on the checklist.

Track 46

Examiner: In this part of the test, I'm going to give each of you two photographs. I'd like you to talk about your photographs on your own for about a minute, and also to answer a question about your partner's photographs. Antonia, it's your turn first. Here are your photographs. They show people doing healthy activities. I'd like you to compare the photographs and say how important you think each activity is for staying healthy. All right?

Antonia: OK, so both photographs show people doing things which might be good for their sanity, sorry, I mean their health. In the first photo, I can see someone who looks as if he's, what's the word, he's commuting by bicycle in busy traffic. So, he's getting some exercise, which must be good for his general fitness. In the second photo, there are some young people who are doing some cooking – well, not exactly cooking because what they're doing is preparing a salad. What I want to say is, they're going to eat something quite healthy. I mean, it's not like eating pizza or hamburgers. So both photos show people doing something healthy – getting exercise and eating a good deeat, sorry, I mean diet. I'd say there are some problems with the idea of health in the first photo because of the danger from the traffic, especially because he's cycling in the night, I mean in the dark, and the, I can't think of the word, but it's a type of smoke which comes from the cars. On the other hand, if you live in the city, it's a good way of getting exercise. In the second photo, the people should remember that they need to eat a mixed, um, sorry, a balanced diet, not just salad and fruit.

Examiner: Thank you.

3 Read the rubric with the students before putting them into pairs or small groups to discuss the questions. Encourage them to support their responses by giving examples taken from the extract. For example, for question 2a the examiner asks a personalised question, but Nikolai responds generally 'cycling is good for people's health'. Once you have elicited the answers, elicit examples of how Nikolai and Peter's responses could be improved, e.g. *I prefer cycling as it is very good*

for my health …; I'd prefer to make salad because cycling is dangerous in my city, where there is a lot of traffic …

Answers
1 Miguel 2 a Nikolai b Miguel c Peter

/P/ Pronunciation: intonation (3)

4 Read the information with the students and remind them that using the correct intonation will help them to sound more natural and improve comprehensibility, which will achieve higher marks in the speaking exam.

4.1 Encourage students to take turns reading the extract out loud as they complete the task.

Answers
OK, so both photographs show people doing things which might be good for their sanity, sorry, I mean their health. In the first photo, I can see someone who looks as if he's, um, what's the word, he's commuting by bicycle in busy traffic.

Track 47
See page 125 of Student's Book for audioscript.

4.2 Allow students to discuss their ideas in pairs before eliciting the answer from the class.

Answers
The speaker is more confident in a. Her voice falls on the final stressed words. In b, her voice rises on the final stressed words, making her sound uncertain.

Track 48
See Track 47

4.3 As an alternative to simply reading the extract, you could ask students to choose which intonation pattern to mimic: confident or uncertain.

4.4 Students work individually, reading the extract out loud as they make their decisions, before comparing their answers in pairs.

Answers
See Track 49 for answers.

Track 49
a I'd say there are some problems with the idea of health in the first photo because of the danger from the traffic, especially because he's cycling in the night, I mean, the dark, and the um, I can't think of the word, but it's a type of smoke which comes from the cars.
b On the other hand, if you live in the city, it's a good way of getting exercise. In the second photo, the people should remember that they need to eat a mixed, sorry, a balanced diet, not just salad and fruit.

4.5 Tell students to adopt a confident intonation pattern when reading the extracts. Monitor and listen for correct intonation. Once students have completed the activity, select a few stronger students to read the extracts to the class.

Answers
Extract b, because her voice falls at the end of phrases.

5 Put students into pairs and ask them to decide who is Student A and who is B. Give them a moment to turn to page 124. Before playing the recording, remind Student A to adopt a confident intonation pattern and B to listen for this when completing checklist point 7. Monitor and write examples of checklist items you hear. Do not carry out whole-class feedback until after students have completed Exercise 6.

Track 50
Examiner: In this part of the test, I'm going to give each of you two photographs. I'd like you to talk about your photographs on your own for about a minute, and also to answer a question about your partner's photographs. Student A, here are your photographs. They show people doing healthy activities. I'd like you to compare the photographs and say how important you think each activity is for staying healthy. All right?

6 Before you play the recording, tell Student A to complete points 3 to 7 of the checklist on page 124 as Student B speaks. Monitor as you did in Exercise 5. After a minute, stop the students and tell Student A to give Student B feedback. Once they have done this, complete whole-class feedback. Praise students for the correct examples you heard in this and Exercise 5, before eliciting error corrections.

Track 51
Examiner: Student B, which activity would you prefer to do to keep healthy, and why?

7 Students work in the same pairs as they did for Exercises 5 and 6. Before students start, ask them to briefly discuss any checklist points from the previous two exercises they intend to improve. For example, Student A may have given Student B the feedback that they spoke with a flat intonation pattern and so Student B may want to improve that this time.

Track 52
Examiner: Now, Student B, here are your photographs. They show two people with minor health problems. I'd like you to compare the photographs and say why it is important for these people to deal with their problems. All right?

8 As with Exercise 6, tell Student Bs to complete points 3 to 7 of the checklist on page 124 as they listen. During whole-class feedback, ask students for two examples of checklist items and two they would like to improve and why.

Track 53

Examiner: Student A, which problem do you think is more serious, and why?

Writing Part 1 (an essay) SB page 126

▶ **Page 192 Writing bank**

Lead in

Tell students to close their Student's Books, then dictate the following questions: *Do you have a healthy lifestyle? Do you consider your diet to be healthy or unhealthy? Are you healthier now than you were when you were younger?* Put students into pairs to discuss their answers. Before they start, remind them to justify their responses by giving examples and reasons. After five minutes, stop the students. Select students to share their group's ideas with the class.

1 As an alternative to each group discussing both the healthy and unhealthy aspects straight away, you could tell half of the groups to discuss the healthy aspects and the other half the unhealthy ones. After five minutes, select students to share their groups' ideas with the class using reported speech. Write students' ideas on the board so they can refer to them when they complete Exercise 2.

2 Point out that they can choose points which were discussed by other groups in Exercise 1, as well as in their own group, and refer them to the ideas on the board.

Answers
Suggested underlining
Modern lifestyles, endanger, health, food, physical activity

3 Read the rubric with the students and ask them to read the essay quickly. Then put them into pairs (AB). Ask them to read the essay again. This time, as they read, Student A should consider the strong points and B the weak. Encourage them to refer to the essay question in Exercise 2 as they read and make notes or underline the parts of the essay which support their feedback. If students are unsure, you could refer them to the essay checklist in the Writing bank on page 203. After five minutes, stop the students and tell them to take turns sharing their thoughts. Remind them to justify their feedback with examples taken directly from the essay rather than giving feedback generally, e.g. *The writer uses a good range of linking language correctly, for example 'although' in the first paragraph to show contrast, 'for instance' to give an example in the second …*

Suggested answers
Strong points: it's clearly written in paragraphs, covers the notes in the task and is well linked together.
Weak points: the writer's opinion is not clear; there is no concluding paragraph.

4 Put students into different pairs. In addition to deciding which is the most suitable, encourage them to discuss why the others are less suitable. If they are unsure, tell them to consider if the conclusions answer the essay question; if they summarise the main ideas; if they introduce new ideas. After a few minutes, elicit ideas from the class. Encourage students to support their ideas with examples from the conclusions but do not provide feedback until after students have completed Exercise 5.

Answer
2

5 Students work in the same pairs as Exercise 4. Once students have completed this task and you have elicited the correct answers, ask them to briefly discuss how similar their feedback (from Exercise 4) was to the teacher's feedback.

Answers
1 c 2 a 3 b

Extension activity

If students have an essay they wrote in Units 8, 5 or 1 available, you could ask them to choose one, read their concluding paragraph and consider what feedback the teacher would give them with respect to *providing a clear opinion; summarising the main points; (not) introducing new arguments.* If you choose to do this, remind students they will also need to read the relevant essay question. Once students have considered their own feedback, put them into pairs and ask them to do the same with the conclusion written by their partner. Then ask them to take turns saying what feedback they would give both to themselves and to their partner.

6 Students work individually before comparing their answers in pairs. During whole-class feedback, encourage students to paraphrase rather than read out sentences word for word.

Answers
1
a an explanation of healthy aspects of our lifestyles
b examples of things which stop people living healthily
2 however (contrasts information and ideas with the paragraph before)

7 Point out that this exercise will help them write opening sentences and apply them to different topics, and allow students time to read the question in full. Remind them that opening sentences are typically quite short and clearly state the topic of the paragraph. To make this point, if students are struggling, read sample answer 4 and ask them to which number it refers. Tell students to work individually and set a time limit of five minutes. Allow them to compare their sentences in pairs, making corrections as they do so before inviting students to write their sentences on the board.

Sample answers
1 There are several advantages of finding medical information online. **2** However, there are also some disadvantages of modern diets. **3** Exercise is important for the following reasons. **4** However, there are some dangers attached to taking too much exercise.

8 Dictate, or write on the board, the essay question from Exercise 9 (excluding the notes). Put students into groups – you will need a minimum of three groups – and give each a large piece of paper. Allocate one point to each group so that the points are divided equally where possible. Ask students to write notes as they discuss their ideas. Monitor and support weaker students. After five minutes, ask students to change papers with a group who discussed a different point. Tell them to discuss the ideas noted on the paper and add their own. Continue once more until each group has discussed each of the three points. Elicit ideas from the class.

9 Read the rubric with the students. If you chose to do the extension activity after Exercise 5, remind them to consider what feedback they and their partner gave them about their conclusion and how they could write a better one this time. In addition, encourage them to think about whether they are going to write a balanced essay, as introduced in Unit 8. As this is an exam task, point out that, although they can refer to Exercise 3 as they write, they should work individually. Set a time limit of forty minutes. Once the time is up, put students into pairs and ask them to swap papers. Tell them to use the essay checklist in the Writing bank, page 203 to give their partner feedback.

Extension activity
If you chose to do the extension activity after Exercise 5, ask students to compare the concluding paragraph they have just written with the one they reviewed earlier. Encourage them to find one thing they improved based on the feedback they gave themselves and were given, and one thing they could improve further. Once they have done this, put them into pairs to briefly share their ideas.

Model answer
Everyone knows that a healthy lifestyle when you are young is essential for staying well as you grow older. However, many young people could do more to look after their health.
Like everyone else, teenagers should take regular exercise. In my town, perhaps half the young people I know go running or play football or do some other form of sport, but I have many friends who only do sporting activities occasionally, so they are not really fit. This may be because of the amount of time they have to spend studying.
On the other hand, it is becoming increasingly common for young people to have a healthy balanced diet, so few people become overweight, which is very important.
Finally, perhaps because cigarettes are very expensive, few of my friends smoke and this is becoming less fashionable.
As a result, I think my generation is healthier than my parents were at my age.
In conclusion, I believe young people take a reasonable amount of care of themselves, although many would benefit from following a regular exercise routine.

Vocabulary

Words connected with injuries and medical issues

go off	break	bug
trip over	cough	throw up
food poisoning	sneeze	scratch
get badly injured	bump	itchy
allergic reaction	sting	bleed

Idiomatic expressions

a little under the weather	taken aback
in my eyes	teething problems
rushed off my feet	thrown in at the deep end
to rub shoulders with	

Vocabulary activity 1

This activity provides students with the opportunity to practise the 2nd conditional whilst recycling medical language from the unit. Put students into groups and tell them they are going to discuss some medical moral dilemmas using the 2nd conditional. If necessary, elicit the 2nd conditional structure: *if* + past simple + *would/could* + infinitive. Then dictate the following questions (and/or your own ideas):

Would you pretend you had a bad cough if you didn't want to present at a business meeting because you hadn't prepared?
If you got food poisoning from a special meal your best friend cooked you, would you say anything?
If you ruined your best friend's favourite jumper by accidently throwing up over it, what would you do?

Monitor and listen for examples of students using the target language and the 2nd conditional both correctly and incorrectly. After five minutes, stop the students and elicit ideas from the class before praising them for the correct examples you heard and eliciting error corrections. If time allows, you could ask students to choose two more words from the list and write two of their own moral dilemma questions to ask another group.

Vocabulary activity 2

Write on the board, *a time when I was …* and tell students they need to think of a time when the following happened, while you dictate or write on the board: *rushed off my feet*; *thrown in at the deep end*; *a little under the weather*; *taken aback*; *having teething problems*; *rubbing shoulders with*. Next, tell students they have five minutes to think of an example for three before putting them into small groups to share their stories.

DIGITAL CLASSROOM

Practice Extra Unit 11

Test Generator Unit 11 test

Test and Train Exam Practice

12 Animal kingdom

Unit objectives

Topic: animals and nature

Reading and Use of English Part 1 (multiple-choice cloze): identifying words in the sentences that refer to something specific in the text

Reading and Use of English Part 7 (multiple matching): understanding why an answer is incorrect

Writing Part 2 (a letter or email): giving advice

Listening Part 1 (multiple choice): deciding on the main idea of each question

Speaking Parts 3 and 4 (collaborative task and discussion): discussing topics related to animals; commenting on the question; expressing other people's opinions; expressing agreement and disagreement

Pronunciation: word stress (3)

Vocabulary: *avoid, prevent* and *protect; check, control, keep an eye on* and *supervise*

Grammar: third conditional and mixed conditionals; *wish, if only* and *hope*

Starting off SB page 128

Look at the photos with the students. To get them started, elicit the animal in each photo before reading the rubric and eliciting an example role and benefit(s) of one animal. For example, in photo 6 the role of the cow might be, *a domestic animal raised to produce dairy products (cheese, milk, etc.) and meat*; two benefits might be *to provide food for human consumption and an income for the farmer.* Then put students into pairs to complete the activity. Remind them that when they discuss their magazine article choices, they must justify their ideas with reasons. Monitor and support weaker students. After five minutes, stop the students and elicit ideas. Finally, hold a class vote on which two photos are the best for an article.

Listening Part 1 SB page 128

Exam advice

Ask students to read the exam advice before asking why it is important to underline the main idea (the recording will not ask a question, only introduce the topic).

1 Ask students to underline the main ideas as they discuss them. When eliciting the answers, encourage them to paraphrase. For example, for question 1 students might say *How does the man think most people feel about exotic birds?* Point out that students should pay particular attention to determiners such as *most* (people) in question 1 and pronouns such as *they* (agree) in question 2, reminding them that the correct choice must answer the question fully.

2 As this is an exam task, students work individually. Play the recording twice. Elicit answers as a class then put students into pairs or groups and ask them to discuss why the incorrect options are incorrect before eliciting responses from the class during whole-class feedback.

Answers
1 B 2 B 3 C 4 B 5 B 6 C 7 C 8 B

Track 54

Presenter: One. You hear a man talking about a type of exotic bird that now lives in the UK.

Man: Visitors to London are often surprised to see flocks of bright green birds with red beaks and a distinctive high-pitched call when they visit the city's parks. However, the ring-necked parakeet is now a common sight. Nobody's sure how these birds, which are native to the foothills of the Himalayas, came to settle in England, but it looks like they're here to stay. While some people fear that they'll cause other bird species to decrease in numbers, most are fascinated to see such exotic birds in their local park.

Presenter: Two. You hear two friends talking about a recent trip to a zoo.

Man: What did you think about the visit to the zoo last weekend?

Woman: I didn't really enjoy it, to be honest. I thought the animals looked a bit fed up – hardly surprising, given the fact that their enclosures were so small.

Man: I was sorry to see that not all of the animal enclosures were open, as it prevented us from seeing some of our favourite animals. They could have at least given us a discount.

Woman: I know what you mean. The entry fee was so expensive. The guide really knew her stuff, though, which made up for it a little.

Man: Yeah, but it wasn't exactly information we didn't know already. I mean who doesn't know that giraffes are the tallest animals in the world!

Presenter: Three. You hear a man telling a friend about his garden pond.

Man: So, this is our garden …

Woman: Wow, it's much bigger than your old one. Oh, I love your little pond!

Man: Yes, I check it regularly for wildlife. There are lots of frogs and newts, and plenty of interesting insects – dragonflies and butterflies …

Woman: You could get some fish for it, too.

Man:	I did consider that, but I think it's a bit too small for fish. We'd need to make it bigger and that would cost a lot of money. I think we'll just add a few more plants and maybe a fountain. Then it'll look really nice. I think we should be able to do that quite easily with a smaller budget.
Presenter:	Four. You hear a man talking about keeping hens in his garden.
Woman:	So, these must be your hens.
Man:	Yes, I've had them for nearly four years now. They're like part of the family.
Woman:	Are they easy to look after?
Man:	Yes, very easy. Some hens are aggressive and peck each other, but mine all get along really well.
Woman:	That's great. And I bet you save lots of money on eggs!
Man:	Well, to be honest, it costs us a lot to feed the hens, but we get plenty of fresh eggs, which are much better than the ones you buy in the shop.
Presenter:	Five. You hear a woman talking about foxes.
Woman:	While foxes traditionally live in the countryside, it's now thought that there are nearly 150,000 foxes residing in the cities of England. Why are so many foxes moving to urban areas? Well, life in the countryside isn't easy for foxes: they struggle to find enough to eat, especially in winter. In cities such as London, there are many tasty treats, including worms from people's gardens, rats and mice. Many people are afraid that foxes will attack them, but in truth, these shy creatures tend to avoid contact with humans. Foxes are aware of potential dangers, such as cars, and stay hidden to protect themselves.
Presenter:	Six. You hear a mother talking to her son about his pet.
Mother:	Please don't tell me you're ordering that for Felix!
Son:	What!? It's good for his development. I read about it on Sarah's blog.
Mother:	Honestly, if you spent as much time on your schoolwork as you did reading blog posts about cats, you'd be top of your class!
Son:	Very funny, Mum! I'm also a bit concerned about his hair loss.
Mother:	Well, be sure to run it by the vet when you see her, which – I hope you haven't forgotten – is tomorrow.
Son:	I know! Do you think she'll be able to do something about it?
Mother:	I'm sure she will. I've watched a couple of videos and it seems to be a common problem for cats his age.
Son:	That's good to know.
Presenter:	Seven. You hear a woman talking about frogs.
Woman:	I volunteer as a frog patroller in my free time. During the spring months, many frogs return to local ponds to breed, but often face danger when crossing roads. In answer to this, the town council has set up frog patrols to help the frogs reach the water safely. Many people have been keen to get involved in this new scheme and there's usually a good crowd on the evenings when we meet. People bring their dogs and children and it's been a nice opportunity for the community to get together while helping local wildlife.
Presenter:	Eight. You hear a woman talking to her husband about their next-door-neighbour's cat.
Woman:	I saw Colin's cat in our garden earlier on. It was hanging around near the bird feeder, where the birds like to eat the peanuts I leave for them. If I hadn't frightened it away, it would have attacked the birds.
Man:	Oh no! It's lucky that you scared it.
Woman:	I think you need to put the feeder in a different place, so that the birds can eat safely.
Man:	That's a good idea. I'll put it in the apple tree. The cat doesn't usually climb that one. I'll keep an eye on the bird feeders from now on and let you know if I spot anything.

Vocabulary SB page 129

avoid, *prevent* and *protect*; *check*, *control*, *keep an eye on* and *supervise*

Lead in

Point to the vocabulary items under the heading in the Student's Book. Tell the students you are going to dictate five sentences (see below) and that you will say each sentence twice. Point out that the vocabulary item in each sentence will be incorrect. Tell them that as they listen, they need to write down the sentences you say but that they need to replace the incorrect vocabulary item with the correct one.

If you can't ***prevent*** *your dog, you should put it on a lead.* (control)

If it's sunny, you need to ***avoid*** *your skin by wearing a sunscreen.* (protect)

Will you ***control*** *my bag while I go to the toilet?* (keep an eye on)

The government is ***protecting*** *the distribution of medicine to its citizens.* (supervising)

Before you travel, ***keep an eye on*** *that you have all your documents in order.* (check)

Once you have dictated the incorrect sentences, allow students a few minutes to compare their answers before you select students to read each sentence to the class, replacing the incorrect word with the correct one. If a student answers incorrectly, elicit the correct word from the class.

1 Students work individually. Point out that these are examples of real candidate errors. Once students have completed the activity and you have elicited the answers, tell them to asterisk (*) any questions they answered incorrectly, then write correct examples in their note books under the heading *common errors*, and refer to their notes when they are revising for the exam.

Answers
1 avoid **2** protect **3** check **4** prevented
5 keep an eye on

2 Students work in pairs. Allow them to use an English dictionary if they are unsure. Monitor and support weaker students. Once they have completed the task, put them into different pairs to compare their answers before eliciting them from the class.

Answers
1 protecting **2** supervise / keep an eye on **3** control
4 prevents **5** checking **6** avoid **7** protect
8 supervise / keep an eye on **9** check **10** control

3 Tell students to read the sentences, ignoring the gaps, before reading them a second time to complete the task. If students are unsure, encourage them to read the sentences out loud as it may help them to choose the correct option if they hear it.

Answers
1 successfully prevented **2** narrowly avoided
3 heavily protected **4** strictly controlled
5 closely supervised **6** avoid; at all costs
7 check; carefully **8** properly protected

Grammar SB page 130

Third conditional and mixed conditionals

▶ **Page 179 Grammar reference**

Lead in
On the board draw a stick man running away from a lion and elicit that it is a lion chasing a man. Then write: *If I had/hadn't … I would/wouldn't have …* Put students into small groups. Tell them they need to think about what the man (or, for fun, the lion) might be thinking the day after this happened and to come up with as many sentences as they can using the structure on the board. Encourage them to be as creative as they like but if they are struggling for ideas, you could give them an example sentence: *If I hadn't got out of the jeep, I wouldn't have needed to run from the lion; If the lion hadn't had such big teeth, I wouldn't have been so scared.* Once the time is up, invite students to write their sentences on the board. If you can, leave the sentences on the board and do not elicit error corrections until after the students have completed Exercise 3.

1 Ask students to underline the third conditional sentence then put them into pairs to complete this task. Tell them that if a statement is incorrect, they should discuss why. When eliciting the answers, if you notice that the majority of students are making errors, allow them time to read the information about third conditionals in the Grammar reference on page 179 before moving to Exercise 2.

Answers
1 T **2** F **3** T

2 Read the rubric with the students and put them into pairs to complete the task. Once you have elicited the answers, you could remind them that the further the tense moves from the present, the further it moves away from reality, i.e. zero conditional is present tense + present tense (generally true), first conditional is present tense + *will* (possible, probable), second conditional is past simple tense + *would* (imagining, improbable), the third conditional is past participle tense + *would have* (imaginary results of something which did not happen in the past).

Answers
1 b **2** a **3** b **4** a **5** b **6** a **7** a

3 Students work individually. Point out that these are examples of real candidate errors. Once students have completed the activity and you have elicited the answers, tell them to asterisk (*) any questions they answered incorrectly, then write correct examples in their note books under the heading *common errors*, and refer to their notes when they are revising for the exam.

Answers
1 would have finished **2** had known **3** would have gone
4 had not been **5** had sat **6** would have enjoyed
7 would not have made **8** had not barked

Extension activity
If you chose to do the Lead in activity and the student sentences are still on the board, select a student to come to the board, then invite the class to call out error corrections as the selected student makes changes.

4 Allow students time to read the questions and consider their answers before putting them into pairs to discuss the questions. Monitor and listen for correct and incorrect examples. During whole-class feedback, praise the students for the correct examples you hear and elicit error corrections.

5 If students are struggling, write the following on the board from the example in Exercise 1: *If I hadn't frightened the cat away, it would have attacked the birds; If it had attacked the birds, I wouldn't be photographing them feed.* Elicit that the first is a third conditional sentence and the second is a mixed conditional sentence, before asking: *Did the speaker scare the cat away?* (yes) *Did the cat attack the birds?* (no) *What is the present result of the cat not attacking the birds?* (the speaker is now taking photos of them feeding). Put students into pairs to complete the exercise. As you elicit the answers in whole-class feedback, ask students to explain what the speaker in each sentence means. For example, in 1 they bought a dog because they do not live in a safe area. Once you have elicited the answers, point out that all conditional structures allow people to imagine or hypothesise about

actions. However, whilst the third conditional is used to imagine a different situation in the past and a different result in the past, mixed conditionals are used to imagine a different situation in the past with a different result in the present or to imagine a different situation in the present with a different result in the past.

Answers
1
a second, refers to present time b third, refers to past time
2
a second, refers to present time b third, refers to past time

6 Read the rubric and put students into pairs. Tell one student to answer questions 1–3 and the other 4–6. Once they have done this, they should tell their partner their answers, discussing and amending any they think may be incorrect. Before eliciting the correct answers, put each student pair with another pair to compare their answers.

Answers
1 had; would have driven
2 had studied; would not feel / would not be feeling
3 did not bark; would have taken
4 had not been; would still be
5 had known; would not have lent
6 had not got; would not have met

7 Read the rubric with the students. As this is a shorter exam style task, set a time limit of five minutes and ask students to work individually.

Answers
1 would have allowed him **2** had left home earlier
3 less frightening, I would have **4** had spoken more slowly

Reading and Use of English Part 1 SB page 132

Lead in
Ask the students whether they like cats. Select a student who does and another who does not to share their reasons with the class.

Read the exam advice with the students. Ask them why they should read the text after they have finished (when they read the text through they may notice errors that they did not notice when they were completing the gaps). Then point to the final bullet point and remind them that it is always better to guess if they do not know an answer: an unanswered question will definitely be wrong. Point out, however, that they should never choose two options for any one question; this will be marked wrong even if one of their choices is correct. Finally, encourage them to read all the options before making their choices.

Exam advice

1 Read the rubric with the students. If you chose to do the Lead in and a significant number of students indicated they did not like cats, you could also ask them to discuss the question: *Why do some people not like keeping a cat as a pet?* You should find that students are giving reasons and examples automatically at this stage of the course. However, to ensure they are, monitor and prompt them for reasons and examples if necessary.

2 Set a time limit of a minute for students to do this activity, before putting them into pairs to compare their answers. When eliciting, encourage students to paraphrase rather than read from the text word for word.

Answers
1.6: kilometres (in length) of the island of Aoshima
0.5: area in square kilometres of the island of Aoshima
120–130: number of cats on the island of Aoshima
13: number of residents living on the island of Aoshima
1:10: ratio of cats to humans on the island of Aoshima

3 Read the rubric with the students. Remind them that as this is an exam task, they should work individually. Set a time limit of ten minutes. After ten minutes, stop the students and elicit the correct answers.

Answers
1 B **2** D **3** A **4** A **5** C **6** D **7** B **8** A

Extension activity
Dictate the following questions: *Did you follow all the Exam advice given in this section? Were you able to answer all the questions in ten minutes? Which questions did you find the easiest and which the most challenging?* Then put the students into small groups and ask them to discuss the questions. Remind them to give reasons for their answers. After five minutes, stop the students and ask them to think of one thing they would do differently the next time they tackle a Reading and Use of English Part 1 task. They could write this in their note books under the heading *Reading and Use of English Part 1* and refer to their notes when they are revising for the exam.

4 As an alternative to pairwork, you could put students into threes. Allocate each student one question. After they have had a minute to consider their response, tell them to take turns giving their answers before inviting the others to agree or disagree with them. If you choose to do this alternative, encourage students to use phrases from the Speaking bank pages 209 and 210 (*Do you agree?*; *Yes, you're right*; *Yes, I completely agree with you*; *I can see what you mean, but …*; *I'm not sure about that*, etc.).

Grammar SB page 133

wish, if only and *hope*

▶ **Page 180 Grammar reference**

Lead in

Write on the board: *I wish I ...* and *I hope I ...* Tell students to look at the photo on page 131: people riding camels in the desert. Point to the last person and ask the students to imagine they are one of the people and must complete the sentences *I wish I ...* and *I hope I ...* so that they are true for them. After a minute, put students into pairs to say their sentences before inviting students to write them on the board. Example sentences might include: *I wish I hadn't agreed to ride a camel; I wish I was at the beach; I wish it wasn't so bumpy; I hope I can get off this camel soon; I hope I can ride a camel again.* It is likely that students will make several tense errors. However, do not elicit error corrections at this stage. Leave the sentences on the board and elicit corrections after students have completed Exercise 1 (or the extension activity if you choose to do it).

1 Allow students time to read the sentences and questions before putting them into pairs to complete this task. If students are struggling, allow them to refer to the Grammar reference on pages 180 and 181 as they work.

Answers
1 b, c, d, e **2** b, c, d **3** b **4** past tense and *would* + infinitive **5** a **6** past perfect **7** f **8** present simple

Extension activity

Point to the photo on page 131 and put students into groups. Ask the groups to imagine that they are riding the camels and to come up with four sentences: one sentence using *wish/if only* + past simple, one with *wish/if only* + would, one with *wish/if only* + past perfect and one using *hope*. Monitor and support weaker students. After five minutes, select students to share their group's sentences with the class before eliciting error corrections. Example sentences might include: *If only I knew how to ride a camel; I wish this camel would walk a bit slower; I wish I hadn't agreed to come; I hope this camel doesn't bite me.* If you chose to complete the Lead in activity, and you have not yet corrected the sentences on the board, point to them now. Tell the students to use the Grammar reference on pages 180 and 181 and the information in Exercise 1 to correct any errors they made with these sentences.

2 Read the rubric with the students and point out that these are real candidate errors. So that the students can identify the errors they are making, tell them to work individually and not to compare their answers after they have finished. After you have elicited the correct answers, tell them to asterisk (*) any questions they answered incorrectly, then write correct examples in their note books under the heading *common errors*, and refer to their notes when they are revising for the exam.

Answers
1 ~~wish~~ hope **2** ~~wish~~ hope **3** correct **4** ~~wish~~ hope
5 correct **6** ~~wish~~ hope **7** correct **8** ~~wish~~ hope

3 As this is similar to a Reading and Use of English Part 4 task and students have practised it a number of times, set a reduced time limit of five minutes. If you have not already done so, point out that they will have seventy-five minutes to answer seven Reading and Use of English parts. Tell them that they will answer some parts quicker than others and that they will need to manage their own time. However, they should aim to spend no longer than a few minutes on each of the fifty-two questions, moving on if they find they are spending too long on one question.

Answers
1 was a better **2** I'd / I had studied harder **3** would make less OR wouldn't / would not make so much **4** hadn't / had not called off the **5** wish you'd / you had met

Reading and Use of English Part 7 SB page 134

Lead in

Write on the board the wild animals mentioned in the reading text: *elephant, scorpion, polar bear, pelican.* Tell the students you are going to describe one of the animals and they must call out which it is. Then describe one of the animals, e.g. *It has a large beak, a bag-shaped throat pouch* and *long feathers* (pelican). Put students into pairs. Tell them to choose an animal and describe it briefly. Their partner must say the animal they have described before taking their turn. Monitor and write down examples of B2-level language you hear (e.g. *paw, feathers, beak, fur, poisonous, trunk, tail, sting*). After a minute or two, stop the students and write the words you heard on the board, eliciting others as necessary. Then ask whether they have seen or would like to see any of these animals. Elicit answers, encouraging students to use the B2-level language from the board and making sure that they give reasons to support their views.

1 How you set this task up may depend on which country(ies) your students are from. For example, if you have students from a wide range of countries you could group them so that a number of different countries are represented in each group. Alternatively, you could elicit all the dangerous wild animals from the class before putting them into groups to discuss the second point. Remind them that as what they do may depend on the animal they see, they should justify their ideas with reasons.

Read the exam advice with the students. To practise the advice in the first bullet point, write on the board *a charging elephant*. Put the students into pairs and ask them to briefly discuss what *charging* means. Elicit one or two ideas but do not comment. Then refer students to line 4 in the text and ask them to use the context to guess the meaning. You should find that they are able to use *crashed through some small trees*, to guess *moving forward quickly* or something similar. Point out that they can also guess meaning by breaking a word down. For example, they could guess the word *eyesight* in line 18 means something about *an eye* or *eyes*. They could then use the adjective *poor* (written immediately before *eyesight*) which suggests something negative to guess that *poor eyesight* means *cannot see well*. As students can worry when they have to guess the meaning of an unknown word, point out that there will be words they do not understand and that approximate meaning is often sufficient for them to answer the question correctly.

Exam advice

2 Students work individually before comparing their answers in pairs. When eliciting the answers, encourage the students to paraphrase the main idea. For example, for question 7 students could say *unhappy with the result of seeing* (a wild animal). Paraphrasing may encourage them to avoid word spotting when they answer the question in Exercise 3.

Answers
Suggested underlining
1 didn't immediately realise, injured **2** unwilling, injure, animal **3** believes, behaviour caused, attack **4** advice, ignored **5** people, lacked, knowledge to help **6** informed, may have missed, opportunity **7** disappointed by, outcome, encounter **8** might not have been injured, another time of day **9** happy at first, to see, animal, attacked **10** surprised, eventually, escape

3 Before students complete the task individually, review the exam advice on pages 34, 56 and 84. Remind students that they have seventy-five minutes to complete the whole Reading and Use of English paper and ask them how long they think they should spend on a single part (as there are 7 parts, approximately 10 minutes). Allow students to compare their answers in pairs before eliciting them from the class.

Answers
1 B **2** C **3** D **4** A **5** B **6** B **7** D **8** B **9** D **10** A

4 Read the rubric with the students. If you want to provide them with some initial ideas, draw their attention to C *Baz Roberts* from the reading text on page 134 and ask them how the polar bears' habitat (the Arctic) could be negatively impacted by tourism. Put them into pairs to discuss this briefly before eliciting one or two ideas (e.g. oil spills from ships; rubbish left by visitors). Then put the students into different pairs, or alternatively small groups, to discuss the question.

Speaking Parts 3 and 4 SB page 135

▶ **Page 209 and Page 211 Speaking bank**

Lead in
Ask students what they would do in the exam if their partner spoke too much or too little. Then put them into pairs or groups to discuss the question briefly before inviting ideas from the class. After elicitation, point out that if a partner is too quiet, it is a good opportunity to gain marks for effective communication by asking for an opinion; and if a partner dominates, it is important that they speak even if it is difficult, as the examiner needs a large enough sample of their language to mark them on.

Read the exam advice with the students. Point to the second point, put students into pairs and ask them to briefly discuss differences between having a conversation and speaking individually. Elicit ideas before pointing out that conversations are interactive; listeners should acknowledge what the speaker has said using verbal and non-verbal communication before they take their turn to speak. Then elicit examples of non-verbal communication, e.g. eye contact; nodding or shaking the head; posture; facial expressions. Remind students that they will gain higher marks in the exam if they balance listening and contributing.

Exam advice

1 Allow students time to read the task, then play the recording twice before putting them into pairs to discuss their ideas. As an alternative, and to prepare students for Exercise 3, you could put them into pairs and tell them to brainstorm two ideas for each prompt before they listen and complete the task.

Answers
1 Javier is doing all the speaking and not giving Sophia a chance to participate
2 Sophia needs to find an opportunity to interrupt.

Track 55

Examiner: Now I'd like you to talk about something together for about two minutes. Some people think that it's a good idea to keep animals as pets, but other people disagree. Here are some things they think about and a question for you to discuss. First you have some time to look at the task.
Now talk to each other about whether it's a good idea to keep animals as pets.

Javier: One big advantage of keeping a pet is the positive impact it can have on a child's development. It teaches children to be more responsible from an early age and helps them to develop important social skills. That being said, I do think that people often rush into getting a pet without really thinking about how it will affect their lifestyle. If you want a dog, say, but work full-time, it can be difficult to manage, and the animal's physical and mental health may suffer as a result. Then there's the important point of costs to consider. There's no point getting a pet if you can't afford to look after it properly, so it's vital to check your household budget and make sure you can put enough money aside each month.

2 Put students into pairs to discuss their answers briefly before eliciting them from the class.

Answers
Sophia uses the phrases:
Yes, I agree. and *That's right.*

Track 56

Javier: One big advantage of keeping a pet is the positive impact it can have on a child's development. It teaches children to be more responsible from an early age and helps them to develop important social skills.

Sophia: Yes, I agree. I think this also helps to improve the child's confidence. Most pets become a child's best friend, too, which means they learn the value of companionship and friendship from a young age.

Javier: That being said, I do think that people often rush into getting a pet without really thinking about how it will affect their lifestyle. If you want a dog, say, but work full-time, it can be difficult to manage, and the animal's physical and mental health may suffer as a result.

Sophia: That's right. If a family simply doesn't have the time to look after their pet, not only will the animal suffer, as you say, but they may also be forced to give the pet up, which can cause all sorts of emotional distress.

3 Before students start this task, you could elicit two or three more phrases they could use to politely interrupt, e.g. *May I add something? Sorry to interrupt but …, Could I just say something?* If you chose to do the alternative in Exercise 1, draw students' attention to this now, telling them to use the ideas they came up with. Monitor and listen for examples of students dominating and interrupting. You may find that students forget to do this once they start talking, so be prepared to stop and re-start the task if necessary.

4 Read the rubric with the students and remind them that they should agree and disagree with each other before offering an opinion of their own. Elicit phrases they could use (*Yes, that's true*; *I can see what you mean but …*, etc.). If students are unsure, refer them to the Speaking bank on page 210. Monitor and listen for examples of the target language.

Track 57

Examiner: Thank you. Now you have about a minute to decide what you think is the best reason for having a pet.

5 Before students listen, ask them to read the strategies (Q1) and, working in pairs, predict which they think Sophia will use and why. Elicit ideas from the class. Once you have played the recording, pairs discuss whether their predictions were correct before you elicit the correct answers. Then, play the recording a second time before they work in pairs to answer questions 2 and 3.

Answers
1 c
2
comment on the question: That's an interesting question; That's quite difficult to answer
introduce other people's opinions: People often suggest …; Some people say that …
say whether you agree or disagree with other people's opinions: I don't share this view; I agree up to a point

Track 58

Examiner: Sophia, do you think animals should be kept in zoos?

Sophia: That's an interesting question. People often suggest that animals have better lives in zoos because they are well looked after by zookeepers, who provide them with food and medicine. I don't share this view, however, as I believe that it's cruel to keep animals in zoos because they don't have the same amount of freedom and space that they'd have in their natural habitat and this can have a negative effect on the animals' mental and physical well-being.

Examiner: Some people argue that animal testing should be banned. What do you think?

Sophia: That's quite difficult to answer. Some people say that animal testing has a positive impact on humans, on account of the life-saving medicine that is developed from these kinds of experiments. I agree up to a point and I don't think it should be banned altogether. However, we must do more to ensure the animals don't suffer as a result, and spend more money on developing alternative methods of testing which means we are no longer dependent on animal experiments.

/P/ Pronunciation: word stress (3)

6 Read the information with the students.

6.1 Students work individually before comparing their answer in pairs.

Answers
See Track 59 audioscript for answers.

Track 59

That's quite difficult to answer. Some people say that animal testing has a positive impact on humans, on account of the life-saving medicine that is developed from these kinds of experiments.

I agree up to a point and I don't think it should be banned altogether. However, we must do more to ensure the animals don't suffer as a result and spend more money on developing alternative methods of testing which means we are no longer dependent on animal experiments.

6.2 After students have listened, elicit that stressed words are pronounced louder, for longer and with a higher pitch; whereas the unstressed words are pronounced more quietly with a lower pitch, and are said more quickly. The latter means that a group of unstressed words are often linked together and may sound like fewer words. To emphasise this point you could say the following quietly, quickly, and using natural linking if you can, and ask students to count the number of words they hear: *on account of the life saving medicine that's developed* (10) . Finally, point out that we can change word stress when we want to change the meaning of a sentence by emphasising a different part of it. For example, in the sentence, *Toby didn't steal Mia's laptop*, the word *Toby* is emphasised to show that it was someone else (not Toby) who stole Mia's laptop; whereas in the sentence, *Toby didn't steal Mia's laptop*, the word *laptop* is emphasised to show that Toby stole something else from Mia (not her laptop).

6.3 If students are struggling to use the correct sentence stress, you could play the recording again, stop it after each utterance and drill the pronunciation with the class, before asking students to read the extracts in pairs.

7 Allow students time to read the questions and consider their ideas before putting them into pairs to discuss the questions. Remind them to justify their ideas by giving an example from their own experience where possible and to agree and disagree with the opinion of others before offering their own opinion.

Writing Part 2 (an email or letter) SB page 136

▶ **Page 194 Writing bank**

Lead in
Ask students when they last wrote an email, who it was to and what it was about. Elicit a few examples from the class.

Tell the students to close their Student's Books and put them into pairs. Then ask them to come up with two examples for each of the following: a friendly phrase to start an email; a friendly phrase to finish an email. Invite students to write their phrases on the board. Finally, ask them to open their books and read the exam advice before briefly discussing whether the advice includes the same or different phrases from the ones they came up with.

Exam advice

1 Ask the students to read the question and exam task before putting them into pairs to complete the activity.

Answers
1 where to go, what to see and the best way of getting around to see scenery and wildlife **2** Students' own answers
3 informal style; it's a letter to a friend and he has written to you in an informal style

2 Students work individually before comparing their plans in small groups. Remind students that their plans should cover each of the three points they need to deal with. Once students have compared plans, allow them a few more minutes to make improvements to their plans before moving to the next exercise.

3 Students work individually before comparing their answers in small groups.

Answers
1 He writes I'm very glad to hear that you're thinking of visiting my country this summer. **2** Yes – advice about visiting Asturias, what to see while there, and hiring a car.
3 yes **4** informal

4 Students work individually before comparing their answers in pairs. Once you have elicited the answers, and as students commonly confuse *advise* and *suggest*, write on the board, *I ('d) suggest you …* and ask students which verb pattern (1–5) follows (2: + infinitive (without *to*). Point out, or elicit, that in this sentence, if the pronoun *you* is omitted, the verb pattern changes to + *-ing* (*I'd suggest visiting …, I suggest going …*).

Answers
1 I'd advise you to go to Asturias
2 You should visit the 'Picos de Europa'
3 If I were you, I'd hire a car to get around
4 The best idea would be to hire it online
5 Make sure that you take warm clothes and a waterproof jacket

5 Ask students to work individually. Monitor and support weaker students before putting them into pairs to take turns saying their sentences. After you have elicited a few sentences, ask students which sentence from Exercise 4 gives strong advice (*Make sure that …*), and elicit another word to give strong advice (*must* – see Grammar reference page 182). Then elicit how sentence 5 would change if they replaced *make sure* with *must* (*You must take warm clothes and a waterproof jacket*).

Extension activity
Put students into groups and tell them to write down three more ways to give advice and make suggestions, e.g. *You could try* + *-ing; You might like* + *to* infinitive; *Why don't you* + infinitive. Elicit examples, correct errors and write them on the board. Next, tell students to work individually and use each of the phrases to write sentences like those in Exercise 5.

6 Elicit from students how long they should spend answering the question (approximately forty minutes). Note: candidates have eighty minutes to answer two writing questions and although students may find they spend longer on Part 1 (the Essay), they should aim to divide the time equally as both questions have the same word count (140–190 words). Point out that as they have already had time to plan, you will reduce the time to thirty minutes. Remind students to refer to their plans as they answer the question and that they should work individually.

Extension activity
Put students into pairs and ask them to turn to the Writing bank on page 203. Ask them to swap their answers to Exercise 6 and check their partner's writing against the email/letter checklist. Encourage them to find and underline specific examples of informal language, phrases to give advice, and opening and closing phrases. Once they have done this, ask them to take turns giving feedback. Point out that they should say two things that their partner did well and two things they could improve.

Vocabulary

Commonly confused words

avoid
check
control
keep an eye on
prevent
protect
supervise

Collocations

avoid … at all costs
check … carefully
closely supervise
heavily protect
narrowly avoid
properly protect
strictly control
successfully prevent

Vocabulary activity 1

In this activity, students are going to recycle the vocabulary for the unit while practising a Speaking Part 3 and 4 task. Write on the board: *Is it a good idea for people to follow a vegan diet?* Elicit five prompts that could go with this question (e.g. animal welfare; education; conservation; health). Once you have elicited ideas and the class have agreed on five prompts, write them on the board. Then put students into pairs and say:
Now I'd like you to talk about something together for about two minutes. Some people think that it's a good idea for everyone to follow a vegan diet, but other people disagree. Here are some things they think about and a question for you to discuss. First you have some time to look at the task (pause for a moment). *Now talk to each other about whether it's a good idea for everyone to follow a vegan diet.*
Monitor and write down examples of target words and phrases from the unit as well as language to agree, disagree, ask for and offer an opinion, and politely interrupt. After two minutes stop the students and say: *Thank you. Now you have one minute to decide the best reason to follow a vegan diet.* Continue monitoring for target language. Once students have completed the task, praise them for the correct examples you heard and elicit error correction.

Vocabulary activity 2

With Student's Books closed, tell the students you are going to write five questions (see below) on the board. Each question will have one gap. Tell them they must complete the gap with a word or phrase from either the *commonly confused words* or *collocations* from the unit.

Whose responsibility is it to properly ____ the habitat of endangered animals? (protect)
When you go shopping, do you ____ buying products packaged in plastic? (avoid)
Do you think governments should ____ large companies to make sure they are reducing their carbon footprint? (keep an eye on)
How can people be successfully ____ from illegally keeping wild animals as pets? (prevented)
Do you agree that agriculture in fragile regions, for example The Amazon, should be strictly ____? (controlled)
Once you have elicited the correct answers in whole-class feedback, put the students into small groups to discuss the questions. Remind them to agree and disagree with the opinion of others before they offer their own opinion.

DIGITAL CLASSROOM

Practice Extra Unit 12
Test Generator Unit 12 test
Test and Train Exam Practice

Unit 11 Vocabulary and grammar review

1
1 stung; to scratch; itchy 2 food poisoning 3 teething problems 4 rushed off my feet 5 coughing/sneezing; sneezing/coughing
2
1 misunderstood 2 disappeared 3 dissatisfied/unsatisfied 4 inexperienced 5 dislikes 6 unaware 7 uncertain 8 unacceptable 9 unreliable 10 dishonest
3
1 whose arm is broken has 2 one the medicine (which/that) / medicine the one (which/that) the 3 whose inhabitants are (all) 4 in a/the way (that/which) 5 from his email what 6 (which/that) Chiaro tells do not / don't

Unit 12 Vocabulary and grammar review

1
1 B 2 C 3 A 4 D 5 A 6 B
2
1 had not/hadn't been 2 was/were 3 wasn't/weren't, would have had 4 would not/wouldn't make 5 lived 6 would be 7 will change/are going to change 8 had studied 9 would have got 10 had eaten
3
1 had not/hadn't left 2 had paid her in 3 have made a/any difference 4 had a better relationship with 5 would help him once in 6 turned him down

13 House space

Unit objectives

Topic: homes

Reading and Use of English Part 5 (multiple choice): identifying options which reflect the true meaning in a text

Reading and Use of English Part 2 (open cloze): understanding which type of words are tested

Writing Part 2 (an article): planning a piece of writing

Listening Part 2 (sentence completion): identifying the required form of the word needed for each gap

Speaking Part 2 (long turn): strategies for answering Part 2 questions

Pronunciation: linking (2)

Vocabulary: vocabulary to describe where you live; *space, place, room, area, location* and *square*

Grammar: causative *have* and *get*; expressing obligation and permission

Starting off SB page 140

1 Read the rubric with the students. Then read the example and elicit which home it is describing (B: mobile home). If you think students will struggle with the property types, elicit these before putting them into pairs to complete the activity (e.g. A: terraced house/town house; B: mobile home; C: contemporary architecture; D: block of flats; E: log cabin; F: detached house).

2 Allow students time to read the list. Then put them into pairs and tell them to discuss what the words and phrases in bold mean, guessing any they are not sure about. As they do this, write down the meaning of any you think might be new. For example, the word *allocated* in 8 means *reserved*. After a few minutes, stop the students and elicit the meaning of new vocabulary from the class before putting them back into pairs to complete the activity. During whole-class feedback, elicit the answers to the matching before selecting students to talk about their list of features, making sure they give reasons and examples to support their ideas.

Suggested answers

Picture A: 3, 6, 10	Picture D: 2
Picture B: 8, 9	Picture E: 1, 7
Picture C: 4	Picture F: 5

Extension activity

To prepare students for Speaking Part 2 on page 146, ask them to choose two photos from Starting off. Then say: *The photos show two different types of home. I'd like you to compare the photographs and say what type of person might choose to live in each of these homes.* Remind students to speak for one minute each. Monitor and write down examples of complex language to make comparisons and target language from the section. After two minutes, stop the students and select one or two stronger pairs to repeat the task in front of the class.

Reading and Use of English Part 5 SB page 140

Exam advice

Read the exam advice with the students. Note: there will be an opportunity for students to practise the point made in the first bullet point in the teacher's notes for Exercise 3.

Lead in

Put students into pairs. Point to the picture on page 141 and ask them to use some of the words and phrases from Starting off, Exercise 2, to describe the homes and/or location in the picture. Point out that they should speculate if they are not sure and use the language in both a positive and negative sense. (e.g. *These homes are likely to have balconies, or a patio or terrace but are unlikely to have gardens.*) Monitor and support weaker students by asking targeted questions, e.g. *Are these properties likely to be cosy? Why / Why Not?*

1 Read the rubric with the students and point to the picture on page 141, or refer students back to it if you did the Lead in. Elicit one or two positive and negative ideas about life in 18th-century Venice from the class before putting them into pairs to answer the question, e.g. positive: stunning architecture; beautiful canal views; negative: may smell terrible in the summer; canal water carries harmful bacteria/disease.

2 Remind students to read the title before skimming the article. Encourage them to underline the parts of the extract that give them the answer. Set a time limit of around one minute. When eliciting the answer in whole-class feedback, ask students to paraphrase. This will help discourage them from word spotting when they tackle the questions in Exercise 3.

Suggested answer

It's conveniently situated close to the Grand Canal; the district is interesting; it's near the city centre

Extension activity

This activity will encourage students to increase their reading comprehension whilst skimming. It works better if it is done immediately after students have skimmed a text. Ask the students to close their Student's Books and quickly write a brief two- or three-sentence summary of the text they skimmed in Exercise 2 (without worrying too much about grammatical accuracy). After a minute, stop the students, put them into pairs and ask them to take turns reading their summaries. Then ask the students what the purpose of reading a text quickly is (to get an overview of it / to understand the general idea). Remind them that if they understand the general idea of a text before they look at the questions and options, they may find they do not need to absorb all the options later on. As three out of four options are incorrect this is likely to be a more time-effective technique than if they read the questions and options first.

3 Read the rubric with the students. Tell them to read each question carefully, underlining the part of the question they should find in the text (e.g. *house typical of Venice* for question 1). Point to the first bullet point in the exam advice and stress that the full meaning of the option must be reflected in the text, otherwise it is incorrect. If students are struggling with this point, you could draw their attention to the words *house typical of Venice* in the first question and ask them to locate the part of the text where this is mentioned: *as is customary in the city* (line 14). Then tell them to decide why a candidate might choose option A, even though it is incorrect. Allow them a minute to do this before eliciting *a door and two entrances* (line 10 and 11) matches with *several ways of entering it* in the option; however, this does not specifically refer to something which is *typical of Venice*.

Answers
1 C **2** B **3** C **4** D **5** D **6** A

4 Read the rubric with the students and point out that they can describe a house, apartment, flat or another form of accommodation. While they are planning, encourage the students to re-read the text from Exercise 3 and find a few words or phrases they could use to describe the property they have in mind (e.g. *cellar*: line 15; (x) *storeys high*: line 18; *elegant arched windows*: line 37; *shutters*: line 38), and choose three or four phrases from Starting off Exercise 2 (e.g. *recently refurbished*; *modern fittings*).

Vocabulary SB page 142

space, place, room, area, location and *square*

Lead in

Tell the students they are going to do a key word transformation task and elicit the process and rules of the task. Then write on the board:

I had trouble finding somewhere to park near the school.
SPACE
It was hard to find ____ park near the school. (a space to)

Our house is too small for a dog.
ROOM
We do not ____ for a dog. (have enough room)

Properties in and around Bristol are expensive.
AREA
Bristol is ____ to buy property in. (an expensive area)

Put student into pairs and allow them a few minutes to complete the answers before eliciting them from the class.

1 Students work individually. After they have completed the activity, tell them to find the sentences in the text on page 141 and check their answers. Once you have elicited the answers, point out that as these are real candidate errors they should asterisk (*) any questions they answered incorrectly. They can then write correct examples in their note books under the heading *common errors*, and refer to their notes when they are revising for the exam.

Answers
1 place **2** square **3** location **4** area

2 Put students into pairs. Encourage them to read the sentences out loud before they decide which option is correct as hearing which options sound incorrect may be helpful, particularly when focusing on the words before and after the gap. If students are confused about the difference in meaning between *space* and *room*, point out that *room* is used to describe a specific enclosed place in a building (e.g. *I'll be in the staff room at 9 am*; *There are three rooms upstairs*); whereas *space* is used to describe an area that is unoccupied and can remain unoccupied (e.g. *There are a lot of green spaces in my city*). However, they can have the same meaning when used to describe the capacity of something (e.g. *There's not enough room/space for a wardrobe next to the bed*). Once students have answered the questions, allow them time to compare their answers in larger groups before you elicit them in whole-class feedback.

Answers
1 space **2** room **3** space **4** location **5** area **6** space
7 square **8** area **9** space **10** place, room

Fast finishers

Write the following sentence halves on the board. Ask students to choose the correct option before completing the sentences so that they are true for them:
The most popular areas/spaces to live in my town or city are …; My ideal holiday location/area is …; If I don't have enough place/room for all my things, I'll … (Answers: areas, location, room)

Encourage students to write their completed sentences

on the board so that you can discuss them, and elicit error corrections from the whole class after everyone has completed Exercise 2.

3 Before students answer this question, ask them to close their Student's Books then write *area*, *place*, *room* and *space* on the board. Invite a student to come to the board and write down collocations as the class calls them out. Once students have run out of ideas, ask them to open their books and complete the exercise, mentally noting any collocations they already knew. Once you have elicited the correct answers, ask students to write down any additional collations in their note books. Other collocations might include *burial place*, *commercial space*, *seating area*.

Answers
1 place **2** space **3** room **4** area

4 Students work individually before comparing their answers in pairs. Once you have elicited the correct answers in whole-class feedback, dictate the following questions and then ask students to discuss them in pairs or small groups:

Do you think employers should allocate free parking spaces to all their employees?

Why do you think homes with open-plan spaces have become so popular these days?

Should local governments restrict the number of picnic areas in green spaces to reduce litter and protect wildlife?

Remind students to justify their ideas with reasons and examples. Monitor and check that students are using the target language and prompt them if they are not.

Answers
1 parking spaces **2** personal space **3** green space
4 spare room **5** meeting place **6** picnic area

Listening Part 2 SB page 142

1 Read the rubric with the students. Ask the students to think of five ways a home can be smart. Elicit (additional) ideas from the class (e.g. smart meters; smart coffee makers; smart personal assistants, e.g. Alexa, Siri).

Refer students to the exam advice. Remind them that they must write the same words they hear in the recording. They don't have to change the word at all. Exercise 2 will practise the first point.

Exam advice

2 Ask students to work individually. If they need support, answer the first question with them. After a few minutes, stop the students. Put them into pairs to compare the questions they answered and complete any they did not have time to finish.

Answers
1 a person **2** a feature of the conference **3** a subject
4 a type of technology **5** a type of problem **6** a type of problem **7** a resource **8** a feature of the conference
9 an activity during the conference **10** an initiative

3 Tell the students that you will play the recording twice, so they should use the second time they listen to check any answers they were unsure of the first time. Ask students to check their answers using the audioscript on page 242 before you elicit them from the class.

Answers
1 personal tutor **2** cost **3** (software) engineering
4 robots **5** privacy **6** environmental **7** leaks
8 workshops **9** contacts **10** group

Track 60

Jason: Hello, everyone. A few weeks ago I missed a few classes because I travelled to Bengaluru, in India, for the Smart Home Exhibition. You might recognise the name because our professor mentioned this event a few months back, remember? It wasn't until I expressed my interest in representing the university at an international conference that my personal tutor suggested I attend this one, and I jumped at the chance, of course, even though I wasn't looking forward to the prospect of the 13-hour journey ahead of me! What I hadn't realised, however, was how expensive it was going to be! I panicked a bit because I didn't know if the university was going to cover the cost, and it was obviously something I couldn't afford on my own. Thankfully, that worked out in the end.

As for the conference itself, at first, I was concerned that I wouldn't be able to keep up with the more technical talks aimed at software engineering graduates, who made up the vast majority of the participants. I needn't have worried, though, as being an architecture student enabled me to look at the subject in a different but equally interesting light.

So, I arrived on the first day and I found myself surrounded by the most advanced and futuristic inventions you could imagine. Smart devices of all kinds – lights, locks, appliances and TVs. One area I enjoyed learning more about was the new solutions being found for charging devices quicker and more conveniently. But the thing that really impressed me was the robots that can cook, mow the lawn and even clean the windows. I hadn't realised how advanced domestic technology had become.

That's not to say I was convinced by everything I saw. Voice-controlled devices are a good example of this. What bugs me the most about these is the fact that they appear to always be listening. I realise that the manufacturers state that all recordings are either anonymised or destroyed, and that this technology can be socially useful in other ways, such as for people with mobility problems. But privacy is still something we should be concerned about, in my view, and I tend to keep quiet around these devices.

Anyway, as shiny and fascinating as all these gadgets and features may be, the real revelation for me at this conference was green technology. We're always talking about how we can protect the environment, for instance by recycling more, consuming fewer resources and travelling less frequently. So it was great to learn more about how smart home features can protect the planet – the measured environmental impacts of this technology shared in the presentations were very impressive. At the stands, I saw several solutions for smart heating that reduce and optimise energy usage, smart water systems that can detect leaks, and even devices that allow you to recycle materials at home! I was so motivated by this to do my bit that I had a smart water system installed as soon as I got back home. I set up a smart vacuum cleaner as well, but I won't pretend that wasn't just because I'm too lazy to vacuum my flat myself!

Overall, I had a great time at the conference. Yes, the location could have been more accessible, but don't forget that they hold it in different countries every year. I attended some really good lectures and workshops, although the latter were a bit beyond me as far as my technical knowledge goes. What made it so special, though, and why I'd encourage everyone to try and go, is that you have a wonderful opportunity to make contacts. The conference attracts people from all over the world, so it's an ideal place to meet other people in the industry.

I feel so inspired after this experience that I might just start a company here in the UK! In the meantime, if anyone is interested in joining the interest group I've just set up, where we meet once a month to discuss new smart home technologies, please let me know at the end of the lecture and I'll sign you up to the newsletter!

4 Elicit the smart technologies that were mentioned in the listening and write them on the board. If students are struggling, refer them to the audioscript on page 242, asking them to find the smart technologies mentioned and call them out. Once you have put the students into groups, tell them that in addition to smart technologies their ideal home would feature, they should also discuss those they would avoid and why. For example, a student may say they would avoid using a smart assistant because they are concerned about the security of their personal data.

Grammar SB page 143

Causative *have* and *get*

▶ **Page 181 Grammar reference**

Lead in

With Student's books closed, write the following two sentences on the board: *Jonas has had his hair cut; Jonas has cut his hair.* Put students into pairs and ask them to briefly discuss the difference between the two sentences. If they are struggling, ask them to consider who cut Jonas' hair. After a few minutes, elicit or tell the class: *In the first sentence someone else (probably a hairdresser or barber) cut Jonas' hair; in the second, Jonas cut his own hair.* Ask students: *When was the last time you had your hair cut?* and elicit a few examples from the class, correcting errors by pointing to the board and asking *Who cut your hair?*

1 Students work individually. Monitor and support weaker students. As you monitor consider how much support the class need for this grammar point. Once you have elicited the answers, either ask the students to raise their hands if they answered incorrectly; or, if you think the students would be uncomfortable admitting this, gauge the students' level from the monitoring you did earlier and allow them time to read the information in the Grammar reference on page 181 as necessary.

Answers
1 B **2** A **2** A, B **3** experts / professionals

Fast finishers

If you find the students' levels are mixed, allow stronger students to complete this activity whilst the others read the information in the Grammar reference on page 181. Tell students you are going to write three professions on the board, and they must write a causative *have/get* sentence for each. If students are unsure, give them this example: (electrician) *I need to have/get my lights looked at as the bulbs keep flickering.* Then write on the board: *Teacher / Decorator / Optician.* Encourage students to write their completed sentences on the board so that you can discuss them during whole-class feedback, eliciting error corrections from the class rather than correcting them yourself.

2 Students work in pairs. Allow weaker students to refer to the Grammar reference on page 181. Put students into different pairs to compare their answers before you elicit them from the class.

Answers
1 to have/get (your passport) renewed **2** had/got (a tooth) pulled out **3** having/getting (the house) painted **4** have/get (it) cut down **5** have/get (it) extended **6** has/gets (all his meals) delivered

3 Encourage students to work individually, and set a time limit of five minutes. When the time is up, allow students to compare their answers in pairs before you elicit them. Encourage corrections from others in the class, rather than providing them yourself.

Answers
1 had my bag stolen while **2** is having/getting his picture taken **3** have/get her hair dyed **4** his application turned down by

Reading and Use of English Part 2 SB page 144

1 First, refer students to the photos at the bottom of the page. Remind them that this home was included in Starting off (on page 140) and ask what words or phrases they can remember using to describe it. Write them on the board as students call them out (*cosy, compact*, etc.). Then put students into pairs to answer the questions, encouraging them to use the words and phrases on the board as they do so. When eliciting answers to question 2, encourage students to use a range of words to talk about benefits and drawbacks, e.g. *positives, (on the) plus side, advantage, strong point; negatives, downside, disadvantage, weak point.*

> Read the exam advice with the students. At this stage of the course, students should be aware of the grammatical items being tested. However, if not, elicit examples of any terms they are unsure about. For example, relative pronouns: *which, whose, who, whom,* etc.; possessive adjectives: *my, your, his, her,* etc.
>
> **Exam advice**

2 Read the rubric with the students and ask them to work individually. Set a time limit of around eight minutes. Allow students to compare their answers in pairs before you elicit them from the class. Once you have done this, refer students to previous Reading and Use of English Part 2 tasks in Units 1, 6 and 10. Ask them to compare the number of questions they answered correctly and note down any grammatical items which consistently cause them difficulties. Finally, put them into groups to briefly share their individual observations before coming up with two things each group member could do to improve their performance. Elicit ideas from the class.

Answers
1 are **2** of **3** as **4** yourself **5** such **6** only **7** due **8** all

3 Allow students a few minutes to read the task. Point out that it is a good idea if they tackle the task by working through one room at a time before they consider the house as a whole. Groups which are creative may like to have paper and coloured pens on which to draw the design for their house; others may prefer to record their ideas using mind maps or to make detailed bullet-pointed notes. Whichever way each group prefers to work, tell them they have twenty minutes to discuss and design their tiny home and that when the time is up, they will need to come to the front of the class and present at least two space-saving design ideas for each room of the house.

Grammar SB page 144

Expressing obligation and permission

▶ **Page 181 Grammar reference**

1 Read the rubric with the students. If any of your students have stayed with a host family, ask them to share their experiences regarding house rules. As students complete the task, monitor for example sentences which include grammatical errors with language to talk about obligation and permission (*should, must,* (*don't*) *have to, supposed to,* etc.) and write them on the board. After a few minutes, stop the students and elicit example lists from the class, adding those with grammatical errors to the sentences you wrote during monitoring. If students call out error corrections at this stage, amend them but if not, leave them uncorrected until after students have completed Exercise 2.

2 Allow weaker students to work in pairs. Once you have elicited the answers, refer students to the Grammar reference on pages 181 and 182 if they are still unsure.

Answers
1
a I have to **b** I can't; They won't let me **c** I can; They let me
2 b

3 Read the rubric with the students and allow them a moment to quickly re-read sentences A–F. Remind them of the dangers of word spotting, before playing the recording once. Put students into pairs to compare their answers before eliciting them from the class. As you elicit, encourage students to say what they heard which helped them to choose the correct option. For example, for question 1 a student should have heard Miguel say, *I can't stay out too late …* which matches with option D, *I'm supposed to be back home early.* If students are struggling, you can play the recording a second time. However, note that you will play it again in Exercise 4 when students will listen for distractors.

Answers
1 D **2** E **3** C **4** B **5** A

Track 61

Antonia: So, what's your host family like, Miguel? Are they friendly?

Miguel: Yeah, they're great fun, especially the mum. She's always making jokes and suggesting interesting things to do. And she's got a couple of daughters my age who never stop laughing! The house is always full of their friends too, so it's like a permanent party, and that's great for my social life. The only drawback is that I can't stay out too late because they all have to be up early the next morning. I don't have to do anything around the house or things like that – though I do help from time to time, just to fit in and make things easier for them. What about you, Irene?

Irene: You sound really lucky with your family, Miguel. I haven't got any complaints, but my family certainly isn't as much fun as yours. I mean, they didn't let me invite a couple of friends to dinner the other day. They told me it just wasn't convenient and I can see that's not unreasonable – it is their house, after all. And anyway, it's not always like that. For example, the other day when I wanted to go down to the seaside for the day, they actually lent me their car. I thought that was really nice of them and very trusting. I mean, I've only just passed my test! Are you living with a nice family, Martyna?

Martyna: Well, we have our ups and downs. The other day, my host told me off because I'd got home a bit late and missed the family dinner. Apparently, I was supposed to phone to say I wasn't coming. Then when I went to see if there was anything left over in the fridge, I got into trouble again. She told me I couldn't just help myself to things without asking her first.

Miguel: So, what did you do? Walk out?

Martyna: No! I apologised for being late and explained that I had to finish some project work at school. She calmed down and said, 'Never mind,' and then she helped me to cook a really nice meal. So we were all friends again.

Nikolai: Great. Still, all your families sound really nice to me.
Martyna: Isn't yours, Nikolai?
Nikolai: Well, they're all right, I suppose. Not very tidy, which is one thing I would complain about. I'm not the tidiest person myself, but I think they're just taking advantage of homestay students by saying that anyone staying in their home must do their share around the house – you know, like clearing up a bit, doing a bit of the hoovering, a bit of the cooking. I needn't clean the bathroom or do any shopping, fortunately, because I wouldn't have the time. But I doubt if they'd let me have my friends in for dinner or anything like that. Not like you, Antonia.
Antonia: Well, I'm lucky. Martyna, you've been round for dinner and so has Nikolai. I had to buy the food and cook it, of course, and they don't allow me to have big parties, but a couple of friends is OK. And they join in too, which makes it really interesting because we have ... I don't know ... like a sort of international evening. It's quite good fun. And I cook traditional Sicilian food, which makes a change for everyone.
Miguel: It sounds as if we're all quite lucky, then. Not like a friend of mine who went back to Peru last year.

4 Students match the sentences to the speakers in pairs before listening again to check their answers. Elicit answers and corrections in whole-class feedback.

Answers
1 Miguel **2** Antonia **3** Antonia **4** Martyna **5** Irene **6** Nikolai

5 Elicit the first phrase *I can* from sentence A (Exercise 2) and categorise it with the students before asking them to work individually to complete the task. As an alternative, put the students into groups and give each group a board pen. Write the table on the board, elicit the first phrase and write it under the correct category. Then allow students a few minutes to underline the phrases before inviting groups to come to the board and complete the table. Encourage students to cross out and 'move' any phrase they think has been categorised incorrectly by another group. Once the class are happy the phrases have been categorised correctly, correct errors and add omissions as necessary.

Answers
obligation (present): I must, I'm supposed to, I have to
obligation (past): I had to, I was supposed to
prohibition (present): I can't, I'm not allowed to, They won't let me, They don't allow me to
prohibition (past): They didn't let me
permission (present): I can, They let me
no obligation (present): I don't have to, I needn't

6 Read the rubric with the students. As this is an exam style task, tell students to work individually and set a time limit of around five minutes. When the time is up, put students into pairs to compare their answers, before eliciting them from the class.

Answers
1 not allow him **2** don't have to **3** am/'m supposed to take **4** are not/aren't allowed (to go) **5** to let Amy borrow **6** not let us use

Speaking Part 2 SB page 146

▶ **Page 206 Speaking bank**

Read the exam advice with the students. Point out that if they spend a few moments thinking about what they want to say before they start, it may help them to organise their thoughts and produce a more comprehensive answer. Also remind them that if they ask the examiner to repeat the intructions, they will not lose marks.

Exam advice

1 Read the rubric with the students. Put them into pairs and ask them to close their Student's Books. Write three headings on the board: *topic words and phrases*; *language to compare and contrast*; *language to speculate*. Tell them they have five minutes to brainstorm five words or phrases for each heading. If they are unsure about the first heading, tell them to think about the vocabulary from Starting off and from the Vocabulary section of this unit but do not elicit any target language or provide additional support. As students are working, write down examples of target language from pages 140 and 142 (e.g. *quiet, peaceful location*) and from Speaking bank page 207 (e.g. *whereas, I guess they probably, They must be ...*) After five minutes, or once students have run out of ideas, stop them and invite pairs to write their phrases on the board, adding your own phrases if necessary. Finally, elicit error corrections from the class. If possible, leave the phrases on the board until after students have completed Exercise 3.

2 Put students into different pairs from Exercise 1 and allow them to use an English dictionary to look up any new vocabulary. Once you have elicited the answers, and if the phrases from Exercise 1 are still on the board, add the vocabulary under the heading: *topic words and phrases*.

Answers
Photo 1: close to nature, fresh air, organic food, a rural setting
Photo 2: hi-tech, sophisticated entertainment, pollution
Both photos: environment, maintain a lifestyle, occupants, spend quality time, social life

3 Read the rubric with the students. At this stage of the course, the students should have a feel for how long a minute is, but if not, monitor and encourage students who dry up too soon to continue speaking.

4 Read the rubric with the students and allow them time to read the checklist items. Tell students you will play the recording twice. The first time they listen they should mark the checklist items true or false. The second time they listen, they should write down examples they hear of the following: topic vocabulary (words or phrases); language to compare and contrast; language to speculate. Once you have elicited answers to the true or false questions, elicit examples of the target language (e.g. *traditional country cottage, smart luxury flat, peaceful, organic food; whereas, on the other hand; I guess, It must be, the people … probably have*)

Answers
1 F **2** T **3** T **4** T **5** T **6** T **7** T **8** F **9** F

Track 62

Examiner: Peter, it's your turn first. Here are your photographs. They show two different places to live. I'd like you to compare the photographs and say what you think it is like for the people to live in each of these places. All right?

Peter: OK. The first photo shows a traditional country cottage with the occupants, a family, standing in the garden where they grow their own vegetables, whereas the second photo shows a young family living in a smart luxury flat with a view of the city. I guess both photos show a lifestyle which the people have chosen and which they like, so for both families it must be very pleasant to live where they do. Living in the country cottage must be very peaceful, with very little stress, no pollution and plenty of physical work, healthy organic food and fresh air. On the other hand, living in the city flat might be quite exciting because you're at the centre of things, with entertainment and friends close by. I think the first photo shows a way of life where money and success in your career are not so important as being close to nature and the countryside. The people living in this sort of environment probably have plenty of time to spend together. The family in the second photo must need to earn quite a lot of money to maintain their lifestyle, which is probably busier and more stressful.

Examiner: Thank you. Tania, which place would you choose to live in?

Tania: I'd choose the city flat because I can only fulfil my ambitions in a city, so I'd have to live there as well.

Examiner: Thank you. Now, here are your photographs. They show …

/P/ Pronunciation: linking (2)

5 Read the information with the students. If they are unsure about linking, write a short sentence on the board that includes two or three examples of the target linking. For example, *I /j/ am going to /w/ Australia after the /j/ exam*. Say the sentence, emphasising the consonant sounds before drilling the sentence with the students.

5.1 Play the recording twice before putting students into pairs to compare their answers.

Answers
a - y /j/ b - r /r/ c - w /w/

Track 63

See page 147 of Student's Book for audioscript.

5.2 As an alternative to reading out loud in pairs, and if students have access to personal recording devices, ask them to take turns recording themselves reading the phrases. Once they have done this, ask them to listen and compare their recording with their partner's, repeating the exercise if they think the consonant sounds are not pronounced clearly.

5.3 Read the rubric with the students. Point out that when two vowel sounds meet, as in, *the /j/ occupants*, we typically insert an extra /j/ /w/ /r/ sound. Elicit from the students what consonant sound is added in the first gap (/r/) before asking students to work individually. Encourage them to read the sentences out loud as they work. Monitor and listen for students who are producing the target pronunciation so they can model the pronunciation in the next exercise. After a few minutes, put students into pairs to compare their answers, completing any outstanding gaps together, before they listen.

Answers
1 further-r-away; the-y-old **2** he-y-ever-r-answer
3 Our-r-aunt; stay-y-at; now-w-and **4** fewer-r-and; our-r-area are-r-open **5** Many-y-of; busy-y-and **6** The-y-end; more-r-exciting

Track 64

See page 147 of Student's Book for audioscript.

5.4 Select one or two stronger students, who you identified when monitoring in Exercise 5.3, to read the sentences before students complete the activity. Alternatively, if your students are weaker on this point, drill the sentences beforehand.

5.5 Students work individually. First ask them to write three sentences, reminding them to include topic related words and phrases, language to make comparisons and language to speculate. Monitor and support weaker students by silently pointing to the parts of the sentence where linking with /w/ /r/ /j/ occurs. Once they have done this, ask them to read their sentences out loud to themselves and annotate them with linking consonants /w/ /r/ /j/. Then put the students into pairs and tell them to take turns reading their sentences out loud, helping each other to make corrections as necessary. Monitor and write down examples of correct linking production you hear. Select stronger students to say their sentences to the class before drilling a few examples with the whole class.

6 Read the rubric with the students. As students will pair with someone who chose the other task in the next exercise, point out they should choose one task between them and not one task per person. If you think all the pairs will choose the same task, allocate task A to half the pairs and task B to the other half. Point out that as this is exam practice, they should not write anything down. After a few minutes, stop the students.

7 Allow students a minute to swap partners and encourage them to work with someone with whom they are less familiar. Monitor and write down examples of correct and incorrect target language and pronunciation production. Once all students have spoken, select a few stronger students to repeat the activity to the class before praising the students for the correct examples you heard and eliciting error correction.

Writing Part 2 (an article) SB page 148

▶ **Page 196 Writing bank**

Exam advice

Read the exam advice with the students. Point to the last bullet point. Then ask the students to re-read the articles they wrote for Unit 2 and Unit 7. As they do this, tell them to consider the advice in the last bullet point, and write down two or three examples of mistakes they repeatedly make. Encourage them to use the article checklist in the Writing bank, page 203 to help categorise their errors. For example, did they cover the bullet points in the task for one, both or neither of their articles? If neither, this may be an example of a mistake they often make. Students could also consider grammatical accuracy, e.g. their use of articles or prepositions. After around five to ten minutes, stop the students, put them into pairs and ask them to take turns telling each other what they believe their common mistakes are.

1 Students will not spend time analysing the question at this stage as they will do this in Exercise 3. Point out that during the discussion they should aim to use target words and phrases from the unit (e.g. *good transport links* page 140; *an area with green spaces*, page 142). After five minutes, elicit ideas from the class, encouraging students to justify their ideas with reasons and examples.

2 Read the rubric and bullet points with the students. Tell students they should take turns to speak for one minute each and should include at least five target words and phrases (see Exercise 1). Tell the student who is listening that as well as thinking of questions, they should also write down examples of the target language they hear and give feedback after their questions have been answered. Monitor and listen for correct and incorrect examples of target language. During whole-class feedback, praise the students for the correct examples you heard and elicit error corrections.

3 Allow students a few minutes to work individually and consider their ideas before putting them into pairs to discuss the questions. During the discussion, encourage students to make notes. Monitor and identify stronger students. During whole-class feedback, select some of the stronger students you identified when monitoring to present their ideas to the class. Elicit any corrections from the class rather than providing them yourself.

Answers
1 readers of the college magazine, i.e. other students, teachers, etc. **2** informal **3** conditional with *would* – it asks you to imagine your ideal home **4** the type of house, its location and features of the house **5** by surprising the reader, by saying interesting things about yourself

4 Students work individually. Allow students a few minutes to read the sample answer and consider their own ideas. Tell them that for question 2 they should find and underline examples in the answer that tell them the candidate has answered each main point in the task. After around five minutes, stop the students and put them into pairs to compare their ideas before you elicit them from the class.

Suggested answers
1 Students' own answers **2** Yes – type of house: small, stylish, modern flat in a historic building; location: Barcelona or Bologna, conveniently close to the centre; features: cosy bedroom, handy kitchen, balcony, etc.

5 Remind students of the importance of writing a plan (it helps them write a more comprehensive answer) before they complete the activity in pairs. When eliciting the answers, encourage students to paraphrase and summarise, rather than read from the sample answer word for word.

Answers
Paragraph 1: Type of flat and location; My present accommodation; Advantages of ideal flat
Paragraph 2: Characteristics of flat
Paragraph 3: Conclusion: room for my things

6 Point out that this task is similar to Reading and Use of English Part 2 (open cloze). Remind them to look carefully at the words before and after the gap and elicit the type of words they are tested on in Part 2, (e.g. parts of verbs, prepositions, relative pronouns). As this is an exam-style task, tell students to work individually and set a time limit of five to eight minutes. When eliciting the answers during whole-class feedback, ask students to say and spell the answer, referring them to the exam advice on page 144 and reminding them of the importance of using the correct spelling.

Answers
1 from **2** where **3** own **4** what/whatever/ anything
5 have **6** few **7** long **8** If

7 Read the rubric with the students and refer them to the article in Exercise 4. Tell them they should find and underline examples in the text for the statements they think are true and making a note of why they identify any

as false. Elicit examples during whole-class feedback. For example, for question 1, ask students to call out examples of adjectives used (e.g. *small*, *stylish*, *modern*, *historic*) and for question 3, elicit or tell students why the writer does not mention all the furniture they would need (if they write long lists of items they will not use a sufficient grammatical range and their writing will be less interesting).

Answers
1 T **2** T **3** F **4** T (She would like to live alone and make her own decisions, she likes history, culture and reading, she wants an active social life.) **5** T **6** F (She lives in a suburban house.)

8 Read the rubric with the students and allow them time to read the bullet points. Before they start, and if you chose to do the exam advice activity, remind students to consider the two or three mistakes they identified at the start of this section. Point out that in addition to working through each bullet point, they should also try and improve at least one of their common mistakes. Set a time limit of forty minutes.

Extension activity
Put students into pairs and ask them to swap their answers from Exercise 8. Refer them to the statements in Exercise 7. Ask them to find and underline examples in their partner's article for statements, 1,2, 4 and 5. If they cannot find an example, tell them to think of one for their partner and write it down. For example, if a student cannot find between five and ten adjectives in their partner's writing, they should look for nouns where suitable adjectives could have been included. So, if a student's article says, *My dream home is an apartment in the city centre* their partner could write down adjectives *open-plan* or *cosy*, which could have been included before the word *apartment* and the adjectives *buzzy* or *lively* or *colourful* which could have been included before the words *city centre*. Once students have done this, tell them to take turns giving each other feedback before eliciting examples from the class.

Vocabulary

Words and phrases to describe your home

allocated car park spaces
balcony
bright
central location
cosy and compact
en-suite bathroom
fully furnished
garden
good transport links
local amenities
modern fittings
open-plan
peaceful
patio
quiet
recently refurbished
residential area
spacious
terrace

Commonly confused words

space, place, room, area, location, square

Vocabulary activity 1

This is a whole-class activity. Students are divided into two teams. One person from each team (the player) comes to the front of the class and sits with their back to the board. Tell the players they are not allowed to look at the board. Write one word or phrase on the board from the vocabulary list. The team members must describe the word without saying it. Encourage them to describe the words or phrases rather than use synonyms (see example below). The players must guess what it is, using the clues given, and say the word out loud. A point is given to the first player to say the correct word. A point is deducted if the team 'accidentally' say the word written on the board. For example, if you have written *balcony* on the board, the team members may say, *It is attached to side of your home, usually on the outside*; *it is not a garden, but it is outside space*; *it must be higher up than the ground floor*.

Vocabulary activity 2

Ask the students to prepare a bingo card with nine squares that are big enough to fit two words in each.
Then write on the board, *hiding*, *reception*, *standing*, *meeting*, *floor*, *play*, *spare*, *parking*, *picnic*, *office*, *personal*, *green*. Ask students to choose nine words and write them on their card. Tell the students you will say words which collocate with the words on the board: these should include the target language *place*, *room*, *space*, *area*, *location* and *square*. When the student hears a word which they think collocates with one (or more) on their card, they write that word under the word they have written. When they have matched all the words, they shout bingo. The first person you hear shout needs to do two things. First, they will give you their nine collocations which must be correct, then they must give you three error free sentences using the collocations correctly. If any of the collocations or sentences are incorrect, you will move to the next student who shouted bingo until there is a winner.

DIGITAL CLASSROOM

Practice Extra Unit 13

Test Generator Unit 13 test

Test and Train Exam Practice

14 Fiesta!

Unit objectives

Topic: festivals and celebrations

Reading and Use of English Part 6 (gapped text): checking the text before and after the gap fits the chosen answer

Reading and Use of English Part 3 (word formation): recognising when negative prefixes and plural forms are required

Writing Part 1 (essay): *it, this, that,* and *they* for reference

Listening Part 4 (multiple choice): using the options to predict what you might hear

Speaking Parts 3 and 4 (collaborative task and discussion): strategies for working with a partner

Pronunciation: improving fluency

Vocabulary: vocabulary for festivals; suffixes to form nouns for people

Grammar: the passive

Starting off SB page 150

1 Read the rubric with the students. Allow them time to read the words in the box and elicit the meaning of any new vocabulary, pointing out the difference between any which could be confused, e.g. *commemorate* and *celebrate* (*commemorate*: showing respect to the memory of an important person or event in the past; *celebrate*: doing something for a special occasion, e.g. eating a special meal at a wedding). Alternatively, encourage students to use the context in questions 1–8 to help them understand the meaning of any new vocabulary and concept check during whole-class feedback (e.g. *Do you commemorate or celebrate your birthday every year?*).

Answers
1 celebrate **2** dress up; perform **3** march; commemorate
4 hold **5** play **6** gather round **7** let off **8** wearing

2 Put students into different pairs to complete this task. Point out that the words and phrases can be used more than once.

Answers
Photo A: traditional costumes; parade
Photo B: fireworks
Photo C: traditional costumes; bands
Photo D: street parties
Photo E: traditional costumes; street performers
Photo F: street performers; disguises

3 Read the rubric with the students. Remind them to use the words and phrases from Exercises 1 and 2 and encourage them to use language to speculate (e.g. *It looks as if, They must be, They're probably* – see Speaking bank page 207, Exercise 6). Monitor and write down correct and incorrect examples of the target language you hear. During whole-class feedback, select stronger students to answer the questions in front of the class. Note: the photos were taken in the following countries (and cities): A Australia (Melbourne); B Canada (Toronto); C Scotland (Huntly); D UK (London); E Mexico (Jalisco); F Germany (Berlin).

4 Give students a few minutes to read the rubric and bullet points and prepare their ideas. Then put them into threes (A, B, C). Remind them that they may be asked questions about celebrations in Speaking Part 1 of the exam. Then tell Student A to ask Student B the questions. As Student B answers, Student C should listen and write down four examples of words or phrases from Exercises 1 and 2. Once Student B has answered all three questions, Student C should give feedback before the students swap roles. The students continue until each student has taken each role.

Listening Part 4 SB page 150

Exam advice

Read the exam advice with the students. Remind them that as well as listening for the speaker to finish talking about a topic, they should also put a line through any options which they know are definitely incorrect as they listen.

1 Allow students time to read the rubric and bullets before putting them into pairs or small groups to discuss. Point out that when discussing the third bullet point, students should consider both the positive and negative aspects of having this job. Monitor and support weaker students. After around five minutes, stop the students and elicit ideas from the class.

Background information
Stand-up comedy is usually performed in front of a live audience by one solo artist. It is thought to have originated in the United States in the 19th century with comic humourists and writers, like Mark Twain, who toured the country at that time. Stand-up comics often draw from their personal experiences or observations for their material and can spend many years studying the art of comedy and mastering their craft.

2 Read the rubric with the students. Remind them that they will have one minute to read the questions before the recording starts so it is important that they utilise the time effectively. Then give them one minute to read the question stems and either make notes in the margin or underline the main points before you play the recording. After you have played the recording twice, allow the students to compare their answers in pairs or small groups. When eliciting the answers, encourage students to justify their choices and say why the incorrect options are incorrect.

Answers
1 B **2** B **3** B **4** C **5** C **6** A **7** A

Track 65

Interviewer: My guest today is comedian Harry McDonald. Welcome, Harry. So, you're currently in the middle of a tour – how's it going so far?

Harry: It's enjoyable and exhausting at the same time. I spend most of the day revising my act and tailoring the jokes for the town or city I'm playing in. I know a lot of comedians write generic material that's applicable to all audiences but, to be honest, I find that lacks the personal touch. It does make things a little trickier, mind, but it's totally worth it when a joke I've just told is met with roars of laughter from the audience – which admittedly, doesn't happen every time.

Interviewer: What made you get into comedy in the first place?

Harry: When I was eighteen, my friends and I went to an open mic night, which is a live show where anyone is allowed to perform on stage. I'd always been the class clown at school. You know, that one person who could put a smile on your face no matter what. So, after a few acts, one of my friends turned to me and suggested that I give it a go. I thought, 'OK, what have I got to lose?' and up I went. Ten minutes later, I was hooked and I knew I had to pursue a career in it.

Interviewer: How did your life change after you won the best new comedian award all those years ago?

Harry: The phone never stopped ringing! I was being asked to do live shows, one-off specials, everything! The thing is, when you're thrust into the limelight like that – you know, appearing in newspaper articles and magazines – people start to build you up as some sort of comic genius. The pressure's immense. Then, when you don't deliver, it seems the whole world is queuing up to have a go at you. I mean I was used to the odd troll online, but this was something else.

Interview: And that led to you taking a bit of time off, right?

Harry: Yes. Three months to be exact. When you're on tour, you don't really get a minute to switch off and observe what's around you – and that's where you find inspiration for comedy. I was writing every day until eventually I had enough material for a new show. I sent copies to all my friends, relatives, basically anyone I could get hold of and used their feedback to make it as good as it could possibly be. Before long, I was back on tour.

Interviewer: Speaking of family, you often reference your parents in your live shows. What do they make of your career?

Harry: Ohhh, my parents ... to be fair I've written so many jokes about them over the years that I'm surprised they're still talking to me! They're forever sending me articles from the local newspaper that they think would be good to include in my act – they just love to help in any way they can. I think it's because they've secretly dreamt of doing the same thing as me, even though they're well into their seventies, just so they can embarrass me as much as I've embarrassed them.

Interviewer: One of your career highlights was when you were asked to perform at the Royal Variety Performance. How did that feel?

Harry: Unbelievable. When my agent called to say that I'd been personally selected by the Prince, I thought he was winding me up at first. It's certainly something I look back on with a great sense of pride. I was nervous, though. I kept thinking what would happen if the royals didn't laugh at my jokes. Thankfully they did, along with the rest of the audience, and I gained about half a million extra followers on social media as a result.

Interviewer: Finally, what advice do you have for aspiring comedians?

Harry: Well, it's a really competitive industry, so you'll need to come up with an act that helps you stand out from the crowd. Some people get their foot in the door by writing jokes for other, more established comedians, which is good for networking, while others try to find fame online. One thing's for certain, though: a lot of the success is down to having the right people around you to organise shows, set ticket prices – that sort of thing – leaving you to concentrate on writing the jokes!

Interviewer: Thanks Harry. That's all from us today ...

Extension activity
Refer students to the audioscript on page 244 and ask them to find and underline words and phrases which could be used when discussing Exercise 1 on page 151. For example, *roars with laughter* for answering the second point, *one-off special* for the first and, *thrust into the limelight, the pressure's immense* for the third. After a few minutes, put students into pairs to compare their ideas, allowing them to check any unknown words or phrases in an English dictionary as they do so. Next, tell the students to briefly discuss the questions in Exercise 1 again, this time using the words and phrases they underlined where appropriate (e.g. *The funniest show I've ever seen was a one-off special called ... It made me roar with laughter ...*)

3 Read the rubric with the students and encourage them to give reasons and examples to support their ideas. If you chose to do the extension activity, remind them to use the words and phrases they underlined in the audioscript where appropriate. Monitor and write down examples of correct and incorrect language use. During whole-class feedback, invite students to share their ideas before praising them for the correct examples you heard and eliciting error corrections.

Grammar SB page 152

The passive

▶ **Page 182 Grammar reference**

Lead in

Write the following two sentences on the board: a) *Someone found my new coat in the classroom;* b) *My new coat was found in the classroom.* Elicit which sentence is active (a) and which passive (b). Then invite a student to come to the board and underline, or call out the passive verb in sentence b (*was found*). Point out that we use the passive form to change the focus of a sentence. Say that in the above example, the active sentence focuses on *someone;* whereas the passive sentence focuses on *finding the new coat.* Then elicit why the passive sentence might be preferred in this example (because the person who found the coat is unknown or because finding the coat is more important than the person who found it).

1 Students work individually before comparing their answers in pairs. Monitor and support weaker students by encouraging them to look for a form of the verb *be* followed by the past participle.

Answers
a where anyone <u>is allowed</u> to perform on stage **b** I <u>was being asked</u> to do live shows **c** when you <u>were asked</u> to perform **d** to say that <u>I'd been personally selected by the Prince</u>

2 Once students have answered the question, ask them to check their answers by referring to the information in the Grammar reference on page 183 before eliciting them from the class.

Suggested answers
1 d **2** c **3** a **4** b

3 Read the rubric with the students and ask them to work individually. As students often incorrectly change the form of the verb when forming the passive, remind them that it is only the form of *be* (or *get*) that changes; the verb (e.g. *found, select, stole*) is always in the past participle. After around five minutes, stop the students and allow them to compare their answers in pairs, completing any that they have not had time to finish, before eliciting the correct answers.

Answers
1 was founded in 1904 **2** has been stolen **3** is being repaired **4** 've been given a place on the course **5** would have been told off (by the teacher)

4 These are real candidate errors so once you have elicited the answers, tell the students to asterisk (*) any questions they answered incorrectly. They can write correct examples in their note books under the heading *common errors,* and refer to their notes when they are revising for the exam.

Answers
1 ~~might be owned~~ might have been owned
2 ~~was going to replace~~ was going to be replaced
3 ~~that is going to be read on the radio a short story by Agatha Christie:~~ that a short story by Agatha Christie is going to be read on the radio
4 ~~if the computer wasn't invented~~ if the computer hadn't been invented
5 ~~has already published~~ has already been published
6 ~~have been using~~ have been used
7 ~~nobody wants to be revealed their private life in public~~ nobody wants their private life to be revealed in public

Fast finishers

Write the following sentences on the board. Put students into pairs and ask them to discuss the questions, using the passive form where possible.

Which festivals are visited most in your city or country?
What food is usually eaten at these festivals?
It's been said that festivals are important for conserving traditions. Do you agree?

During whole-class feedback, select students to share their ideas, encouraging the use of passive sentences, e.g. *(X) is visited by large numbers of people ...*

5 Read the rubric with the students and set a time limit of one minute for them to complete this task. When eliciting the answer, encourage students to paraphrase rather than read directly from the text.

Answers
People go out in the open air in the early morning; young men swim in the Nile; they eat traditional foods.

6 Students work individually before comparing their answers in pairs or threes. When comparing, encourage students to discuss any answers they do not agree on, giving reasons to support their choices.

Answers
1 are **2** as **3** been **4** to **5** is **6** being **7** by **8** have **9** doing **10** were (Note: fish can be singular or plural, depending on the context.)

7 Read the rubric with the students and allow them time to read the example sentence and questions (1, 2, 3) carefully before they work in pairs to complete the task. Alternatively, if students are overwhelmed by the passive with reporting verbs, tell them to complete question 1 and elicit the answer before asking them to complete question 2 and so on. The Grammar reference on page 183 covers this point in detail, so give students time to refer to this if they need support.

Answers
1 a
2 A large number of contemporary Egyptian traditions are said to have their origins in very ancient times.
For example, offerings of fish are believed to have been made to the ancient gods ...

> **3** It is said that a large number of contemporary Egyptian traditions have their origins in very ancient times. For example, it is believed that offerings of fish were made to the ancient gods.

8 Remind students that they must use the words given and tell them to work individually. Monitor and support weaker students. During feedback, invite students to write their sentences on the board and conduct peer correction from the whole class, praising students for accurate sentences and providing error corrections for any that are still incorrect.

> **Answers**
> **1** It is thought that Sham el Nessím marked the start of the spring festival in ancient Egypt. **2** It is known that eating salted fish was a custom of the ancient Egyptians. **3** Five thousand people are reported to have joined in the festivities. **4** Our festival is said to have the best fireworks in the world.

9 As this is an exam-style task, ask students to work individually and set a time limit of around six to eight minutes. Remind them, however, that in the exam they will be tested on a range of grammatical and lexical structures.

> **Answers**
> **1** is believed to have originated **2** expected to be chosen **3** said that the festival is **4** is thought to be **5** is considered to be **6** to go/date back more than

Reading and Use of English Part 6 SB page 154

1 Allow students a few minutes to complete the quiz. Point out that teams should try to reach agreement when selecting options for questions 1, 3 and 4. After eliciting the answers, ask students which answers most surprised them and why, and if time allows, encourage students to come up with one or two creative ideas for recycling tents and materials for costumes using the passive form, e.g. *Tents could be repaired and donated to charity, tent material could be made into something else* (e.g *a kite*), *metal tent pegs could be made into jewellery*.

> **Answers**
> **1** b **2** plastic bottles, tents, materials from costumes **3** c **4** b **5** onsite recycling sites, deposits for reusable cups, water pipes for refilling water bottles

2 Ask students to raise their hand if they have any additional ideas they wish to share, encouraging them to give full responses using the passive form where appropriate, especially when talking about reducing waste, plastic, etc. (see examples in Exercise 1).

> **Exam advice**
> Invite a student to read the exam advice to the class. Point out that as the sentence after the gap must follow on logically from the sentence they have selected, checking the words before the gaps but neglecting those after can cause them to select the wrong option.

3 Read the rubric with the students. This activity works best if it is divided into two parts. First, tell the students to read the text quite quickly, writing the topic of each paragraph in the margin as they do so. Remind them that often, but not always, the topic is introduced in the first sentence of a paragraph (the topic sentence). Once students have done this, elicit the answers to the first bullet point before moving on. Next, read the second bullet point with the students and draw their attention to the underlined word *unfortunately*. Then elicit how this word might refer to the missing sentence (it suggests something negative). When eliciting the answers to the second bullet point, ask students to say how they think the words or phrases they underlined refer to the missing sentences.

> **Suggested answers**
> Paragraph 2: How festivals can damage the environment
> Paragraph 3: The concept of green festivals
> Paragraph 4: Reducing waste and traffic emissions
> Paragraph 5: Reusing clothing
> Paragraph 6: Lessons for festival organisers

4 Allow students a minute to re-read the exam advice. Tell them to work individually and set a time limit of between fifteen and twenty minutes. Elicit the answers from the class.

> **Answers**
> **1** C **2** D **3** B **4** A **5** G **6** F

5 Remind students to check that the words after the gap logically lead on from the sentences they have selected and allow them a few minutes to make changes before eliciting the answers.

> **Extension activity**
> Put students into groups and tell them to justify why each answer is correct or incorrect, paying particular attention to the words after the gap. This works well if students have come up with different answers to the same question. For example, a student may have incorrectly connected the words *travel to festivals by car* and *increased pollution … surrounding area* before gap 2 with the words *more public transport … in order to reduce the impact of vehicle transmissions* in sentence A; while other group members may be able to point out that *plastic drinks cups, water bottles …* after gap 2 does not logically lead on from this and that the correct sentence for gap 2 is D, where *And then there is all of the waste that they produce* introduces the following list of examples of a different source of impact.

6 Allow students a few minutes to read the bullet points and consider their ideas before putting them into pairs to discuss the questions. During whole-class feedback, encourage students to give examples and reasons to support their ideas.

Reading and Use of English Part 3 SB page 155

Read the exam advice with the students. Remind them that identifying the form of nearby verbs and paying attention to the use of articles (*a, the*) will help them decide if they need a plural or singular form of a noun and that linking words and phrases, e.g. *however, at first*, will help give them a sense of the text around the gap and whether a positive or negative form is required.

Exam advice

1 Read the rubric with the students and tell them to work individually. When eliciting the answers, ask how students know the answers are plural nouns (the plural verb form *have* and the phrase *a number of* for question 1; the lack of articles *a* or *the* for question 2).

Answers
1 organisers **2** designers

2 Allow students a few minutes to work individually before putting them into pairs. For weaker students, elicit common noun suffixes for people, e.g. *-ist, -ant, -or, -er*, before they start the activity.

Answers
1 tourist **2** novelist **3** researcher **4** collector **5** survivor **6** consultant **7** motorist **8** comedian **9** salesman/saleswoman/salesperson **10** specialist **11** refugee

3 Read the rubric with the students. Remind them that as this is an exam task they should work individually, and set a time limit of around eight to ten minutes. As question 1 is an example of a plural form and question 4 a negative prefix (mentioned in the exam advice on page 155), during whole-class feedback elicit how they knew these forms were required. (question 1: the plural verb form *begin*; question 4: *at first* before the gap, followed by to *his pleasant surprise* after the gap suggests the writer initially thought something negative before he went on to think something positive).

Answers
1 preparations **2** organised **3** initiative **4** unpopular **5** participated **6** energetic **7** surrounding **8** unusually

Speaking Parts 3 and 4 SB page 156

▶ **Page 209 and Page 211 Speaking bank**

Ask students to close their Student's Books. Tell them you are going to dictate five statements about Speaking Parts 3 and 4 and they must decide if the statements are true or false. If the statement is false, they must discuss why. Then dictate:
You must discuss all five prompts. (false: it is better to discuss a few in more detail).
It is important to allow your partner to express his/her ideas. (true)
You will lose marks if you and your partner do not reach agreement. (false: you should try but don't have to reach agreement)
In Part 4 you should support your opinion. (true)
You should comment on what your partner says as well as agree or disagree. (true)
Put students into pairs to briefly discuss the statements before telling them to check their answers by reading the exam advice on page 156.

Exam advice

1 Read the rubric with the students and pair them with someone they are less familiar with. Allow them ten to fifteen seconds to look at the diagram before playing the recording. As Exercise 4 focuses on strategies for working with a partner, monitor and listen for examples of how the students react to what the other has said and make a note of the phrases you hear. Pay particular attention to how students comment on each other's ideas (e.g. *That's a good point*), support each other and invite the other to speak (e.g. *Is that what you mean?*). You will refer to these notes when students have completed Exercise 4. After two minutes, stop the students and move straight to Exercise 2.

Track 66
Examiner: I'd like you to imagine that you are going to do a class project on festivals around the world. Here are some aspects of festivals that you could investigate and a question for you to discuss. First, you have some time to look at the task. Now talk to each other about what you can learn about different places by studying these aspects of their festivals.

2 Read the rubric with the students before you play the recording. Continue to monitor and write down examples of how the students comment on what the other has said. After one minute, stop the students and move straight to Exercise 3.

Track 67
Examiner: Now you have about a minute to decide which two aspects you and your partner should work on together.

3 Keep students in the same pairs as for Exercises 1 and 2. After you have played the recording once, allow the pairs a few minutes to discuss the question before stopping them and moving to Exercise 4.

Track 68
Antonia: OK, let's see. What can we learn from studying their clothes and costumes?
Nikolai: Well, I think it shows how people carried things in the past.
Antonia: You mean, how they dressed in the past?

Nikolai: Yes, thank you, how they dressed in the past, which perhaps shows the sorts of activities they did and the materials which were available.

Antonia: That's a very good point. I think we can learn how they looked in the past, um …

Nikolai: Good, and let's move on to the food. What do you think we can learn from that?

Antonia: Um, well, I, um …

Nikolai: I mean, do you think it might show us what food was available on special occasions in the past?

Antonia: Yes, it probably does, so we can learn about their past eating habits and perhaps also what they think is still important in the present.

Nikolai: Yes, that's a good idea, because of course festivals change …

Antonia: You mean they evolve.

Nikolai: Exactly, they evolve. I mean I think of festivals in my country, and the customs and traditions have changed over the years.

Antonia: An interesting point. You must have studied this a bit.

Nikolai: Yes, I have a bit. What about dances and music?

Antonia: Well, I think this is very interesting because I'm a musician myself –

Nikolai: Oh great!

Antonia: – and I think by playing and listening to traditional festival music we learn about what is beautiful. What was lovely in the past can still be lovely for us today.

Nikolai: I think that's a very interesting general idea about all these things: that festivals really – what's the word – join the best things from the past with the best things in the present?

Antonia: In other words, combine the best things!

Nikolai: Exactly, combine the best things, so that, so that, um …

Antonia: So that, well, that's evolution, isn't it? When the best aspects of the past and present take us on to the future.

Nikolai: Well, we're getting philosophical. I think what you're trying to explain is how we can learn about progress by looking at how festivals change, um, but what about these special activities …

4 Allow students time to read the rubric and points 1 and 2 before playing the recording a second time. Put students into pairs to compare their ideas before referring them to the audioscript on page 245 to check their answers. As students do this, look at the examples you wrote down when monitoring in Exercises 1 and 2, and once you have elicited the answers during whole-class feedback, praise the students for the examples you heard.

Answers

1
(Suggested answer)
They help each other with vocabulary and expressing ideas, they react to what the other person says, they invite the other person to speak and express ideas. This is important because they should try to have a normal conversation.

2
a That's a very good point; Yes, that's a good idea; An interesting point; I think that's a very interesting general idea ...
b You mean … ; In other words
c I mean … ; So that … (Antonia continues when Nikolai runs out of ideas)

5 Before students complete this task, give them a moment to look at the phrases noted in Exercise 4. Monitor and listen for examples of the target language but do not provide feedback until after students have completed Exercise 6.

Track 69

Examiner: Now I'd like you to talk about something together for about two minutes. Some people think that it's a good idea for towns and cities to put on festivals but other people disagree. Here are some things they think about and a question for you to discuss. First you have some time to look at the task. Now talk to each other about whether it's a good idea for towns and cities to put on festivals.

6 Do not change pairs for this task. Remind students to use the phrases they asterisked (*) in Exercise 5, focusing on those which they have not already used. If they have used all the phrases asterisked give them a moment to identify one or two additional phrases from Exercise 4 they wish to practise. Then play the recording. After a minute, stop the students. During whole-class feedback, elicit examples of the target language you heard when monitoring.

Track 70

Examiner: Thank you. Now you have about a minute to decide what you think is the best reason for putting on a festival in a town or city.

7 Read the rubric with the students. So that students do not read the extracts in Exercises 8.1 and 8.4, ask them to keep their Student's Books closed for the task. Tell them that as they listen, they should write down what benefit(s), and examples in support of their ideas are mentioned by Antonia and Nikolai. Elicit answers in whole-class feedback.

Track 71

Examiner: Antonia, how do towns and cities benefit from having festivals and other celebrations?

Antonia: Hmm, that's a good question. / Some people say that it's good for, / what's it called, / community spirit, but I think the main benefit is for local businesses / because tourists and visitors are attracted to the town / to spend their money in shops and restaurants.

Examiner: Nikolai, do you agree with Antonia?

Nikolai: Yes, I partly agree with her. / I think in many places, / people spend a lot of time during the year preparing for their festival / and I think it really encourages a feeling of cooperation / and a community feeling.

Examiner: And, Nikolai, do you think festivals should be organised more for tourists or more for local people?

/P/ Pronunciation: improving fluency

8.1 Encourage the students to read the extracts out loud, underlining the words they think are stressed before they listen and check their answers.

8.2 Either play the recording and ask students to mark the intonation as they listen, or alternatively, ask them to mark the intonation before they listen and then check their answers.

8.3 Remind students that pausing effectively helps the listener to follow and understand what is being said. Point out that it is unnatural to pause between a set phrase or collocation and between an adjective and noun, e.g. after *good* and before *question* in the first sentence. Elicit the first pause with the students before they work in pairs. Encourage them to read the extract out loud as they work, focusing on phrases, collocations and adjective + noun pairs, as this may help them hear where they should pause.

Answers
8.1, 8.2 and 8.3
See underlining, pause marks and intonation arrows in recording script for Track 72.

Track 72

Antonia: Hmm, that's a good question. / Some people say that it's good for, / what's it called, / community spirit, but I think the main benefit is for local businesses / because tourists and visitors are attracted to the town / to spend their money in shops and restaurants.

8.4 Tell students to work individually and allow them around five minutes to complete the task. Once completed, put them into pairs to compare their answers, taking it in turns to read the extract using word stress, rising and falling intonation and pausing where they think appropriate. Monitor and support weaker students. Then, play the recording so students can check their answers. During whole-class feedback, invite a stronger student to read the extract to the class.

Answers
See underlining, pause marks and intonation arrows in recording script for Track 73.

Track 73

Nikolai: Yes, I partly agree with her. / I think in many places, / people spend a lot of time during the year preparing for their festival / and I think it really encourages a feeling of cooperation / and a community feeling.

8.5 Pair students with someone they are less familiar with to do this task. Monitor and support weaker students by drilling sentences where students are not using the correct word stress, intonation or pausing. During whole-class feedback, invite a stronger pair to read the extracts with one student reading Antonia (8.1) and the other reading Nikolai (8.4).

8.6 As an alternative to working in pairs, put students into fours (A, B, C, D). Ask Students A and B to answer the question, while C listens for two examples of suitable stress and two examples of suitable intonation and D listens for two examples of suitable pausing and two examples of phrases to comment on what a partner has said from Exercise 4 (e.g. an interesting point). Monitor and write down correct and incorrect examples of the target pronunciation and language you hear. After around a minute, stop the students and tell C and D to give A and B feedback before the students swap roles while you continue monitoring and writing down examples. During whole-class feedback, invite students to share the examples they heard before you praise the students for the examples you heard and elicit error corrections.

9 Remind students to give examples to support their ideas, agree and disagree with the opinions of their partner, and use phrases to encourage and help each other as well as using suitable stress, intonation and pausing. Encourage the 'examiner' to give feedback before students swap roles.

Writing Part 1 (an essay) SB page 158

▶ **Page 192 Writing bank**

Lead in
Ask the students if they have ever been, or would like to go, to see their favourite singer or group play live. Select students to share their ideas, encouraging them to give reasons and examples.

Exam advice
Read the exam advice with the students and elicit why it is important to write a plan (so that they write a more complete answer) and how long they should spend writing a plan (around five to ten minutes).

1 Allow students time to consider the first two bullet points individually before putting them into pairs to complete the task. When eliciting the answer to the second bullet point, invite a student to come to the front of the class and write the lists of advantages and disadvantages on the board as the students call them out. If possible, leave them on the board until after students have completed Exercise 2. Once you have elicited all the answers, hold a class vote on whether it is better to listen to live or recorded music.

Answers
Suggested underlining
better to listen; live; recorded music; quality of the music; convenience; own idea

2 Read the rubric with the students. If the list(s) of advantages and disadvantages are still on the board, refer students to them as they choose which ideas to use. Set a time limit of between five and ten minutes for students to write their plans. When comparing plans, they could highlight which part of their plan refers to which of the notes (in the essay question), which part to the introduction and which the conclusion, or where the plan outlines reasons for their point of view.

3 Allow students time to read the rubric and questions before they read Ulli's essay. Encourage them to make notes as they work. After five minutes, put students into pairs or small groups to discuss their answers.

4 Read the rubric with the students. Elicit some examples of correct comma use (e.g. after introductory clauses, phrases or words that come before a main clause, e.g. *Yesterday, I went to the park*; *Although it was hard, I passed the exam*); to separate independent clauses joined by a coordinating conjunction (e.g. *and, but, for …*: *The class had finished, but the students wouldn't leave*). As these are examples of real candidate errors, encourage students to work individually. Monitor and support weaker students. When you have elicited the answers, ask students to asterisk (*) any incorrect sentences and write them in their notebooks under the heading *common errors*. They can then refer to these when they are revising for the exam.

Answers
Although people can listen to recorded music on their devices when they are travelling**,** working or studying, music festivals and concerts are becoming more and more popular. This is because**,** I believe**,** they offer two main advantages.
The first advantage is that the quality of the sound is much better at live concerts**,** where the music and voices come directly from the performers. This makes it a much more emotional experience because you have direct contact with the musicians and you react to them and they react to you.
The second advantage is the atmosphere. Instead of listening to a recording alone on your personal device, you are listening with a huge crowd of people and enjoying the music together**.** This means it is a social as well as an artistic experience.
The main disadvantage is that you cannot listen to live music whenever you want**,** like you can on a personal device. In addition to that, the noise from the audience sometimes spoils the quality of the sound. In my opinion**,** however**,** the best way to enjoy music is the spontaneous atmosphere of a live concert. It is more exciting because you are surrounded by other enthusiastic fans.

Extension activity
You may find that your students make punctuation errors by incorrectly overusing commas and creating what is known as a comma splice: this is a type of run on sentence where independent clauses that do not include conjunctions (*but, so*, etc.) are incorrectly separated by commas. If your students do this, point out that independent clauses are clauses which form complete sentences and can stand alone. As such, they should be separated by full stops. Then write the following on the board and ask the students to replace commas with a full stop where appropriate.
On the other hand, a drawback of the theatre is the price of the tickets, they are often very expensive, if they were cheaper, people would go more often. (correct: On the other hand, a drawback of the theatre is the price of the tickets. They are often very expensive. If they were cheaper, people would go more often).

5 Read the rubric and the example with the students before putting them into pairs to complete the activity. Once they have completed the task, put them into groups of four to compare their answers before you elicit them.

Answers
2 music festivals and concerts are becoming more and more popular **3** music festivals and concerts **4** the music and voices come directly from the performers **5** listening to music at live concerts **6** the musicians **7** listening with a huge crowd of people and enjoying the music together **8** the main disadvantage is that you cannot listen to live music whenever you want **9** a live concert

6 Point out that *it*, *this* and *that* are used when we want to introduce more information about a topic that we have already mentioned. Tell them that although *this* and *that* are similar, *that* typically shows some sort of distance from the topic, either in time or physical space (*I went to New York last year and before that Chicago*; *I want that one over there, please*). If students are confused between *it* and *this*, point out that although both can be used to refer back to personal opinions (question 1), *this* is more often used to refer back to whole parts of a text or an entire idea (e.g. question 6) and *it* to refer back to non-human nouns (e.g. question 2). As these are examples of real candidate errors, ask students to work individually before comparing their answers in pairs. Once students have completed the activity and you have elicited the answers, tell them to asterisk (*) any questions they answered incorrectly. They can then write correct examples in their note books under the heading *common errors*, and refer to their notes when they are revising for the exam.

Answers
1 It/This **2** it **3** they **4** they; that **5** that **6** This **7** that/this **8** that/this

7 Read the rubric with the students. Tell them that in addition to the correct use of commas, they should aim to use six examples of *it, this, that* and *they* in their answer. Point out that students should spend five to ten minutes writing an essay plan before they start writing. Then wish the students luck and set a time limit of forty minutes.

Model answer
Films are now as popular as they were when my grandparents were young. However, with the internet and DVDs, we now have much more choice about when and where we can watch them.
There's no doubt that for the quality of the experience, the best place to watch a new film is in the cinema on a wide screen with excellent sound. What's more, you can see films which everybody is talking about because they have only recently been released.

The drawback of the cinema is the price of the tickets. If they were cheaper, people would go more often. This means that if, like me, you are a cinema fanatic, you have little choice but to download films from the internet if you want to see them frequently. I also believe that it is worth seeing a good film several times. The best way of doing this is to see it first in the cinema, then later at home, when you can appreciate different aspects of the film.
For me, however, going to the cinema is a far better experience, because it is a special location.

Extension activity

Put students into pairs and give each pair a copy of the sample answer. First, ask them to find and underline examples of *it, this, that* and *they*. Once they have done this, tell them to find and say what each of the underlined words refers to. For example, in the first and fourth sentences *they* refers to *films*; whilst in the sixth sentence *they* refers to *tickets*. In the seventh sentence the word *this* refers to the idea of *tickets being too expensive*. After you have elicited the answers in whole-class feedback, students complete the task again but this time with their partner's answer to Exercise 7. If students believe any of the examples found are incorrect, they should make a note of the correction to provide during peer feedback, as well as praise for correct usage. Monitor and support students who are unsure, or who cannot agree whether a target word has been used correctly or incorrectly.

Vocabulary

Festivals and celebrations

bands	gather round	play
celebrate	hold	street parties
commemorate	let off	street performers
disguises	march	traditional
dress up	parade	costumes
fireworks	perform	wearing

Collocations

avoid … at all costs	narrowly avoid
check … carefully	properly protect
closely supervise	strictly control
heavily protect	successfully prevent

Vocabulary activity 1

Tell the students to close their Student's Books and put them into pairs. Tell them they have two minutes to write down as many words and phrases as they can remember to talk about festivals and celebrations. When the time is up, elicit the words from the class and write them on the board. If they did not remember the complete list, add the remaining words and phrases. Next, tell the students to imagine that they have bumped into each other at a festival and are going to 'chat' about what they did before they saw each other and what they plan to do next. However, instead of 'chatting' they are going to transcribe the conversation in their notebooks. Point out that this will give them time to focus on grammatical and lexical accuracy and that they will read out their conversations later. They should aim to use at least ten words or phrases from the list on the board. If students are unsure, start them off by dictating (or saying) the following:

A: Hey, [student's name]! I didn't know you'd be here celebrating.
B: Oh hi [student's name]. I love a good street party, so I wasn't going to miss it. Did you see those performers earlier?
A: Yeah, they were great. It was amazing to see the traditional costumes …

Allow students time to write full dialogues (around ten minutes). Once the majority have finished, go around the class and invite the pairs to read out their dialogues to the class. As they do, tell the remainder of the class to count the number of target words or phrases they hear.

Vocabulary activity 2

One student has to describe a word or phrase without saying it and the other has to guess what they are describing. Once the student has guessed the word correctly, they must make up a question using the word for their partner to answer, e.g. Student A: *a group of musicians that play music together.* Student B: *a band.* Student B: *Who do you think the most influential rock band of all time was?* Student A: *Well that's an interesting question. In my opinion …*

DIGITAL CLASSROOM

Practice Extra Unit 14

Test Generator Unit 14 test

Test and Train Exam Practice

Unit 13 Vocabulary and grammar review

1
1 space 2 room 3 location 4 location 5 area 6 place 7 space 8 square 9 room 10 place
2
1 since 2 made 3 out 4 than 5 enough 6 there 7 one 8 What
3
1 have a tennis court built 2 you have the car checked 3 to clear up 4 have to do 5 are supposed to pay 6 are not allowed to speak

Unit 14 Vocabulary and grammar review

1
1 lawyer 2 possibilities 3 especially 4 suitably 5 responsibility 6 appropriately 7 demanding 8 representative
2
1 reputation 2 safety 3 amazement 4 dissatisfaction 5 existence 6 truth 7 width 8 addition 9 difference 10 obligations
3
1 is expected to arrive 2 had broken into 3 are reported to have 4 has not/hasn't been serviced for 5 is said to be living 6 cake was/had been eaten

Answer key

Grammar reference

1 Present perfect simple and continuous

1
1 have/'ve been preparing; have/'ve not finished 2 have you been doing 3 have/'ve been looking; have they been working 4 have not/ haven't/'ve not finished; have/'ve been chilling 5 have/'ve been doing; have/'ve damaged 6 have/'ve been 7 has/'s become 8 have/'ve been working
2
1 Correct 2 Correct 3 I have/'ve finally learnt 4 he has/'s been eating 5 Correct 6 Correct 7 They have/'ve been browsing 8 I have/'ve been going
3
1 Scientists have discovered vaccines to cure many fatal illnesses. 2 He has not/hasn't put his recent qualifications on his CV yet. 3 Wake up! You have/'ve been sleeping for over two hours now. 4 I'm not surprised you're thirsty because, as usual, you haven't drunk enough during your run. 5 She has/'s known him since he was a small child. 6 It has been snowing heavily all morning and as a result, the roads are slippery now.

2 Making comparisons

1
1 worst 2 more often 3 most complicated 4 most memorable 5 cheapest 6 more irregular
2
1 the **most** ~~more~~ hard-working student 2 **more** ~~most~~ effective than 3 Correct 4 Correct 5 **hotter** ~~hot~~ than 6 **more** casual clothes than 7 **the most** ~~more~~ accurate 8 By far **the most** efficient way
3
1 His ambition has always been greater than his brother's. 2 Her analysis of the financial situation was as accurate as the report in the magazine. 3 The lecturer is less available to her students since she started work on her thesis. 4 His skills are not developing as fast as people predicted. 5 My interest in the project is considerably greater now than it was at the beginning. 6 My motivation is not quite as high as I would ideally want. 7 There are slightly fewer people living in the town than ten years ago. 8 It's considerably more tiring to travel by car than by train.

Adjectives with *-ed* and *-ing*

1
1 fascinated 2 irritated 3 amusing 4 exhausted 5 tired; depressed 6 disgusting
2
1 appealing 2 fascinating 3 involved 4 astonishing 5 disappointed 6 irritating 7 disgusting 8 prejudiced

3 Past simple, past continuous and *used to*

1
1 used to worry 2 socialised 3 was scuba diving 4 discarded 5 deteriorated 6 rang
2
1 were putting / rang 2 was winning / claimed 3 was serving / noticed 4 was strolling / ran 5 entered / were drawing / (were) jumping 6 asked / was heading

at, in and *on* in time phrases

1
1 f 2 d 3 c 4 a 5 b 6 e
2
1 **on** ~~in~~ Tuesday morning 2 **in** ~~at~~ August. 3 Correct 4 Correct 5 **in** ~~at~~ a relatively short period of time 6 **at** ~~on~~ night

Past perfect simple and continuous

1
1 had/'d been waiting 2 had/'d been cheating 3 had/'d built 4 had/'d handed 5 had already put 6 had picked up
2
1 had not/hadn't ordered 2 had/'d committed 3 had/'d fallen 4 had/'d been riding 5 had/'d been watching 6 had/'d lived

4 *so* and *such, too* and *enough*

1
1 much 2 few 3 such 4 such a lot of 5 so 6 so
2
1 They were **so** ~~such~~ thrilled 2 Correct 3 He's **too** ~~to~~ exhausted 4 Correct 5 she had **so** ~~much~~ little time left 6 She designed **such** ~~so~~ fabulous clothes
3
1 F 2 C 3 E 4 D 5 B 6 A

5 Zero, first and second conditionals

1
1 will get 2 get 3 are 4 takes 5 If 6 won't win
2
1 is/'s; will/'ll have to 2 were; would/'d buy 3 come; will see 4 had; wouldn't be 5 study; will/'ll pass 6 would/'d buy; won
3
1 if the neighbours **stopped** having parties 2 We**'ll take** a taxi 3 Correct 4 I **won't** either 5 We definitely **won't** cancel the beach party, unless it pours with rain./ We definitely will cancel the beach party, **if** it pours with rain. 6 Correct

6 Countable and uncountable nouns

1
1 suitable **accommodation** 2 our **luggage** 3 **Pollution** caused by plastic 4 listen to **advice** 5 Correct 6 extremely valuable **works** of art
2
1 coffee 2 any 3 cardboard; paper 4 was 5 equipment; is 6 damage

Articles

1
1 a; the 2 the; the; a; the 3 an; the; the 4 the 5 The 6 a; the
2
1 the 2 The; the; the 3 The; the 4 The; the; the; the 5 a 6 – ; –

7 Infinitive and verb + *-ing*

1
1 He decided **to make** a high offer 2 Correct 3 They persuaded me **to apply** 4 Correct 5 Can I remind you **not to drive** 6 The lawyers advised him **to say**
2
1 to speak 2 following 3 joining 4 celebrating 5 taking up 6 watching 7 to do
3
1 d 2 c 3 f 4 b 5 e 6 a
4
1 to buy 2 carrying 3 taking 4 to stay/staying 5 Analysing 6 paying

8 *at, in* and *on* to express location

1
1 on 2 at 3 in 4 in 5 in 6 on
2
1 **at** ~~on~~ the back door 2 **in** ~~at~~ the queue 3 **in** ~~on~~ the world 4 Correct 5 Correct 6 **on** ~~in~~ that cruise ship
3
1 on 2 on 3 on 4 at 5 in; on 6 at

Reported speech

1
1 worked 2 was having 3 had never done 4 had got; had eaten 5 would call; had woken up 6 could; couldn't
2
1 A 2 A 3 B 4 B 5 A 6 A
3
1 Correct 2 He **promised** ~~promises~~ me 3 how long **I had** ~~had I~~ been employed as a receptionist.~~?~~ 4 when **she would** ~~would she~~ be available for an interview.~~?~~ 5 what time **we finished** ~~did we finish~~ work.~~?~~ 6 Correct
4
1 given him clear instructions about what to do the previous day. 2 they had discovered her missing sports gear in the washing machine that morning. 3 he was working on the following day. 4 his essay was extremely confusing. 5 she had done the previous day. 6 had noticed any of his belongings there.

9 Modal verbs to express certainty and possibility

1
1 must 2 must 3 can't 4 must 5 can't 6 couldn't
2
1 d 2 c 3 b 4 f 5 a 6 e
3
1 may/might 2 couldn't have 3 can't 4 can't 5 must have
6 might not / may not

10 *as* and *like*

1
1 **as** a dental receptionist 2 he looks **like** a professional player 3 **As** far as I can tell 4 such **as** onion soup 5 Correct 6 **As** she stole a bottle of perfume
2
1 as; as 2 like 3 as 4 as 5 like 6 as; as

Modal verbs to express ability

1
1 Could 2 couldn't 3 can 4 was able to 5 can't 6 can't
2
1 I wasn't able **to** translate 2 fortunately I **was able to** ~~could~~ use 3 I am afraid I **can't** ~~couldn't~~ accept 4 Correct 5 Correct 6 He **was able to** ~~could~~ run the marathon

11 Relative pronouns and relative clauses

1
1 which 2 whose 3 which 4 where 5 who 6 who
2
1 that/which 2 where 3 that/why 4 that/who/whom 5 that/who
6 whose

12 Third conditional, Mixed conditionals

1
1C 2C 3C 4A 5B 6B
2
1 hadn't arrived; wouldn't have missed 2 had/'d gone; wouldn't have woken up 3 had/'d enrolled; might have got 4 had/'d been; would have learnt 5 hadn't gone; would/'d never have met 6 would/'d have taken; had/'d had

wish, *if only* and *hope*

1
1 had 2 could 3 would stop 4 would start 5 were 6 wouldn't keep
2
1 He wishes he **had** chosen 2 I hope you **make** lots of money 3 Correct
4 He hopes **to** get a job 5 We all hope you **managed** to get a visa
6 Correct

13 Causative *have* and *get*

1
1 am going to get/have; cut 2 had/got; delivered 3 have/get; dry cleaned
4 had; stolen 5 get/have; serviced

Expressing obligation and permission

1
1 have to 2 must 3 must 4 supposed to 5 should 6 ought 7 can
2
1 You are not **allowed** to park 2 Correct 3 Correct 4 I **needn't have done** 5 Correct 6 Correct 7 he **was** recognised

14 The passive

1
1 The safe was opened for me by a member of the hotel staff.
2 Lots of bargains can be found at the market. 3 Tickets for the event can be bought online. 4 It was thought that children were to blame for the damage to the trees. 5 My phone was taken out of my jacket pocket.
6 The winter tyres on my car have been replaced.
2
1A 2C 3C 4B 5C 6A
3
1 Some football supporters **are** reported 2 Pele **is** considered to have been 3 Homeless people are **known** to sleep 4 The manager is understood **to** have praised the technicians 5 Correct 6 Correct

used to, *get/be used to*

1
1 didn't use to enjoy 2 didn't use to do 3 used to spend 4 used to own
5 Did he use to go 6 didn't use to like
2
1 Correct 2 I **used to** work / I worked in a steel factory 3 she **used to** enjoy / she enjoyed riding 4 I **used to** live in New York State 5 Correct
6 Correct
3
1 is/'s used to 2 to get used to 3 am/'m not used to 4 to get used to
5 am/'m getting used to 6 get used to
4
1 was not used to living 2 is/'s getting used to 3 used to be 4 would relax

The position of adverbs and adverb phrases

1
1B 2B 3A 4B 5A 6A 7A 8B
2
1 He spoke **seriously** 2 Correct 3 personal problems **frankly**
4 They will **hopefully/Hopefully** they will be 5 was **clearly** not 6 Correct

Future perfect simple and future perfect continuous

1
1 will have been driving 2 will have been 3 will have been living
4 she will have been working 5 will have reached 6 will have retired 7 will have been cooking 8 will you have been studying 9 will have known
10 will have earned
2
1 I will have **learnt** ~~been learning~~ 2 Correct 3 we **will** have been waiting
4 Correct 5 we will have **walked** ~~been walking~~ 6 They will have **been travelling** ~~have travelled~~ all day

Phrasal verb builder

Communication

1
1 up 2 out 3 down 4 to 5 up 6 up
2
1 shut 2 dealt 3 got 4 gave 5 noted 6 is looking
3
1 **for** ~~to~~ 2 **into** ~~in~~ 3 Correct 4 **up** ~~in~~ 5 **out** ~~over~~ 6 Correct

Education

1
1 out 2 out 3 through 4 up 5 up 6 off
2
1b 2a 3f 4c 5d 6e
3
1 He dropped out **of** university 2 she needed to read up **on** ~~in~~ 3 Correct
4 Correct 5 They have taken **up** ~~over~~ drama 6 Can you all listen **up** ~~on~~

Travel

1
1 get away 2 check into 3 booked; into 4 set out 5 took off
6 stop over
2
1f 2e 3c 4d 5a 6b
3
1 into 2 over 3 up 4 on 5 out 6 away

Writing bank

Part 1: An essay

2
Question: Will environmental problems be worse in 20 years?
Ideas: pollution, climate change and your own idea

3
It includes the extra idea of a growing population.

5
Ideas 1, 3, 4, 6, 8

6
1 sentence 1 2 sentences 3, 6 3 sentences 4, 8

7
1 B. It makes general statements to introduce the topic and the arguments which will be developed in the essay.
2 C. It sums up arguments on both sides, and expresses a personal opinion.

9
1 as 2 in my opinion 3 In addition to this 4 Firstly 5 such as 6 as a result

11
Model answer
Cycling is becoming a very popular way of getting around cities nowadays, and a lot of big cities have cycle schemes which allow people to use public bikes. But there are advantages and disadvantages to bikes as a form of city transport. On the one hand, cycling is good for your health. It provides good exercise, and can help you to lose weight and keep fit. It is also cheap, because if you have your own bike, it does not cost you anything to travel around the city. A third advantage is that cycling is good for the environment, because it does not cause any pollution. On the other hand, cycling on busy streets can be dangerous. Car and lorry drivers do not always notice cyclists, especially when it is dark, and this can lead to accidents. On balance, I would say that cycling is an excellent form of transport in cities during the day and when the weather is nice. However, when it is dark or the weather is bad, it is better to use another form of transport.

Part 2: An email/letter

2
You should write an email to a friend, Jo. You should write about your new home, things there are to do in the city and your new friends.

3
Yes, it answers all the questions in Jo's email. The tone is informal.

5
1 false 2 true 3 true 4 false 5 true 6 false

6
Sentences 2, 5, 6 and 8. They are suitable because they are formal.

7
1 Dear Ms Copeland 2 in response to 3 currently 4 would be interested in working 5 studied different aspects of 6 was employed 7 gained some experience as 8 customer satisfaction 9 I would be grateful if you would 10 I look forward to hearing from you.

9
Model answer
Dear Ms Simpson,
I am writing in response to your job advertisement, which appeared in the Weekly News last week.
I am interested in applying for the job of receptionist at your hotel this summer. This role interests me particularly because I am a very friendly and outgoing person, and I would enjoy meeting guests and helping them feel welcome. As I am currently studying English, it would also be a good opportunity for me to practise using the language.
I have experience of working as a hotel receptionist, as I spent last summer working in a hotel in Ireland. I am therefore used to taking reservations, helping guests check in and check out and dealing with problems they may have. I am cheerful and hardworking, and I understand the importance of providing good customer service. I am also a good team worker, which I know is a very important quality for working in a busy hotel. I have a good level of English, and I am able to communicate well in the language. I hope you will consider me for this role, and I look forward to hearing from you.

Part 2: An article

2
You should write an article about your hobby. You should say what it is, when you started doing it, and why you enjoy it. People will read your article in an English-language magazine.

3
1 yes 2 four 3 one 4 informal

5
B is the best. The title is interesting and makes the reader think. The sentence is a question which engages the reader and makes them think for themselves about Mandela's achievements.

6
1 d 2 e 3 a

7
1 fascinated by 2 packed 3 huge 4 freezing 5 terrifying 6 essential

8
2 I like is 3 that really surprised me was 4 I will never forget is 5 I noticed was

10
1 For 2 in 3 as 4 which 5 What 6 tell

Model answer
<u>A healthy life is a happy life</u>
Can you be happy if you're not fit and healthy? For me, the answer to this question is definitely no, and keeping fit and healthy is an important part of life.
Firstly, a good diet is vital if you want to maintain a healthy lifestyle. This means eating plenty of fruit and vegetables, and avoiding foods high in fat and sugar. It can be difficult to achieve this if you eat out in restaurants, where portions tend to be large and the food is often rich. However, it is possible to maintain a balanced diet if you make careful choices.
The second important part of a healthy lifestyle is exercise. There are obviously hundreds of different ways to exercise, from running and hiking to playing football and tennis, but in my opinion, the most important thing is to find a form of exercise that you enjoy. After all, no one can motivate themselves to do something every week if it isn't fun!
By eating sensibly and doing regular exercise, it is possible for anyone to improve their health, and remember – healthier people are happier people!

Part 2: A report

2
The report is for the group leader of some English-speaking students. The report should include: the best time of year to visit your city, interesting places to visit and the best way to travel around the city.

3
Yes, it covers all the points in the input.

5
1 c 2 a 3 b

6
B. The information is relevant to the topic of the report and uses personal experience to support the recommendation.

7
Introduction: C. It explains the aim accurately and uses formal language. (A is too informal; B is not accurate, as the report does not discuss disadvantages.)
Conclusion: A. It gives a clear recommendation and uses formal language. (B is too informal; C does not give a clear recommendation.)

8
1 is often recommended 2 is considered to be 3 is expected 4 has been suggested 5 are recommended

10
1 The aim **of** this report 2 In **addition** to this 3 college**. M**oreover, the ones 4 I have no hesitation in **recommending** 5 All things **considered**, the 6 In conclusion,

12
Model answer
<u>Introduction</u>
The aim of this report is to look at the shops in a popular shopping centre in Oxford and make recommendations for additions.
<u>Green Cross Shopping Centre</u>
Green Cross is a large and popular shopping centre near the city centre. It has nearly 150 shops as well as several cafés and restaurants.
<u>Popular shops</u>
The most popular shops are the large clothes shops, especially those selling well-known brands of clothing. A lot of these shops offer significant discounts throughout the year, which makes them popular with shoppers who are searching for bargains. The more exclusive stores offer additional services such as fashion advice, which makes them attractive to customers who are looking for something special.
<u>Recommendations for improvements</u>
Some smaller independent shops would be a good addition. There are very few of these at present, and they would offer shoppers a good alternative to the big High Street names.

Conclusion
To sum up, Green Cross is a busy and successful shopping centre, which already has plenty of popular shops. It could be improved by having some smaller stores offering more unusual alternatives to the standard brands.

Part 2: A review

2
You should write a review of a film you have seen. You should say what it is about, say why you did or didn't enjoy it, and say whether you think other people will enjoy it. People will read your review in an English-language magazine.
3
1 yes 2 yes 3 anyone except young children 4 informal and friendly
5
Plan A is better. Each paragraph has a clear topic and gives the reader useful and helpful information; it starts with a general introduction with factual information; it gives good points and problems about the website/product; it ends with a clear recommendation. Plan B contains information that is not relevant for the reader, e.g. the writer needed a new tablet, how the writer found the website; the third heading is not appropriate, as the focus should be the product you bought, not games that you play; it doesn't end with a clear recommendation.
6
1 incredibly 2 ridiculously 3 rather 4 brilliantly 5 extremely 6 very 7 absolutely 8 really
7
1 c 2 f 3 a 4 e 5 d 6 b
8
1 spite 2 though 3 despite 4 Although 5 However
10
1 than 2 disappointing 3 will 4 miss 5 using 6 advise

12
Model answer
Playa de Oro
Last summer, I spent a week with my family in a holiday resort called Playa de Oro in the south of Spain. This is a popular tourist area, but we were keen to choose a quiet resort where we could just relax on the beach or by the pool.
The resort had some positive points. The apartment buildings were attractive, and our apartment was spacious and well-equipped. The resort had two swimming pools, and both were extremely clean and well-maintained. The staff were also incredibly friendly and helpful.
However, we were disappointed to find that our resort was surrounded by several other, much bigger resorts. The beach was therefore absolutely packed with people every day, and it was almost impossible to find a place to sit. Even worse, the advert said that the resort was peaceful, but in fact there were two nightclubs nearby which were open every night until four o'clock in the morning! We hardly slept, and came home exhausted.
This resort might be OK if you want a week-long party, but my advice is to avoid it if you want a peaceful, relaxing holiday.

Speaking bank

Part 1

3
1 a 2 c 3 e 4 a 5 b 6 d 7 d 8 c 9 e 10 b
4
Yes, she does.
5
She uses contracted forms.
7
1 past 2 present 3 future 4 present 5 future 6 past
8
1 C 2 A 3 B 4 B 5 C 6 B
9
adding extra information: also, as well, plus, too
giving a reason: because, the reason for this is that
giving an example: for example, for instance, like, such as
10
1 The reason for this is that 2 too 3 because 4 like 5 For instance 6 also

Part 2

3
The topic is holidays. You have to say why the people have chosen these holidays.
4
Yes, for both photographs.
5
1 Both 2 different 3 whereas 4 other 5 difference 6 as
6
1 c 2 e 3 a 4 f 5 b 6 d 7 h 8 g
7
Speaker 1 – B Speaker 2 – D Speaker 3 – A

Track 79

Student 1: These two photos both show people cooking food. I prefer the first photo because it shows a dad cooking with his children. I think they might be making a cake or something. He looks very happy, and the children are both looking very serious, so I guess they're concentrating on what they're doing. I think that when they eat the cake, they will all feel very proud that they made it together. I think it's really nice for parents to spend time in this way with their children. The second photo shows a chef in a restaurant.

Student 2: Both photos show people preparing food. The first photo shows a dad cooking with his children, whereas the second photo shows a professional chef cooking in a restaurant. The main difference between the two photos is that the dad is cooking for pleasure, whereas the chef is cooking because it's his job. The dad probably only cooks from time to time. On the other hand, the chef probably cooks every day. The people in both photos look quite happy, although the children look a bit serious. The chef looks as if he enjoys his work, but I think it's much more fun when you're cooking just for pleasure, rather than cooking as a job. I think the professional chef must get very hot sometimes, and he might get a bit fed up with his job sometimes, because chefs often have to work late at night. I would prefer to just cook at home, for fun, or to cook meals for my friends..

Student 3: The first photo shows a dad with his children. I think they're at home, and they're making a cake together. The dad is smiling and he's looking very relaxed and happy. The two children look a bit serious, but I'm sure they're looking forward to eating the cake. Personally, I love making cakes at home. The second photo shows a chef in a restaurant. He's cooking a big pan of something, but I can't see what it is. He looks like he is concentrating on what he is doing, so I think he is taking a lot of care with the food he's preparing. I wouldn't like to be a professional chef because I think it's very hard work!

8

Track 80

Student: Both photos show people working, but their jobs are very different. The first photo shows two factory workers making a car, whereas the second photo shows a doctor treating a child. The factory workers might be quite bored. I guess this kind of work is quite boring because you probably do the same thing all day, whereas a doctor's job changes all the time. I think the doctor's job is quite sociable, whereas the people in the first photo are working with a piece of machinery rather than with people. I think that in both jobs the people have a lot of responsibility. I think the factory job must be difficult because you have to concentrate a lot, to make sure you do it properly, but it isn't very interesting. I think the doctor's job is more difficult because sometimes you see people who are very ill, which might be upsetting.

Part 3

3
You have to discuss how the different ideas might attract more guests to a hotel. There are five prompts to discuss.
4
They discuss all the prompts. Yes, they both express their opinions.
5
Yes, they do.
6
Pair 1 – C Pair 2 – A Pair 3 – B

Track 89

Narrator: Pair 1
Student 1: Shall we talk about the swimming pool first? I think …
Student 2: Yes, I think the swimming pool is a very good idea because most people enjoy …
Student 1: I agree. Everyone loves swimming when the weather's hot, so …
Student 2: But I don't think that tennis courts are a very good idea because most people …
Student 1: But I think a lot of people like playing tennis!

Narrator: Pair 2
Student 3: I think that entertainment would be a great idea. Do you agree?
Student 4: Yes. For example, there could be films for children to watch, and maybe shows later in the evening. Children always love watching films, especially with their friends, and I think older people like watching shows, like comedy shows, for example.
Student 3: Yes, that's a good idea. Or maybe live music in the restaurant. I think that might be popular, because most restaurants don't have live music.
Student 4: Yes. I think that entertainment would definitely attract more guests, especially if people don't have to pay for it. Not many hotels offer entertainment, do they?
Student 3: No, so it would make this hotel a bit different, and I think people would choose it for that reason.
Student 4: OK, shall we quickly talk about the other ideas?
Narrator: Pair 3
Student 5: Well, personally I think that reduced prices would be a very good idea because price is the most important thing for a lot of people. I also think that evening entertainment would be popular with guests, and that would attract people.
Student 6: I would say that an award-winning chef would be a good idea, because it would improve the experience that people have in the hotel. I also think a swimming pool would attract more guests because most people enjoy swimming, especially in the summer.
Student 5: But I don't believe that tennis courts would be very popular because only a small number of people play tennis, and they don't always want to play when they're on holiday.

7
1 b 2 e 3 a 4 c 5 d
8
1 Do 2 do 3 Would 4 Do
9
1 think 2 that's 3 right 4 agree 5 mean, better 6 sure 7 but
10
a 2 and 4 b 5

Part 4

3
Yes, they do.
4
B
5
Pair 1 – D Pair 2 – A Pair 3 – B

Track 91

Narrator: Pair 1
Examiner: Tania, what places are popular for holidays in your country?
Tania: Well, there are a lot of beaches in my country which are very popular for holidays, for local people and for people from other countries. There are also —
Peter: Everyone wants to go to the beach in the summer! For example, in my country …
Narrator: Pair 2
Examiner: Bruno, what is the advantage of going on holiday with friends, rather than with family?
Bruno: I think it's definitely more fun to go on holiday with your friends.
Examiner: OK. Sofia, what do you think is the advantage of going on holiday with friends, rather than with family?
Sofia: I agree with Bruno. I prefer to go on holiday with friends. I don't like going on holiday with my family.
Narrator: Pair 3
Examiner: Marina, some people say that tourism is bad for an area. What do you think?
Marina: Well, I agree in some ways, because tourism can cause pollution and it can also make places very crowded. For example, if a beach is full of tourists, it isn't much fun for local people. But, on the other hand, tourism brings money into an area, and that's very good for it.
Examiner: What do you think about this, Pablo?
Pablo: Sorry, what did you say? Were you talking about tourism?

6
Student 1: Why? Student 2: Where? Student 3: When?

Track 92

Narrator: Student 1
Examiner: Do you like eating in restaurants?
Nicola: Yes, I really enjoy eating in restaurants. One reason is that I'm not a very good cook, so the food is much better in restaurants. Also, I think it's difficult to relax and enjoy food if you have to prepare it and then clean up afterwards. So I prefer to eat in restaurants if I can.
Narrator: Student 2
Examiner: Do you think people should try to eat food that is produced locally?
Alex: Yes, I think it's important to eat food that's produced locally. For example, where I live in Italy, the farmers grow a lot of different kinds of fruit and vegetables, and I think the people who live there should try to eat this food, to support the farmers.
Narrator: Student 3
Examiner: Some people think that advertising junk food should be banned on TV. Do you agree?
Bruno: Well, junk food is obviously bad for people, especially children, and I definitely think that advertising it should be banned early in the evening, when children might be watching TV. For me, it isn't so bad later in the evening, because I don't think that advertising has such a big influence on adults.

8
Student 1 – 2 Student 2 – 1 Student 3 – 3

Track 93

Narrator: Student 1
Examiner: Which are the most popular sports in your country?
Peter: Well, sport is very popular in my country, and a lot of people play sport or watch it on TV. I think the most popular sport is probably football because when there's a big match, for example if our national team is playing, nearly everybody watches the game.
Narrator: Student 2
Examiner: What could schools do to encourage healthy eating habits?
Tania: Well, that's a very interesting question. Let me see. I would say that they could sell healthy snacks, and of course they could serve healthy food at lunch time. Another thing is to teach children about why healthy food is important. I think schools should do all of these things.
Narrator: Student 3
Examiner: Is it better to exercise alone or with other people?
Sofia: Well, on the one hand, I think maybe it's better to exercise alone if you are serious about getting fit, so you can really focus on your own fitness. But on the other hand, I think it's probably more fun to exercise with other people, in a class or in a team sport. So, I think this is probably better.

Workbook answer key with audioscripts Units 1–14

Unit 1 A family affair

Grammar

Present perfect simple and continuous

1
1 haven't been 2 have/'ve been organising 3 have/'ve changed 4 have/'ve been staying 5 have/'ve been sleeping 6 has/'s been helping 7 have/'ve loved 8 have/'ve found 9 have been 10 have/'ve spent 11 have/'ve been going /'ve been 12 have/'ve seen 13 have/'ve decided 14 have/'ve (already) spent 15 have/'ve looked

2
1 Have you found an apartment yet? 2 Have you visited the Statue of Liberty? 3 Have you been eating healthily? 4 What Broadway shows have you seen? 5 Have you been taking the subway everywhere?

3
1 No, I haven't. 2 Yes, I have. 3 No, I haven't. 4 (I have/'ve seen) The Lion King. 5 Yes, I have.

Vocabulary

Phrasal verbs

1
1 C 2 F 3 B 4 D 5 E 6 A

2
1 turn (the information) into 2 turn up 3 made up 4 hang out 5 carry on 6 count on

Collocations with *make* and *do*

3
1 do 2 make 3 did 4 make 5 make 6 did 7 made 8 make 9 done 10 make

Listening Part 1

1 C 2 B 3 B 4 A 5 C 6 C 7 A 8 A

Track 2

Narrator: One. You hear a young man talking about his friend's new haircut.
Man: My best friend recently dyed her hair pink. Not just a few light pink highlights, but a hot pink – the kind of thing that people stare at in the street. It does look striking and it rather suits her, but I thought she was crazy getting it done, as we've both just graduated and have been looking for jobs. It's really taking a chance having such a loud hairstyle if you want someone to hire you, but she's just got a fantastic job working for a fashion magazine. She told me she thought her hair was why she got the job – it made her stand out. I don't know about that, though.
Narrator: Two. You hear a man talking to his daughter about meeting her mother for the first time.
Daughter: Dad, how did you first meet Mum?
Father: We went to university together. One day I needed a book for an assignment. There was just one copy left in the library, but before I could get to it this girl reached up and grabbed it off the shelf.
Daughter: So you read the book together, then?
Father: No, actually she'd already read it. She'd used her university identity card as a bookmark and had left it inside. She laughed when she shook the book and the card fell out. I realised then that she hadn't meant to be rude – she told me later that she was worried about losing her card. I think I'd have felt the same.
Narrator: Three. You hear a girl talking about getting driving lessons from her father.
Girl: When I turned 17, I was really keen to get my driving licence, but lessons were so expensive. So my dad offered to teach me in his car. I was a bit hesitant at first because I remembered my mum had said that when he taught her to drive years ago, he'd got really annoyed with her because she took so long to learn. But that wasn't the case. Even when I slammed on the brakes or took a corner a bit too fast, he kept his cool. He actually taught me so well, I passed the test first time.
Narrator: Four. You overhear a man and a woman talking about a new café.
Man: I went to that new café on the corner yesterday for lunch.
Woman: It's nice to have a local café again, isn't it?
Man: I thought so too, but it was so crowded! I couldn't get a table and just ordering a sandwich to take to the park took twenty minutes.
Woman: I was there on Tuesday and I had no problems getting served or finding a seat. Oh well. It's good for business if it's popular. The one there before was always empty – that's why it closed down.
Man: You certainly can't keep a place like that open if nobody actually goes there. I think I was practically the only customer in the old place.
Narrator: Five. You hear a woman talking about a tree in her neighbour's garden.
Woman: My next-door neighbour has a huge tree growing in his garden and one of the branches was pressing up against my bedroom window. I asked him to cut the branch down, which he did yesterday, but now it's lying on the grass in my garden and I can't get in touch with him. What do you reckon I should do? I certainly don't want to get into an argument with a neighbour, but I have a feeling he thinks it's up to me to get rid of it. It's enormous, so there's no way I can manage it by myself. I hope he calls me soon.
Narrator: Six. You hear a husband and wife planning a holiday.
Man: Let's go to Greece again this summer. We had such a good time there last year.
Woman: As a matter of fact, I was thinking we could go somewhere more exotic this year.
Man: Really? But you said it was the most memorable holiday you'd ever had.
Woman: Sure I did. But I get hardly any time off and I really want to make the most of it. We can't just keep going back to the same place. I've never been to Asia, for instance.
Man: OK, fine – on the condition that we go somewhere with a beach. I don't feel like I've had a holiday unless I've spent some time away from the city.
Narrator: Seven. You hear two friends talking about a photograph.
Boy: Who's this in the photo here?
Girl: It's a picture of my grandmother when she was a teenager.
Boy: It's a great photo.
Girl: Yeah, it is, isn't it? I didn't know her when she was that age, of course, but the photo tells me she's been the same type of person all her life. She looks so cheerful and full of energy. It'd be great to go through life just as she has – she's always seen the good side of everything, despite any difficulties she's had. Of course, she looks different now – she's elderly – but I instantly recognise the woman I know in this photograph.
Narrator: Eight. You hear a man talking about buying a new car.
Man: I'm looking around for a new car at the moment. I don't really want to get rid of my current one, but as it's eight years old, I think I should sell it now before it completely loses all its value. My kids are growing up fast, so I could probably do with a larger model anyway. I've never been a car person – as long as it gets me from one place to another without breaking down, I don't really care about anything else. I don't want to pay a fortune for it – you'll never see me in a luxury car – but if I need to pay a bit extra for the right car, I'd be happy to.

Reading and Use of English Part 2

1 such 2 of 3 the 4 to 5 with 6 been 7 by 8 if / though / when

Writing

My sisters and I
I am so glad ~~Im~~ **I'm** not an only child. Of course, my parents are ~~grate~~ **great**, but they don't always understand the problems of being young. ~~Thats~~ **That's** when I ~~appreciete~~ **appreciate** having sisters. I'm in the middle of two sisters and we spend all our time together. They are my best

friends and we get on really well. Of ~~corse~~, **course**, we sometimes fight – for example, if I borrow a sister's ~~cloths~~ **clothes** without ~~permision~~ **permission** or if our bedroom gets ~~to~~ **too** messy. They are much ~~tidyer~~ **tidier** than me. We ~~do'nt~~ **don't** usually have many problems but if I argue ~~whit~~ **with** one sister, there is always the other one to talk to~~?~~ . We have the same ~~taist~~ **taste** in music, too. I think that without my ~~sisters'~~ **sisters**, life would be very boring. ~~would~~ **Would** I like to have a brother, too? I'm not so sure. I think I like having sisters more.

Unit 2 Leisure and pleasure

Grammar

Making comparisons

1
1 much hotter 2 much more difficult 3 more, a better 4 more
5 much 6 far 7 much faster, more easily 8 as good as

2
1 as relaxing as / more relaxing than 2 correct 3 as expensive as
4 correct 5 even faster 6 less complicated than 7 (much) more enjoyable than 8 correct

Adjectives with *-ed* and *-ing*

3
1 boring 2 astonished 3 worried 4 puzzled 5 motivating
6 irritated 7 exhausting 8 excited

4

Adjective	Verb	Noun
bored/boring	to bore	boredom
confuse/confusing	to confuse	confusion
embarrassed/embarrassing	to embarrass	embarrassment
excited/exciting	to excite	excitement
exhausted/exhausting	to exhaust	exhaustion
irritated/irritating	to irritate	irritation
motivated/motivating	to motivate	motivation
worried/worrying	to worry	worry

Vocabulary

Phrasal verbs and expressions

1
1G 2H 3E 4A 5B 6C 7F 8D

2
1 ended up 2 came across 3 thrown herself into 4 count on
5 went on 6 came along 7 ran out of 8 came up against

Listening Part 2

1 hobby 2 cool 3 street 4 space 5 bookshop 6 pottery 7 (good) (video) camera 8 100,000 9 (very) wealthy 10 (TV) (production) company

Track 3

Narrator: You will hear a man called Michael Flannery talking about his work restoring and selling antique furniture. For questions 1 to 10, complete the sentences with a word or short phrase.

Man: I restore and sell mid-century furniture for a living. You know the type I mean – Scandinavian-style wooden furniture from the 1950s and 60s. It all started as a bit of a hobby when I bought my house but had no money for furniture. My house dates from the 1950s, so when my grandparents let me take some things from their attic, I found they really suited the style of the house. What I first thought of as old-fashioned was actually quite cool. When people saw the furniture, they were so impressed with how I'd brought it all back to life with sandpaper and a bit of paint that they started giving me pieces they came across. Soon my friends were arriving at the house with a chest of drawers or a side table, saying, 'Look what I found in the street! I thought you might like it.' I think people are tired of good solid furniture going into landfill just because they don't have the space for it. They also realise that there might be someone else who has a need for it.

It got to the stage where my house was not only furnished, but I had too much furniture, so I tried selling some of it on a weekend market stall. I couldn't believe how well it went, and the prices that people were willing to pay for things that had cost me virtually nothing. Eventually I took the risk of giving up my job at a bookshop because I no longer had my weekends free to restore the furniture. That meant I could work on the furniture during the week, and then sell it on Saturdays and Sundays. My mum even reduced her hours at the factory where she works, so she could lend a hand at the weekend when it got busy.

To make my stall look unique, I started buying mid-century pottery from other dealers at the market. This really worked, and my sales almost doubled. I think sometimes people need style ideas to boost their imagination, and adding items to the furniture, such as cushions on chairs, or lamps on top of sideboards, helps people imagine how the furniture could look in their house.

I wanted some equipment to film the furniture projects while I did them – something a bit more professional than just a phone – so the next thing I did was buy myself a good video camera. Then I started an online channel with how-to guides on restoring furniture and information on how I get my stock. I can't just rely on people giving me stuff now, though it does still happen. I get most of the furniture from garage sales, and I film myself walking around them buying things. Strangely enough, people find these videos really relaxing to watch and I have more than 100,000 subscribers. It's amazing how quickly it happened – I was thrilled when I first reached ten thousand!

The problem with a business like this is that I no longer have any time for anything but work. There's always something to do – like picking up furniture that someone has phoned me about. When your passion becomes your job, it's difficult to know when you're working and when you're relaxing. Perhaps that's a good thing. I really love what I do and I'm actually now quite famous.

I'm never going to be very wealthy, but I do get a lot of views on my channel, which is starting to bring in extra income to add to the money I get from the furniture sales. Recently, I was approached by a production company about appearing in some sort of restoration and design programme. And a talent agent wants to represent me. I'm going to film the first episode in the summer and see if any TV networks are interested in it. I'm feeling very positive about my future.

Reading and Use of English Part 5

1D 2B 3A 4C 5C 6B

Reading and Use of English Part 4

1 asked me to buy (her) OR asked (me) if I would/could/'d buy (her)
2 taste nearly as good 3 run out of milk so 4 as much money as me
5 it hadn't been for 6 didn't/did not mean to break

Writing Part 2 (An article)

1
1 Each week we go to a different place because we like to vary the landscapes we paint. 2 I enjoy the company of the other artists and I create some lovely paintings, too. 3 I would suggest it to others because it's a good opportunity to experience the natural environment. 4 I didn't have much experience but the teacher taught me how to use colours and draw the outlines. 5 I saw a poster advertising landscape painting lessons and I decided to enrol on the course. 6 I would never give it up because I have made so many new friends and it helps me to be creative. 7 I really love spending time outside but if it's raining, we paint in the studio.

2
A 5 B 4 1 C 7 2 D 3 6

Suggested order of the text:
I saw a poster advertising landscape painting lessons and I decided to enrol on the course.
I didn't have much experience but the teacher taught me how to use colours and draw the outlines. Each week we go to a different place because we like to vary the landscapes we paint.
I really love spending time outside but if it's raining, we paint in the studio.
I enjoy the company of the other artists and I create some lovely paintings, too.
I would suggest it to others because it's a good opportunity to experience the natural environment. I would never give it up because I have made so many new friends and it helps me to be creative.

Unit 3 Happy holidays?

Grammar

Past simple, past continuous, past perfect simple and past perfect continuous

1
1 went 2 knew 3 woke up 4 was raining 5 decided 6 hoped 7 heard 8 was listening 9 stopped 10 was parking 11 was getting 12 arrived 13 were looking forward to 14 set off

2
1 had been driving 2 had already taken off 3 hadn't travelled 4 had forgotten 5 hadn't been doing 6 had already paid

3
1 decided 2 had been working 3 realised 4 had packed 5 had sailed 6 hadn't brought 7 hadn't taken 8 felt 9 hadn't planned 10 found 11 was getting 12 bought

at, *in* or *on* in time phrases

4
1 at 2 in 3 on 4 in 5 on 6 at

Vocabulary

Travel words

1
Across 1 business 3 overnight 6 travel 7 way 8 trip 10 holiday 12 weekend
Down 2 sightseeing 4 village 5 agent 9 journey 11 abroad

Suffixes

2
1 colourful 2 reasonable 3 successful 4 energetic 5 natural 6 adventurous 7 doubtful 8 thrilling 9 accessible 10 crowded 11 mysterious 12 friendly

Listening Part 3

1 G 2 C 3 H 4 A 5 E

Track 4

Narrator: Speaker 1

Speaker 1: It was the first day of our holiday in Spain. I'd taken the family down to the beach to the umbrellas and chairs we'd rented for the whole week. We couldn't have had a better position, right up the front and almost at the water's edge. I was just settling into my chair when someone greeted me by name. I looked across and who was it but my next door neighbour! Not only was his beach chair and umbrella right next to ours, but he was also staying at the same hotel! He didn't seem that surprised but I was speechless. It's a small world.

Narrator: Speaker 2

Speaker 2: I was on holiday in Venice with a friend and we were doing a tour of a four-hundred-year-old palace where the ceilings were covered in amazing paintings. My friend suddenly burst out laughing and started photographing something in the corner of one of the rooms. I asked her what was going on, but before she could tell me I'd spotted it myself. A chubby little cherub in the painting was peering over the edge of a cloud and its face looked exactly like mine – I couldn't believe it! I still have a photo and people I know always look out for it when they go to Venice.

Narrator: Speaker 3

Speaker 3: I was coming back from a holiday in the USA after a really tiring rock-climbing tour. My flight was going from Dallas to London – and I wasn't looking forward to the ten-hour trip. As I was checking in, I was told there were too many people booked in on the flight and would I take a plane the next day instead. This really wasn't part of my plan, but I agreed, and the airline put me up in a very nice hotel overnight. When I checked in the next day, they told me I'd been upgraded to Business Class. I'd suspected this might happen as I'd done the airline a favour.

Narrator: Speaker 4

Speaker 4: I've always been very active in the conservation movement, and I love helping to record where and when particular birds are seen. I recently went on holiday to Scotland in the hope of tracking down one species of bird people feared had died out. I can still hardly believe it, but when I was in the garden of the hotel, I suddenly saw one sitting on a branch above my head. By the time I'd raced up to my room and come back ready with my camera, it was nowhere to be seen. It was fantastic to discover it hasn't become extinct, even if I don't have proof of that.

Narrator: Speaker 5

Speaker 5: I was walking along the beach on holiday in Nova Scotia in Canada when I nearly tripped over something sticking out of the sand between the rocks. On closer inspection, I saw it was an old bottle sealed with a cork. I got it open at the hotel and pulled out a rolled-up piece of paper with nothing on it but a name and address to contact, which I did when I got back home. Amazingly, the person was still living at the same address. The bottle had been put in the water by a schoolboy in Cornwall 30 years before as a science experiment. He was now grown up and could hardly believe it when I got in touch.

Writing Part 2 (A report)

1 The purpose of 2 In terms of 3 It is also a benefit 4 Disadvantages 5 In addition 6 I would highly recommend 7 Although

Reading and Use of English Part 7

1 B 2 D 3 B 4 C 5 A 6 D 7 B 8 C 9 D 10 A

Unit 4 Food, glorious food

Grammar

so and *such*, *too* and *enough*

1
1 enough 2 enough 3 too 4 such 5 so little 6 so few 7 such a 8 sweet enough 9 too 10 so many

2
1 ~~much~~ many 2 correct 3 ~~too much~~ so much 4 ~~there is enough~~ there are enough 5 correct 6 correct 7 ~~such expensive~~ so expensive 8 correct

Vocabulary

Food and diet

1
1 diet 2 dish 3 meal 4 dish 5 organic 6 food 7 filling 8 fresh 9 meals 10 simple

2
Across 4 convenience 5 tasty 6 recipe
Down 1 balanced 2 lifestyle 3 nutrition 4 catering 6 raw

Reading and Use of English Part 1

1 C 2 A 3 A 4 D 5 C 6 C 7 B 8 D

Reading and Use of English Part 6

1 D 2 C 3 B 4 F 5 A 6 G

Listening Part 4

1 A 2 B 3 C 4 B 5 A 6 B 7 C

Track 5

Narrator: You will hear a radio interview with a man called Mike Jones, who has recently been a contestant on a TV cooking show. For questions 1 to 7, choose the best answer (A, B or C).

Interviewer: I have here in the studio Mike Jones, who's recently been a contestant on the TV cooking show Stars of the Kitchen. How did you get on the show, Mike?

Mike: Well, it was completely unexpected as it was my sister who entered me into the competition. She likes my cooking and thought I'd be a good contestant. When the production company phoned me, I thought it was a joke. It wasn't something I'd ever considered doing as I'm normally quite introverted, but when it comes to cooking, I'm a lot more self-assured. I thought it might be quite a stressful experience, but it ended up being really fun.

Interviewer: Have you ever worked in a professional kitchen?

Mike: No, but I've always had the feeling that I'd open my own restaurant one day because I'm always praised for my cooking skills. The closest I'd got to that was occasionally eating out in a restaurant. I've been cooking since I was a child, although it's only recently that I've become more creative with it. So I suppose that helped.

Interviewer: What was the first day in the studio like?

Mike: It was a bit nerve-racking. I hadn't read the email that had been sent to me properly and so I didn't know I'd have to cook for the judges that day. I thought we'd just be learning how the show worked and doing sound tests. I had to come up with something then and there, so I baked a cake that I could remember how to make by heart. It was a bit on the easy side, so I thought there was no way I'd get through to the next round. But the judges thought it was delicious and said I was in.

Interviewer: Is being on the programme as stressful as it looks on the TV?

Mike: In some ways, yes. We had the same time limits as you see on the show. We usually had an hour to cook something, but that wasn't too bad. I think it seems more stressful on the TV because of the dramatic music they use. We didn't have that, but having to get used to all the equipment was tough. I'm used to hanging out in my own kitchen where I know the oven temperature and where all the knives are.

Interviewer: Do people stop you in the street now?

Mike: Sometimes - and there's not much I can do about it. I still find it strange that people know who I am. With adults, it's different. They don't remember me from the show exactly, but they recognise my face without knowing why. People are more confused than anything. It's a bit embarrassing, but I know it's not going to last for very long.

Interviewer: What was the best thing about being on the show?

Mike: I have to say I learnt a lot about food and came out a much better cook than I went in. Above all, though, I'll always cherish the friendships I made. When the show's on TV, they make it look like we are all really competitive and don't get on, but that's not true at all. I'm still in touch with quite a few contestants and we've become really close thanks to our shared interest in food.

Interviewer: So, did you win Stars of the Kitchen in the end?

Mike: Well, the final episodes haven't gone to air yet so I have to keep it to myself – that's part of the contract. Let's just say it's going to get very exciting and there are a few shocks as well! So I'm afraid you'll just have to wait and see like everyone else. The next episode's on Wednesday night. We're going to be cooking Spanish food.

Interviewer: I'll be watching for sure. Thanks so much for coming in, Mike.

Writing Part 2 (A review)

1 such 2 enough 3 meals 4 so 5 recipes 6 dish 7 food 8 too

Unit 5 Study time

Grammar

Zero, first and second conditionals

1
1 weren't 2 go 3 will/'ll need / needs 4 finish / have finished 5 choose 6 complete / have completed 7 wouldn't do 8 will/'ll try 9 don't pass 10 got / had got

2
1 correct 2 I would/'d spend more time practising 3 She will / 'll have trouble finding a job 4 he has studied / he's studied / studies too late 5 would I need to take an advanced maths course 6 correct 7 I am going to travel / I'm going to travel / I will travel / I'll travel 8 correct

Vocabulary

Phrasal verbs

1
1 look back at 2 got away with 3 puts off 4 handing back 5 live up to 6 turned out 7 pointed out 8 get over

find out, get to know, know, learn, teach and *study*; *attend, join, take part* and *assist*

2
1 ~~unite~~ join 2 ~~known~~ learned 3 ~~learn~~ study 4 ~~join~~ attend 5 ~~know~~ find out 6 ~~learned~~ taught 7 ~~know~~ get to know 8 ~~join~~ take part in

Study words

3
Across 2 career 4 degree 5 prospects 7 revision 8 tutor 9 marks
Down 1 research 2 course 3 admission 6 lessons

Suffixes

4

-tion	-ence	-ment	
intention investigation qualification	existence preference	adjustment agreement assessment	development involvement

-ance	other	
appearance	advice behaviour comparison	confusion feeling response

5
1 agreement 2 comparison/confusion 3 investigation 4 preference 5 response

Listening Part 1

1 C 2 A 3 A 4 B 5 B 6 A 7 B 8 C

Track 6

Narrator: One. You hear a father talking to his son about university.

Son: Dad, why didn't you go to university?

Dad: I did go for a couple of years. Didn't I ever tell you that? I started doing a degree in Accounting and I didn't do too badly in the early part of the course. Then your grandfather got ill and I had to come home to run the family business. I always intended to go back and finish it at some stage, but then I met your mum and you kids came along. I suppose it's a shame I didn't manage to finish my degree, but I would have ended up doing the same work anyway, so it didn't really change much.

Narrator: Two. You hear two students talking about the university library.

Female: When do you go to the university library? I've never seen you there.

Male: I don't go much at all. I prefer to do all my research online. It's easier than having to ask the librarian to collect books and material for me. I have to wait, and then I take a look at them and find they don't contain the information I want at all. It drives me crazy wasting so much time. It's a good thing the papers I need for my research are available free online, otherwise I'd be in the library as much as you.

Narrator: Three. You hear a student talking to a friend about his new school.

Girl: How are you enjoying studying overseas?

Boy: Well… it is one of the best schools in Britain, and it'll give me lots of options for my future education. Winning that scholarship to go away to school has made my parents so proud. But I really struggle being so far from them and all my old friends here in New Zealand.

Girl: That's not so good. Are the lessons tough?

Boy: Oh no, my old school must've been good, because I don't feel I'm behind in any way. Actually, I'm ahead in maths. I sometimes feel I really don't need to be there, but I wouldn't want to disappoint Mum and Dad by not giving it a chance.

Narrator	Four. You hear a student talking to a friend about a history report he has written.
Male:	Can you check this report for me?
Female:	But you know we don't cover this subject on my course.
Male:	I just need someone to read it through to make sure it sounds OK. My friend Isobel and I wrote different sections each, and I'm worried it's not very clear. It'd be useful to get an objective opinion to make sure it's understandable. Please! You've always helped me in the past.
Female:	OK, but I won't be checking any facts.
Male:	That's OK. Thank you so much. Feel free to write any comments you have on it. I'm sure Isobel will be just as happy as me to have another person look at it.
Narrator:	Five. You hear a girl leaving a phone message for a friend.
Female:	Hello Eliza, I got a bit of a shock in my first literature lecture today. I didn't know we were supposed to read all the books on the syllabus before the semester started. I've read one or two, but there are more than ten and I haven't even bought them all yet! In our first tutorial I have to give a talk on three of Shakespeare's history plays and I'm not sure which ones they are. I was just wondering how you coped with all the reading when you did this course last year. I don't know if I'll be able to catch up – everything seems to be moving so fast.
Narrator:	Six. You hear two students talking about using tablets at school.
Girl:	Do you use tablets at your school? We all have to have one next year at ours.
Boy:	Yes, I've been using one since I started high school. It's great not having to carry a big bag of books around all day. All my books are e-books on the tablet, though there's nothing like the feeling of holding a real book in your hand, is there?
Girl:	Well, my parents aren't too happy about having to pay for the tablet – they cost a lot!
Boy:	Tell them not to worry. E-books are much cheaper than paper books, so over the years you save money.
Girl:	Great! I'll tell them that.
Narrator:	Seven. You hear a man talking about a book.
Speaker:	Take this book, for example. The cover makes it look like it's one of those blockbusters you buy at an airport, and the title doesn't really explain what it's about at all. It was a colleague's recommendation that eventually made me decide to get it, despite my first impressions. Often when I start reading a book, after the first few pages, I think, 'Why have I bothered?', and I was expecting the same with this one. But this book turned out to be far better than I'd expected. Until I finished it, I blocked out the world and entered another one as if it were my own.
Narrator:	Eight. You hear a boy talking to a friend about studying after school.
Girl:	How do you manage to study when you have to work in your mother's shop after school?
Boy:	I do most of my homework there. I don't really have much to do in the shop – I only serve customers if I'm needed.
Girl:	Don't you find people coming into the shop all the time distracting?
Boy:	It annoys my mum that sometimes I don't even hear the bell when people come in because I'm concentrating so hard. I'm completely used to people coming in and out. In some ways, it's less distracting being in the shop. There's no TV or video games, for instance. I really get a lot done.

Reading and Use of English Part 3

1 repeatedly 2 interested 3 differences 4 unmotivated / demotivated
5 comparison 6 information 7 creativity 8 knowledge

Writing Part 1 (An essay)

2

Giving your opinion	Expressing contrast
in my opinion	However
I believe	on the other hand
Introducing other people's opinions	**Putting your ideas in order**
Some people think that	Firstly
	Furthermore
Introducing an argument	**Introducing your conclusion**
There are several reasons	To sum up

3

1 F (You must do the essay in Part 1.) 2 F (You must cover the two points given and include your own idea as well.) 3 F 4 T 5 T 6 T
7 F (Your essay should be between 140 and 190 words.) 8 T

Unit 6 Good job!

Grammar

Countable and uncountable nouns

1

2 scenery – U 3 idea – C 4 favour – C 5 luggage – U 6 music – U
7 trip – C 8 food – U

Articles

2

1 - 2 - 3 the 4 a 5 an 6 - 7 - 8 a 9 the 10 the 11 the 12 a
13 - 14 a 15 a 16 - 17 a 18 - 19 the

Vocabulary

work or *job*; *possibility*, *occasion* or *opportunity*; *fun* or *funny*

1

1 fascinating 2 part-time 3 manual 4 outdoors 5 tiring/tough
6 well-paid 7 responsible 8 hard 9 challenging 10 demanding
11 worthwhile 12 permanent

2

1 I couldn't find any **information** online about the company. 2 correct
3 correct 4 If you get the **opportunity/chance**, call me tonight. 5 I spent all weekend doing geography **homework**. 6 Do you have any decorating **equipment** I can borrow? 7 I need (**some**) advice on how to prepare for a job interview. 8 Is there any **possibility/chance** you could babysit for me this evening?

Writing Part 2 (An email or letter)

1

1 T (The word limit is 190 words.) 2 T (There are no contractions, phrasal verbs or informal expressions.) 3 F (Each main point from the advertisement should be dealt with in a separate paragraph in the letter.)
4 F (The formal greeting and sign-off are *Dear Mr Davis* and *Yours sincerely*. A formal greeting should contain the surname and not the first name. If the greeting contains a person's name, the sign-off is *Yours sincerely*; if it is *Dear Sir or Madam*, the sign-off is *Yours faithfully*.) 5 T 6 F (There is no mention of the candidate's ability to communicate in English.)

2

1 H 2 D 3 F 4 C 5 B 6 G 7 E 8 A

Listening Part 3

1 E 2 C 3 G 4 A 5 D

Track 7

Narrator:	Speaker 1
Speaker 1:	After I graduated, I got a job as an accountant with a very big international firm. I'd go around to different companies checking their financial records to make sure they were paying the right amount of tax. It annoyed me when people said the job sounded boring. I remember I loved the variety and the salary was more generous than I'd expected. I was working at a different company every month and it was really rewarding to be able to use everything I'd learned at university. I don't work for that firm any more, but I'm still an accountant.
Narrator:	Speaker 2
Speaker 2:	I used to work as a lifeguard at the beach during my summers when I was at university. I had to do a short course to qualify and I also needed to know first aid. There weren't many waves and the water wasn't very deep, so not many people got into trouble. As a result, it did have its dull moments. For me, it was an excuse to hang out in the sunshine for the whole summer and get paid for it. The money wasn't great, but I met a lot of people, and on a few occasions, I was able to help people in the water.

Narrator: Speaker 3

Speaker 3: I had trouble finding a job in the field I'd studied for. I eventually got hired as a drama teacher, but until that happened I worked in a call centre for about three years. It certainly wasn't my dream job, talking to people who were complaining about their wi-fi going down, but it paid the bills at the time. It also taught me how to deal with angry customers and bring some calm to very negative situations. After a while, I just got used to it, as I knew that every call I got was an emergency situation for someone. It became easier to deal with.

Narrator: Speaker 4

Speaker 4: I worked in a nursing home for old people. It's not a job I would have done my whole life, but I'm glad I had the experience. Nursing homes struggle to fill these positions, so I had no problems in finding work. It certainly wasn't all fun and games, but I mainly remember the lovely old people that I cared for and how I tried to find time for them when they needed someone to talk to. I've always been a good listener. It can be difficult for people to move into a nursing home, and sometimes a bit lonely, especially in the evenings when there are fewer people for them to talk to.

Narrator: Speaker 5

Speaker 5: Cleaning people's houses was a great way to pay the bills when I was studying. It was relatively straightforward, but it was hard work. I had to clean the bathrooms and kitchens, and do all the floors. I would put on my headphones and listen to music though, and the time would fly. I could just switch off and daydream. It was a good way to stay in shape, too – I remember enjoying that a lot. These days I have my own house cleaned once a week because my job means I don't have time to do it myself.

Reading and Use of English Part 5

1A 2C 3C 4D 5A 6B

Unit 7 High adventure

Grammar

Infinitive and verb + *-ing*

1
1 to show 2 sitting 3 being 4 to get 5 training 6 to reduce
7 to start 8 playing 9 Joining 10 not to try

2
1 admitted 2 thought 3 failed 4 succeeded 5 avoided 6 allowed
7 expected 8 decided

Vocabulary

Verb collocations with activities

1
1 going 2 doing 3 compete in 4 playing 5 do 6 held

look, see, watch, listen and *hear*

2
1 to see 2 watching 3 heard 4 don't listen 5 looked 6 watching

3
1 ~~saw~~ looked 2 correct 3 correct 4 ~~listen to~~ hear 5 ~~watched~~ saw
6 ~~listened to~~ heard 7 correct 8 ~~watched~~ saw

Reading and Use of English Part 4

1 suggested taking | an 2 win | despite having 3 any people / anybody / anyone | swam there 4 find it | annoying 5 gets by | on 6 had his | blood pressure checked

Listening Part 4

1B 2A 3B 4C 5A 6B 7A

Track 8

Narrator: You will hear an interview with a motorcycle racer called Darren Beanhill. For questions 1 to 7, choose the best answer (A, B or C).

Interviewer: Today I'm interviewing the young motorcycle racer Darren Beanhill. Welcome Darren. You've been racing for a few years now. Can you remember your first ever race?

Darren: I grew up on a farm in Australia, so I was riding motorcycles from the age of seven. When I was 12, there was a race put on in my town for under-16s. I thought, well, I'm under 16 so I should qualify. All the boys there were bigger and had really expensive, new bikes. I just turned up with one we had used on the farm for years and everyone thought it was hilarious. They didn't tease me for long, though. I ended up winning the race, despite my age.

Interviewer: This is your third year on the international circuit. How is it different from your first two years?

Darren: I think people know now that I stay in the middle of the pack for most of the race and then start overtaking in the last ten minutes. The first year I was the new kid in town and that was a big advantage. I've been threatening to get into the top five for the past couple of years, so now other riders see I'm real competition for them. I don't worry about what the other riders think of me – I'm concentrating too hard on getting to the finish line as fast as I can.

Interviewer: You had some trouble with your tyres last year. How is it going this season?

Darren: Last year they were new tyres for me, and I had some problems with the grip, especially in the rain. I'm slowly getting used to them, and that's given me added confidence on the bends. It's amazing how much a tyre can affect your whole performance, but I suppose they're my only point of contact with the track – it all starts from there, doesn't it?

Interviewer: You spend much of the year at races around the world. How do you cope with the lifestyle?

Darren: Apart from the racing, I live a pretty normal life. My wife and my son, Ricky, travel with me, and we tend to avoid hotel rooms and find somewhere to stay that is more like home. Sure, we're not in one place for very long, but there's something very calming about having both of them with me. I don't know what's going to happen when Ricky has to start going to school, but that's not for a year or two yet.

Interviewer: How would you describe a typical motorbike racer?

Darren: Well, we all seem to have a way of blocking fear. I'm aware of the dangers, but all the riders at this professional level love speed and none of us is concerned about coming off, or even crashing into fellow riders, for that matter. If I suddenly became anxious about going out there, I'd have to quit racing. I've seen it happen to some of my peers. It's meant the end of their careers.

Interviewer: Do you have an age you'd like to retire at?

Darren: I'm 24. Nowadays people are racing until they're nearly 40. Who knows where I'll be and what I'll be doing at that age. Right now, I love it, and I'm just living from season to season. I certainly don't want to think about quitting before I've won a championship. But there's not just yourself to consider when you're married. My wife and I will determine that together, when the time comes.

Interviewer: The forecast says it's going to be 38 °C for the race on Sunday. Will that affect your performance?

Darren: It'll probably help me, in fact. All the races in this championship are in hot places – we follow the sun around the world all year and our bikes are designed to cope. Add in the fact that I'm Australian and grew up in the heat, so I'm used to racing in high temperatures. It's a positive factor for me, unlike the riders who come from cooler climates – I don't have to adapt. In fact, it's when it's cold and raining that my performance is weakest.

Interviewer: Thank you for coming in today.

Darren: Thank you.

Writing Part 2 (An article)

1 In addition 2 As a result 3 As well as 4 By doing this 5 Moreover
6 also

Unit 8 Dream of the stars

Grammar

at, *in* and *on* in to express location

1
1 on, at 2 at, in 3 in 4 on 5 at 6 on 7 at 8 in

Reported speech

2
2 It's the funniest film I've ever seen. 3 I've never heard of it. 4 I'll/I'd definitely watch it again. 5 I can't see it because I don't live near a cinema. / I couldn't see it because I don't live near a cinema. 6 I didn't really enjoy it because it was too long.

Reporting verbs

3
2 promise 3 admit 4 apologise 5 recommend 6 agree 7 warn

4
2 Oliver admitted that it was him who had broken the mirror. 3 My husband agreed that we could go out that night. 4 Julia apologised for not seeing my performance the day before / yesterday. 5 William promised that he would be on time the next day / tomorrow. 6 Angelo recommended that I/we should stream the TV series. 7 Lisa warned us not to buy concert tickets from strangers.

Vocabulary

Describing entertainment

1
Across 4 play 5 gripping 8 stage 12 audience 14 famous 16 edge of your seat 17 scene 18 musical
Down 1 rerun 2 twist 3 part 6 predictable 7 performance 9 act 10 spectators 11 binge watch 12 audition 13 hilarious 15 hooked

Listening Part 2

1 father 2 communication 3 level 4 style 5 contacts 6 reputation 7 tips 8 novels 9 flexible 10 professional

Track 9

Narrator: You will hear a woman called Margie Levine talking about her job as a Hollywood agent. For questions 1 to 10, complete the sentences with a word or short phrase.

Speaker: I've been an agent for actors in Hollywood for nearly 30 years and I've worked with the best in the world. I had an interest in acting from a young age. Show business was in the family – my aunt was a backing dancer in several classical musicals in the 50s. I even tried to pursue a career in musical theatre myself – against the advice of my father – but that came to an end pretty quickly as I wasn't that good at singing or dancing.
But I never lost my desire to work in a creative industry, I just needed to find something that matched my skills. Effective communication has always been one of my strengths and a friend who was working as a talent agent said this quality would make me perfect for that role. You're dealing with dozens of people on a day-to-day basis, so you have to be able to express yourself clearly. I had to learn to be a little more diplomatic, especially when turning actors down, but this came with time.
So I started at the bottom, as a receptionist for a big firm in Los Angeles. Then I became an assistant, then an agent, then a head of department. By holding various positions at each level of the firm, I got to understand completely how it operated. It was a long, slow learning process, but I got the best possible training in the industry.
I never had the intention of starting my own agency, but I kept meeting actors that I liked who were really talented and that I wanted to represent. However, they didn't fit in with the company's style. So I took a chance and started out on my own. It was a bit of a culture shock at first, working alone and not having anyone else to rely on. However, since I had so much experience and so many contacts in the industry, it didn't take me long to become established and get offered lots of assignments.
Once I was working with actors whose abilities I was sure of, I was able to get them plenty of work. This helped me develop my reputation as a talent agent and gain the trust of casting directors, who knew I would only send actors of a high standard.
Young actors are always asking me for tips on how to succeed in Hollywood. I usually give them three. The main thing is that you need to keep developing your skills. Just because you've finished drama school, it doesn't mean your training is over. You never know what you're going to be cast in as an actor and you have to be ready for anything. If you're well-prepared, you'll be less nervous.
Take regular acting classes, learn languages, learn to ride a horse, learn to fight, familiarise yourself with the most recent novels.
Secondly, you have to bear in mind that the best actor doesn't always get the job, so selling yourself well is the first step. By selling yourself, I mean not just showing that you're talented when you audition, but that you're a team player and can get on well with people. Most importantly, however, you have to show that you are flexible when the need arises. The most successful Hollywood actors are the least demanding. That's no coincidence. Casting directors give jobs to people who are going to make their lives easier and not cause problems.
The third suggestion is to make the most of your promotional materials. Don't get your photographs taken by a friend – go to a professional. Amateur-looking photos create a terrible first impression. Keep your biography up to date. After you have an audition, the people in casting will look at your social media. Does it represent the sort of person a film or TV production would want to hire?
So if your agent gives you advice, take it. It's in their interest to find you work, so trust what they say. They know the business.

Reading and Use of English Part 7

1C 2B 3B 4C 5D 6A 7D 8C 9B 10A

Reading and Use of English Part 1

1B 2D 3B 4A 5C 6A 7C 8D

Writing Part 1 (An essay)

1 One of the main reasons is 2 Because of this 3 for this reason 4 Because / Since 5 That is why 6 because / since

Unit 9 The power of the mind

Grammar

Modal verbs to express certainty and possibility

1
2 She might/could/may be out with her friends. 3 He might not/may not speak English. 4 That must be fun. 5 It can't be him driving that car. 6 Her parents must have been very proud of her. 7 They can't have bought another one. 8 My mother might have/may have/could have cooked it for me when I was young. 9 She can't have been able to write. 10 They might/may/could have thought I couldn't afford it.

2
1 can't 2 might/could 3 can't 4 could 5 must 6 may/might

Vocabulary

achieve, *carry out* and *devote*; *stay*, *spend* and *pass*; *make*, *cause* and *have*

1
1 spending 2 stay 3 spend 4 stay 5 passed 6 spend

2
1f 2a 3d 4e 5c 6b

3

achieve	carry out		devote
an ambition an objective success	an improvement an instruction an objective an order	research a test a threat	energy to one's life to time to

Reading and Use of English Part 4

1 can't | be switched 2 I came | across 3 is much | tastier than
4 warned me | not to go 5 will go on | until 6 shouldn't | have borrowed

Listening Part 1

1B 2C 3A 4C 5B 6A 7B 8C

Track 10

Narrator: One. You hear a man talking about drinking coffee.
Man: One of the great pleasures in my life is my first coffee of the day. I'm quite fussy about it. Of course, it can't be instant coffee – in fact, I'm not very keen on any coffee I make myself. I've experimented with most home gadgets and machines, and found that nothing comes close to what a café coffee machine can produce. Luckily, there's a café in my street that I can go to every morning. If I want to fit in a coffee before work, it has the added benefit of making me get up and get dressed on time.
Narrator: Two. You hear a father talking to his son.
Father: Wake up, Jack! It's ten o'clock already and it's a beautiful day outside.
Son: Aaagh ... Dad, it's Sunday – let me sleep in. It's the only day I can do it.
Father: I think you're wasting the day. I know you have to study a lot, but why waste the free time you do have lying in bed?
Son: This is the only day I've got that's truly mine. I love sleeping in...
Father: I've been up since six. I've already taken the dog for a walk and done a load of washing. You've lost half the day already.
Son: Come on, Dad! I'm sure you loved sleeping in when you were my age.
Narrator: Three. You hear a woman talking about doing yoga.
Woman: When I tell people how much I love yoga, I always get the feeling they think it's some kind of passive relaxation therapy. The reality is that the hour I spend twice a week in my yoga class really pushes my body to the limit – it calls for a lot of energy and movement. Everyone knows that all that stretching releases chemicals in the body called endorphins that have a real calming effect. But the body reacts in this way for a reason: it needs to balance out the stress that it undergoes when you hold a yoga position for a long time.
Narrator: Four. You hear a man and a woman meeting after a long time.
Woman: Is that you, James?
Man: Christine? Wow, how long has it been? It must be ten years!
Woman: Yes! Is this your usual supermarket? How strange I've never run into you in here before.
Man: I only moved back to the area last month. I realised I could do my job anywhere and I was getting sick of city life. I've been wondering who still lives here.
Woman: I'm still living with my parents. I travel a lot for work, so it hasn't been worth getting my own place. There aren't many from our class still in the village, though.
Man: That's a shame. It would have been nice to catch up with old friends.
Narrator: Five. You hear a man talking about a favourite pair of trainers.
Man: I think I've had these trainers for about ten years, and I'd love to wear them every day. They've faded quite a bit, so you can tell they aren't new, but they haven't got any holes or tears in them. The fact is, though, that they don't exactly look like they've just come out the box, I don't mind. The most important thing is they're comfortable. I can put them on and know I'm not going to have any problems with them. Unfortunately, they aren't smart enough for work. I mean... I don't care how I look, but the boss does.
Narrator: Six. You hear a man and a woman talking about a film they've just seen.
Man: I'm not sure if it was worth spending three hours of my time watching that film.
Woman: I loved the storyline. I think it was really clever how they revealed who the murderer was.
Man: I guessed who it was quite early, actually. The guy who played the main role did really well – he has such an expressive face.
Woman: He did give a very impressive performance. I loved the music, too.
Man: I'm not sure about having a classical soundtrack in a film like this, but I can see why you liked it. For me, it just didn't work in this film.
Narrator: Seven. You hear a student who's worried about planning her study time.
Woman: I'm just under so much stress at the moment. I have university exams coming up and I really don't know how I'm going to study properly for everything. I still have classes to go to and I'm working every evening as a waitress. I need to ask my boss if I can take some time off to study, or at least reduce my hours, but I'm worried I might lose my job. Strange that I'm more anxious about my part-time job than university – my exams really need to come first. I should consider a less demanding job.
Narrator: Eight. You hear a woman giving a talk about meditation.
Woman: I was suffering terrible mood swings and was always exhausted, so a friend suggested I try meditation. Even though I was doubtful it would help, I was willing to give it a go. It wasn't easy getting in a comfortable position or clearing my brain of my thoughts. Some days I suspected I was wasting my time, but eventually I was able to do it. It might not be the solution for everyone, but it really calmed me down. Not just that, but my memory improved – I started planning my life more effectively and generally felt more positive. Now I wish I'd taken that up years ago.

Writing Part 2 (A report)

1
Sentences 2, 3, 5 and 6 should be ticked

2
1 to find 2 opening 3 repairing 4 to close 5 to attract 6 building

Unit 10 Spend, spend, spend

Grammar

as and *like*

1
1 as 2 correct 3 correct 4 like 5 correct 6 correct 7 as 8 like

Modal verbs to express ability

2
1 can't / 'm not able to / won't be able to 2 couldn't / wasn't able to
3 can 4 haven't been able to 5 could already / was already able to
6 Will I be able to 7 could have 8 am always able to / have always been able to / can always

Vocabulary

arrive, get and *reach*

1
1 arrived 2 reached 3 arriving 4 get 5 arrives 6 arrive / get

2
1 bargain 2 brand 3 sale 4 competitive 5 consumer 6 available
7 stock 8 purchase 9 counter 10 debit card

Phrasal verbs

3
1 for 2 in 3 over 4 into 5 up 6 out 7 up 8 up 9 down
10 around 11 out 12 up

Reading and Use of English Part 2

1 into/in 2 so 3 what 4 even 5 having 6 front 7 there 8 been

Listening Part 4

1A 2C 3A 4A 5B 6B 7C

Track 11

Narrator: You will hear a radio interview with a personal shopper called Amanda Houseman. For questions 1 to 7, choose the best answer (A, B or C).

Interviewer: Today, I have with me Amanda Houseman, who will be talking to me about her job as a personal shopper. First of all, Amanda, what does a personal shopper do?

Amanda: I help busy people who need to buy clothes but never get the chance. Finding time to go shopping is tough for many professional people today, so my principal role is solving that problem. I put together a selection of clothing, usually a mix of luxury, high-prized designer items and everyday brands, which I take to clients to try on. Then they choose what they'd like to buy and I take the other clothes back to the shop.

Interviewer: What kind of experience do you need for the job?

Amanda: Well, time spent employed in the fashion industry is a good start. I began by working in a department store. That doesn't sound like much, but apart from serving customers I built up a lot of skills, including getting to know the work of different designers and learning about sizes and fabrics. Some people have a degree in fashion, and I imagine that would be useful, too.

Interviewer: How did you make the change to being a personal shopper?

Amanda: A customer at the place I was working wanted some advice on what she should take on a business trip. What I chose for her must have been right because not only did she buy everything I suggested, she also offered to pay me to choose clothes for her regularly. I started shopping for her in my spare time, and people began asking her where she got her clothes. That's how it started. She passed my name on to anyone who was interested and I slowly built up a business.

Interviewer: How do you know what clothes to take to clients?

Amanda: Often I'll just get a picture in my head of what they need, or I may spot something in a shop and think that's perfect for a particular person. But in the beginning, much of it is getting to know the individual. I always sit down with them and ask questions about their work and lifestyle. I like to visit clients at home as I can usually learn more about their tastes from the way their house is decorated than from what they're wearing. Just doing that, you get to know a lot about them.

Interviewer: What problems come with the job?

Amanda: It sometimes worries me having to handle clothes that are worth so much. The clothes are my responsibility once they leave the store, so there's quite a bit of trust involved with clients. I once had a client who didn't pay me for the clothes that she'd kept, so that has made me rather cautious. Since then I've only worked for people who have been recommended to me by other clients.

Interviewer: Do you ever take the clients shopping with you?

Amanda: They sometimes ask, but I try to avoid it – above all because when I'm out shopping it's usually for more than one person, so it wouldn't be an efficient way for me to work. Also, if you're in a shop with a client, you lose control of the situation and they can start trying on things that aren't right for them. I don't discourage them from making their own selections, it's their money after all, but it does mean that I have to find something there and then which suits them better.

Interviewer: What advice would you give someone who wants to be a personal shopper?

Amanda: You need to have confidence in your ability to choose the right clothes and be able to guide people without pushing them too hard. On the other hand, you can't forget you have to be flexible, too. If a client doesn't like what you've brought them, it can be quite tough turning round and going out shopping for them again. You need to be ready to admit you might have got the selection wrong. In the end, the client has to want to wear the clothes you've chosen.

Writing Part 2 (A review)

1

2 It was the cover of the book that 3 What I found out when I started reading it was that 4 It was the description of life in New Orleans that 5 What I really liked about this book was that it 6 What I want to read next is

2

1 What I really need at the moment is a new tablet. 2 It was Michael who stole the book from the shop. 3 What happens is the main character loses his job. 4 It was last year that she took out a bank loan. 5 It was the black shoes which I liked the most. 6 What I don't know is what time the department store opens.

Unit 11 Medical matters

Grammar

Relative pronouns and relative clauses

1a

1 which 2 whose 3 who 4 which 5 where 6 which 7 which 8 whose 9 who 10 which

1b

5 I like going to places like the beach in winter, where I know there won't be many people. 7 The city's football team, which is at the top of the league, has more fans than any other.

1c

The relative pronouns can be replaced by *that* in 1, 3, 4, 6, 9 and 10.

1d

The relative pronouns can be omitted in 4 and 10.

2

1 f 2 c 3 d 4 a 5 e 6 b

Vocabulary

Words relating to health

1

Across 1 itchy 4 bumped 7 sneezing 8 broke 9 reaction 10 feet 12 coughing

Down 1 injured 2 stung 3 weather 5 poisoning 6 bug 8 bled 11 hurt

Word formation

2

1 ability 2 awareness 3 certainty 4 experience 5 formality 6 happiness 7 helpfulness 8 honesty 9 patience 10 possibility 11 predictability 12 reliability 13 satisfaction

3

dis-	im-	in-	un-	
dishonest dissatisfied	impatient impossible	inexperienced informal	unable unaware uncertain unhappy	unhelpful unpredictable unreliable unsatisfied

Listening Part 3

1 F 2 C 3 H 4 D 5 B

Track 12

Narrator: Speaker 1

Speaker 1: At around the age of ten I wanted to be an Olympic swimmer. Hours spent in the pool had me getting some really good times for my age and I was competing at regional level. The dream ended, however, after a stay in hospital for a particularly nasty ear infection. It left me almost unable to hear in one ear. The doctor told me it was simply too risky getting back in the pool again, so I had to give up swimming. Still determined, I took up cricket instead, and with the same crazy enthusiasm I'd had for the pool. I got better and better, and now I play for my county.

Narrator: Speaker 2

Speaker 2: You know lice, the little insects that live in your hair? I had them when I was seven. When I turned up at school with an extremely short haircut and parents were told that they needed to check their kids' heads, fingers were soon pointed at me. School was a nightmare after that. Nobody would play with me and some kids were even afraid of me. I was miserable. I really think the teacher should have stepped in at this point and explained to the class that I didn't have lice any more. It wasn't until I went to secondary school that it was all forgotten.

Narrator: Speaker 3
Speaker 3: Children can get vaccinated for it now, but when I was young, chickenpox was a disease everyone got at some point in their childhood. I woke up one morning covered from head to toe in itchy red spots. It made them worse if I scratched them, but I just couldn't resist it, so my mum had to wrap my hands in bandages to stop me. The one thing that worked was lying in a cool bath. Nothing else seemed to help. I was ill for about two weeks – it was terrible. I think it's great that kids don't suffer as much from this illness these days.
Narrator: Speaker 4
Speaker 4: My parents always made me put on sunscreen at the beach, as I had really fair skin. But one day I went with a friend and his family and though Mom had sent me off with a bottle of sunscreen, I forgot to put it on. I had to spend the next three days lying on my stomach as my back and shoulders were really badly sunburnt – I got incredibly painful blisters. I certainly learnt my lesson. Now, when it's hot, I don't leave the house without putting sunscreen on. I never want to go through that again!
Narrator: Speaker 5
Speaker 5: One morning, I woke up completely unable to speak. I had laryngitis, a throat infection. It didn't hurt and I felt OK, so I went to school anyway. My parents didn't think to give me a note for the teacher. Probably because I looked fine, she wasn't convinced that I had really lost my voice, and thought I was just playing games with her. As the morning went on and I still didn't speak, she lost her patience with me and sent me to the headteacher. It wasn't until the headteacher had phoned my parents that I was allowed back into class.

Reading and Use of English Part 6

1G 2E 3A 4C 5F 6D

Writing Part 1 (An essay)

1 due to 2 despite 3 Although / Even though 4 however 5 whereas / while 6 While / Whereas 7 Even though / Although 8 but

1
1 in spite of knowing (that) 2 While it's important to 3 even though they know (that) 4 the fact that temperatures drop

Unit 12 Animal kingdom

Grammar

Third and mixed conditionals

1
1 hadn't gone, wouldn't have found 2 wouldn't have seen, hadn't taken 3 wouldn't have discovered, hadn't offered 4 wouldn't be, hadn't quit

wish, if only and *hope*

2
1 If only 2 hope 3 wish 4 hope 5 hope 6 wish 7 If only 8 hope 9 wish 10 wish

3
1 correct 2 hadn't had the binoculars with her 3 I wish I/we had seen more elephants 4 correct 5 so I hope 6 correct 7 it hadn't rained 8 we could stay

Vocabulary

avoid, prevent and *protect*; *check, control, keep an eye on* and *supervise*

1
1 protect 2 supervised 3 prevent 4 avoid 5 control 6 check 7 keep an eye on

Reading and Use of English Part 7

1C 2D 3B 4A 5C 6A 7C 8A 9D 10B

Reading and Use of English Part 1

1A 2C 3A 4D 5B 6D 7B 8C

Listening Part 1

1C 2A 3A 4A 5B 6B 7A 8C

Track 13

Narrator: One. You hear a man speaking to his friend about a neighbour's pet bird.
Woman: What's that whistling sound?
Man: It's the bird that lives upstairs. The lady that owns it puts the cage out on her balcony if it's a nice day. That's why you can hear it.
Woman: Why would anyone want to have a bird? It seems cruel to me, never letting it out of a cage.
Man: Does it sound unhappy to you? It sings like that all day. My neighbour lives by herself and she says it keeps her company. She told me she sometimes lets it out of the cage and it flies round the house. Apparently, it goes back to its cage on its own when it's had enough.
Woman: Really?
Narrator: Two. You hear a mother talking to her son about an incident at the beach.
Mother: Why are you back from the beach so early? Are you OK?
Son: Well … I was sitting on my surfboard in the water when a shark started circling me. I was too afraid to use my arms to get back to shore, so I had to wait for the next wave and surfed in on my stomach.
Mother: That's unbelievable! You weren't in the water on your own, were you?
Son: Of course not. I shouted to my friends and they got out quickly as well.
Mother: I thought they fly a helicopter over that beach checking for sharks.
Son: Only at the weekend.
Mother: Well, you're not to go there unless it's the weekend, then.
Narrator: Three. You hear a man talking to his friend about a dog walking service.
Man: I've recently started using a dog walking service.
Woman: Oh really, what's it like?
Man: Well, I was a little hesitant at first because it's surprisingly pricey, but then I made a few savings elsewhere and that made it more manageable. But it gives me peace of mind to know that someone's looking after my dog while I'm busy at work, so it's worth every penny. I do have to go a little out of my way to drop the dog off every morning before heading to the office, but it's lovely when I come back and see her so happy in the evening.
Narrator: Four. You hear two friends talking about their exam results.
Boy: So, how did you get on?
Girl: Pretty good overall, I think. I wasn't expecting to do as well as I did in maths. I didn't feel at all confident coming out of the exam.
Boy: That was one of my worst results, to be honest – although it's hardly surprising given how little time I had to prepare for it.
Girl: But you still passed! So you must feel pretty good about that.
Boy: You're right, I suppose. I'm just glad it's all over and I won't have to sit an exam again for a while.
Girl: I couldn't agree with you more on that. Now we can enjoy the rest of the summer.
Narrator: Five. You overhear a father and daughter talking on the train.
Father: I'm glad we decided to go by train today. I'd forgotten how stunning the countryside was around here. You don't see this from the motorway.
Daughter: Yes, it's nice, I suppose, but what are we going to do when we get to the station?
Father: We'll take the underground. It's not far to Covent Garden.
Daughter: Well, at least you don't have to pay for parking.
Father: True, although I knew the train tickets wouldn't be cheap. But this way, I don't have the stress of getting stuck in traffic and arriving late. We couldn't have driven into the centre anyway – it's just not worth taking the car to London these days.

Narrator:	Six. You hear a woman talking on a radio programme about personal challenges.
Woman:	I'd been practising for months, but I was still concerned I might not be successful. My instructor told me not to worry – all I had to do was control my nerves on the day and I'd be fine. I just kept thinking of all the things that could go wrong, though. But as soon as I went outside and got behind the wheel, I felt a boost of confidence, and everything I had been practising just came naturally. The next 40 minutes flew by and when the examiner told me I'd passed, I felt so relieved – I wouldn't have been able to start my new job without my licence.
Narrator:	Seven. You hear a blind man talking about his guide dog, Lola.
Man:	I've had this guide dog, Lola, for eight years, so she's getting near retirement age. She's my fourth guide dog and I think she's the best one I've had. She never gets distracted when we're out in the street. She even ignores children trying to feed her. I have the option of keeping her here with me after I get a new dog, and in the past I've done that and had two dogs at the same time, one working and one in retirement. But I don't think I'll be able to manage this time. I'm too old now to look after two dogs.
Narrator:	Eight. You hear a man talking to an employee of a cruise company.
Man:	I'd like to change one of the names of the travellers in my booking. My wife has to work and can't come with me, so I'm taking my son instead.
Woman:	Certainly. Can you tell me the name of the passenger who's currently booked?
Man:	Yes, it's Jane Sinclair. And my son's name is Hamish Sinclair.
Woman:	OK, that shouldn't be a problem. There'll be a fee of £200 to alter the booking.
Man:	Did you say £200? You're just typing my son's name into a computer? Can't I change it myself online?
Woman:	I'm afraid that's not possible, sir.
Man:	In that case, forget it. That's simply ridiculous!

Writing Part 2 (An email)

2
1 ✓ She thinks it's a brilliant idea. 2 ✓ She suggests a dog. 3 ✓ good exercise and teaches responsibility 4 ✓ She thinks it's a good idea but warns him that pets are a big commitment.

3
Suggested places for paragraphs to begin:
[Getting a dog …, [I don't think you should get a pet…, [So, overall, I think … , [Let me know…

4
The email is too long: it is over 190 words. It should be between 140 and 190 words. There is a greeting ('Hi Jonathan') and a sign-off ('Write soon').

5
1 B 2 D 3 G 4 H 5 A 6 E 7 C 8 F

Unit 13 House space

Grammar

Causative *have* and *get*

1a
2 She needs to have/get the floor carpeted. 3 She'd like to have/get the windows cleaned. 4 She has to have/get the light fixed. 5 She wants to have/get some pictures hung. 6 She is going to have/get some furniture delivered.

1b
2 She has (already) had/got the floor carpeted. 3 She has (already) had/got the windows cleaned. 4 She has (already) had/got the light fixed. 5 She hasn't had/got any pictures hung (yet). 6 She has (already) had/got some furniture delivered.

Expressing obligation and permission

2
1 I don't let my children 2 don't have to 3 needn't have planted 4 are not supposed to 5 shouldn't 6 weren't allowed to 7 can't 8 are allowed to

Vocabulary

Describing where you live

1
1 residential 2 central 3 neighbours 4 outside 5 peaceful 6 en-suite 7 open-plan 8 balcony 9 links 10 amenities

space, place, room, area, location and *square*

2
1 area 2 room 3 space 4 place 5 location 6 square 7 place 8 space

Listening Part 2

1 mother 2 training 3 certificate 4 honesty 5 financial situation 6 (current) owners 7 patience 8 plumbing 9 2.5 million 10 lawyers

Track 14

Narrator:	You will hear a woman called Julie Marshall talking about her work as an estate agent selling houses and other properties. For questions 1 to 10, complete the sentences with a word or short phrase.
Speaker:	Hello, my name is Julie Marshall and I'm here today to talk about my job as an estate agent. I'd often thought about doing the same kind of work as my father – he was an estate agent for 30 years – but it was when we were selling the house that belonged to my grandmother that my mother convinced me I'd be really good at it. Some people are in it for the money, of course, and that can be a great part of the job, but I was initially interested in my company because they provided training, which meant I wouldn't have the expense of going to university. After just 12 months, I finished my course and passed all my exams. The company was really pleased with my performance and my boss hung my certificate on the wall in the office. This gave me the incentive to try for a bonus by selling properties for higher than the expected price. The thing I love most about working with my colleagues in the agency is that we have such good communication. They're always teaching me new sales techniques and better ways to work with clients. And honesty with clients will always work in your favour. People will come back to you the next time they want to buy or sell a house because they have that connection. Sometimes I need information from clients that can be quite private, but thankfully personal questions about their profession are largely irrelevant nowadays. One thing I can't avoid, though, is enquiring about their finances if I want to show them houses they can afford. When I'm showing the houses, I'm always amazed by what the buyers want to know. Apart from the value of the home, you'd think they'd want to know about the condition of the house, but usually they want to know about the current owners. Some people spend ages deciding which house they want to buy and often ask to go back for multiple viewings. I understand that. After all, buying a house is the biggest expense most people have in their lives and they want to make the right decision. So patience is something I have to have a lot of, even if I don't always have the enthusiasm. If you pressure people to make a decision too early, they might decide to go to another agency instead. Sometimes people expect you to know everything about a building. I once had a couple who were very interested in an apartment I was showing them in the city centre. They had the electrics checked, and those did need some work before the purchase, but two months after they'd moved in, they had problems with the plumbing and expected me to take care of it. It took a lot of explaining before they understood it wasn't actually my responsibility. The most expensive place I've sold was a huge beachside residence, but that needed a lot of work doing to it, so it took a long time to sell. Eventually the right buyer came along and we did the deal. I was thrilled because the agency's record for a sale was 2 million and I managed to close for 2.5 million. It was still a bargain for the buyers because the property was originally listed for 3 million before I talked the owners into dropping the price.

I think that the most difficult part of being an estate agent isn't dealing with the homeowners, or even with the sometimes very demanding buyers, but the people that work for them. The banks can be very hard to deal with, but the toughest are the lawyers who inspect the contracts. They always want to change something, which means we need to get legal advice, too. But there isn't anything I can't manage – I love matching people with their perfect home and can't see myself ever doing a different job.

Writing Part 2 (An article)

1
1 No, the title is not catchy or interesting as it repeats the words in the question. 2 ✓ (It includes a question in the first paragraph.) 3 ✓ 4 ✓ 5 ✓ It gives an opinion in the third paragraph, but there could be a better balance between comment and description. 6 ✓

2
1E 2C 3B 4A 5D

Reading and Use of English Part 5

1C 2B 3D 4A 5C 6A

Unit 14 Fiesta!

Grammar

The passive

1
1 has been held 2 is surrounded 3 was set up 4 was built 5 be cultivated 6 were grown 7 were employed 8 is still held 9 were worn 10 were hidden 11 are still worn 12 is attended 13 are sold 14 are also crushed 15 has now been converted / is now converted

The passive with reporting verbs

2
2 It is believed that the escaped prisoner is still in the area. / The escaped prisoner is believed to still be in the area. 3 It is expected that unemployment will fall next year. / Unemployment is expected to fall next year. 4 It is thought that storms will probably hit the coast on Sunday. 5 Maria Callas is considered to be the most popular opera singer ever. 6 It has been confirmed that a man (who has been) missing for 10 years has been found on a desert island. / A man missing for 10 years is confirmed to have been found on a desert island.

Vocabulary

Describing festivals and celebrations

1
1 dress up, wear 2 celebrate, commemorate 3 march, gather round 4 hold, let off 5 perform, play

Suffixes

2
1 motorist, tourist, economist, refugee 2 researcher, collector, survivor, investigator 3 consultant, conductor, assistant, contestant 4 salesman/woman, sportsman/woman, businessman/woman, manager 5 specialist, novelist, comedian, pharmacist 6 waiter, sailor, farmer, miner

Listening Part 4

1B 2C 3B 4B 5C 6A 7B

Track 15

Narrator: You will hear an interview with Margaret Blake, a teacher who organises a poetry festival for young people. For questions 1 to 7, choose the best answer (A, B or C).

Interviewer: Welcome, Margaret. This year's Youth Poetry Festival starts next week. Didn't it all begin with a group of your students?

Margaret: Yes, it did. About ten years ago, I came across some poetry online and recognised the names of a few of my secondary school students, who seemed to have some sort of poetry club. They weren't doing it as classwork, so I had no idea that it was going on. Apart from them putting the poems online, what really amazed me was they were also reading poems to each other at meetings they organised. There was really no other means for them to do this.

Interviewer: Is this what made you come up with the idea for a poetry festival?

Margaret: That's right, it got me thinking. I had a group of students who were writing poetry because they wanted to! I wondered if there was a greater movement of teens writing poetry, hungry for an audience. Perhaps we could set up some sort of writers' festival? I went online to where the young people's poetry was being uploaded and asked anyone who'd like to be involved in a festival to contact me.

Interviewer: Did you get much response?

Margaret: I was completely overwhelmed with emails. I found out that there was a huge community of young poets out there. I received enquiries from all over the country but wasn't expecting so much interest from people in the local area. People were just so thankful for the opportunity. I even had emails from a number of poets offering to promote the festival for me, although this wasn't necessary as a colleague had already promised to set up a website.

Interviewer: So how did the first year of the festival go?

Margaret: In our first year, we had fifty young poets performing and got a lot of interest from the media. Most of the poets were from the UK, but a few had come from all around the world. That's when I knew that we were really onto something big, knowing that so many young poets were willing to come all that way to read their poems in a café. It also turned out to be a wonderful opportunity for them to meet and exchange ideas, so not only was it well received by the audiences, but the poets really got something out of it, too.

Interviewer: So, do you think the festival will change in the future?

Margaret: We're the biggest youth poetry festival in the country, and the event continues to grow. We've increased the number of venues to include five more coffee shops. We could include larger venues as well, but then we'd risk losing the personal atmosphere that you get in a small setting. There's been some call to incorporate short stories and songwriting, but I think we'll leave that to other festivals. What would be really useful, though, is to extend the duration of the festival – we're starting to struggle to fit everyone into the schedule.

Interviewer: If listeners can't get to the festival, is there anywhere they can read the poems?

Margaret: Each year we publish a book with all the poems from that year's festival, along with a short biography of each young poet. The tenth edition came out yesterday, and you can order it online. Be quick, though, as copies usually run out quite quickly. But I really think that people should come along to the performances and hear them in person.

Interviewer: And what about your original poets from ten years ago?

Margaret: Some of them are involved in the organisation of this year's festival. You have to be between 15 and 25 years old to enter, so they can't take part as they're beyond the age limit. They all tell me they still write poetry. I'm not sure whether they still meet to read it – I should ask. But if anyone's interested, the opening night is this Saturday. Just go to our website to check the venues. It's youngpoetsfestival.com.

Interviewer: It all sounds very exciting. Thank you for coming in, Margaret.

Reading and Use of English Part 6

1B 2E 3G 4D 5A 6C

Reading and Use of English Part 3

1 competition 2 innovative 3 fashionable 4 responsibility 5 artistic 6 annually 7 achievements 8 exchange

Writing Part 1 (An essay)

1D 2B 3A 4C

Acknowledgements

The authors and publishers acknowledge the following sources of copyright material and are grateful for the permissions granted. While every effort has been made, it has not always been possible to identify the sources of all the material used, or to trace all copyright holders. If any omissions are brought to our notice, we will be happy to include the appropriate acknowledgements on reprinting and in the next update to the digital edition, as applicable.

All the texts, photographs are used from the Student's Book.

Front cover photography by m-imagephotography/iStock /Getty Images Plus and Howard Kingsnorth/ Stone/Getty Images.

Illustration

Zacharias Papadopoulos (Hyphen S.A.)

Audio

Audio production by IH Sound Ltd.

Typesetting

Typeset by Hyphen S.A.